HD
2328
.D78
1992

THE NEW SOCIETY
THE ANATOMY OF INDUSTRIAL ORDER

D0209321

BELL LIBRARY-TAMU-CC

THE NEW SOCIETY
THE ANATOMY OF INDUSTRIAL ORDER

PETER F. DRUCKER
WITH A NEW INTRODUCTION BY THE AUTHOR

TRANSACTION PUBLISHERS
New Brunswick (U.S.A.) and London (U.K.)

New material this edition copyright © 1993 by Peter F. Drucker. Originally published in 1950 by Harper & Brothers.

All rights reserved under International and Pan-American Copyright Conventions. No part of this book may be reproduced or transmitted in any form or by any means, electronic or mechanical, including photocopy, recording, or any information storage and retrieval system, without prior permission in writing from the publisher. All inquiries should be addressed to Transaction Publishers, Rutgers—The State University, New Brunswick, New Jersey 08903.

Library of Congress Catalog Number: 92-5075
ISBN: 1-56000-624-2
Printed in the United States of America

Library of Congress Cataloging-in-Publication Data

Drucker, Peter Ferdinand, 1909—
    The new society: the anatomy of industrial order/Peter F. Drucker; with a new introduction by the author.
    p.   cm.
    Originally published: New York: Harper, 1950.
    Includes index.
    ISBN 1-56000-624-2
    1. Industry. 2. Industrial relations. 3. Industrial organization. I. Title.
HD2328.D78   1992   92-5075
306.3'6—dc20   CIP

This book is dedicated to my children,
Kathleen, Vincent, Cecily and Joan.
May theirs be a world free from fear.

CONTENTS

NINTH PART: The Principles of Industrial Order: The Labor Union as a Citizen

CONCLUSION: A Free Industrial Society

Introduction to the
Transaction Edition

The New Society was the third and last of my books analyzing and diagnosing the industrial society that emerged out of World War II. It followed *The Future of Industrial Man* (1942) and *The Concept of the Corporation* (1946), both also reissued by Transaction Publishers. The first of these attempted to develop a social theory of society in general and of the industrial society in particular. The second analyzed and presented a major industrial enterprise—the world's largest and (then) most successful manufacturing company, General Motors in the United States. It did so from the inside, as the result of an eighteen-month investigation during which GM opened itself to my inspection. This, the third book, then distilled the conclusions of its two predecessors into a systematic, organized analysis, both theoretical and practical, of industrial society, its constituent elements, its major institutions, its social characteristics, its problems, and its future. Nothing like this had been done before; and, indeed, nothing like this has been attempted since. For *The New Society* not only presented analyses of the major institutions—large business enterprise, government, the labor union—it also attempted to place the individual within this social context; and it equally tried to relate the sociology of an industrial society to the political principles of a free society.

One of the insights of this book which might surprise today's reader, is the chapter entitled "Can Unionism Survive?" To most readers forty years ago this was a silly question and a good many reviewers said so. Unions then were the entrenched rulers of industrial society, the real winners, the real powers. But it was evident to me even then, having worked with major unions for a few years, that their power base was extremely narrow and that the question of their real function in an industrial society had yet to be answered. That management, having power, needs a countervailing power, this book clearly stated—and I believe in this as firmly as I

xi

did forty years ago. But that the union as we inherited it from the nineteenth century—with or without Marxist flavor—is the right way to do that job, this book doubted. Events since then have amply validated the author's conclusion that unionism as it existed in 1949—which is still the only unionism we in the United States really know—can survive. Today's reader may feel that unions are given too much space in the book and are taken too seriously. But the basic question then raised, which is really the question of the basic *political* structure of an employee society, still has to be answered.

But while unions loom larger in this book than they might loom in a similar book today, one major element of modern society is conspicuously absent in this book. And no one in 1949—and I do mean "no one"—then saw it: the knowledge worker. I became the first one to see knowledge work and the knowledge worker. Indeed I did coin the term, but only eight years later, in my next book on society and social analysis, *Landmarks of Tomorrow* (1957; also being reissued as a Transaction book). In retrospect it is amazing that all of us, without exception, failed to see the emergence of the educated employed middle class, the knowledge worker, who became the center of society within another ten or fifteen years. The event that produced this shift had already occurred: the G.I. Bill of Rights of post-World War II America had opened the doors of colleges and universities to millions of returning veterans. Some of us did indeed realize even then that this was a dramatic innovation. I recall a paper I wrote at the time that pointed out that such a policy would have been unthinkable after World War I, and, indeed the World War I veterans would not have considered such a reward a "benefit" at all and would not have availed themselves of it in any numbers. But that this policy signified a fundamental shift in social values and, ultimately, in social structure escaped every observer including this one and yet, in retrospect it should have been obvious.

The Industrial Society that this book depicted was then at its peak. It looks different today. In the first place, the economic center of gravity in developed countries has shifted from manufacturing industry to service industries of all kinds. And within industry it has largely shifted from the very big business that was the success story of the 1930s and 1940s—and of the 1950s as well—to medium-sized business. In the second place the center of *social* gravity no longer clearly lies in business; the non-profit "third sector" has become increasingly important in every developed country (excepting only Japan.) And, as already said, the basic social problems of a developed country are no longer industrial workers; they have become secondary. Increasingly our concerns will center on the productivity of knowledge work and on the dignity of service work, neither known to *The New Society* or to the time in which it was written.

Still, with these adjustments the basic approach, the basic analysis, the basic conceptual frame of this book still apply today—its discussion of basic institutions; of the role and limits of management; of the need for individual independence and yet also of community within the institutions of a developed society; of labor as a resource, the first such in the literature; and so on. And perhaps it is relevant to report that *The New Society* was the first of the author's books to have major impact on Japan, in its discussion of the role and function of profit, management, and, above all, of labor as a resource and of the need to create a plant-community. It is still considered in Japan to have been the guide to the restructuring of Japanese industry; to the development of modern Japanese management; and, above all, to the radical reform in the 'fifties' of Japan's employment and labor policies and practices.

Peter F. Drucker
Claremont, California

PREFACE TO THE 1962 EDITION

THIS book has two main themes. First, that the industrial society of the twentieth century is a new and a distinct society, world-wide rather than "Western" or "Capitalistic," and that it is both little known and well worth knowing. Second, that this new society has a specific social institution: the industrial enterprise with its management, its plant community and its Siamese twin, the labor union.

When this book first appeared, these assertions seemed startling and novel to a good many people. Today, only a dozen years later, they are commonplace. Any good Marxist for instance, would have scoffed then at the very idea of management, let alone at the thesis that there are by the nature of the industrial system unavoidable and permanent cleavages between the objective needs of production and the personal needs and desires of the individual employee—under socialism and communism as well as under capitalism. To say this aloud is still inadvisable in the Soviet Union today. But since Stalin's death the organization and function of management has become the most debated domestic problem of Russian politics and economics, with the discussions startlingly similar to those of the top management people in our "decadent capitalist" system; and these problems, as well as the attempts to solve them, are undistinguishable from those which concern the top managements in our giant corporations. Institutionally, in other words, this new society of ours presents everywhere the same appearance and has the same characteristics of structure, with the differences (and they are very great) being political and moral rather than institutional. Similarly, the resolution of the conflict between the impersonal logic of the organization and the drives and visions of the individual has become a popular theme for the Soviet novelist and playwright.

In the United States we now hear a good deal about the "organization man," that is, about the imposition of the industrial community on the employee. But ten years ago the main criticism of American society and business, especially among the "liberals," was of its too "individualistic" nature.

Yet this book, upon rereading, appears to be especially pertinent to the sixties. There are no pat solutions here. The aim is rather to understand,

XV

and this, apparently, appeals more to readers today than it did a scant
ten or twelve years ago. The concept of the one big solution that would
put everything right was then very much the fashion. We had learned
by bitter experience that the one simple remedy of outlawing the
"Demon Rum" did not, as promised, cure all the ills of society, family
and person. But the yearning for the one big shining panacea in the large
economy package that led us to accept Prohibition after World War I,
was still very much in evidence after World War II. Only the labels had
changed. They read then "communism" or "free enterprise," the "labor
movement" or "world government." There were even a good many intelligent people who believed that the new "absolute weapon," the atom
bomb, would by itself guarantee world-wide peace, if not democracy
and prosperity. The Korean War (it broke out in June 1950, only a
few months after this book had appeared) was such a deep shock to the
American people largely because it dissolved this particular illusion,
among others. And with this began the disillusionment with the big,
simple cure-all.

Today the quest is for understanding, especially among the younger
generation, the people who have grown up since World War II and who
are ready to assume leadership in government and politics, in the professions and in the sciences, in the arts and in business. That there is no one
easy answer to any real question we now know and accept. We realize
that there are facts to be faced and chores to be done. There are risks,
difficulties and compromises. There are problems and opportunities. We
(and this "we" embraces at least all the developed nations of the world)
are becoming non-utopian and even anti-utopian, in the sharpest possible
contrast to our parents and grandparents. To be sure, we are as prone to
being naively complex (as for example in a good deal of "modern literary
criticism" and in some of the super-refinements and super-complications
of present-day personality psychology) as an earlier generation was prone
to being naively simple. And the one is as dangerous as the other. But
at least we are no longer frightened by the fact that the world comprises
a great deal more than can be handled by good intentions. And this is
the central asumption of "The New Society," which is avowedly anti-
utopian and non-utopian.

This re-issue of *The New Society* as a Harper Torchbook cannot have
the shock impact the original edition had. But precisely because it is
unlikely to shock, the book may mean a good deal more to the new

readers for whom this edition is primarily intended. It might—at least this is the author's hope—make them say "I don't know whether I agree or disagree, but at least I understand."

PETER F. DRUCKER

INTRODUCTION: The Industrial World Revolution

THE world revolution of our time is "made in U.S.A." It is not Communism, Fascism, the new nationalism of the non-Western peoples, or any of the other "isms" that appear in the headlines. They are reactions to the basic disturbance, secondary rather than primary. The true revolutionary principle is the idea of mass-production. Nothing ever before recorded in the history of man equals, in speed, universality and impact, the transformation this principle has wrought in the foundations of society in the forty short years since Henry Ford turned out the first "Model T."

Though "made in Detroit," the impact of the new principle is not confined to the United States or to the old industrial territory of the West. Indeed, the impact is greatest on the raw-material-producing, pre-industrial civilizations. The sweep of mass-production technology is undermining and exploding societies and civilizations which have no resistance to the new forces, no background or habit-pattern of industrial life to cushion the shock. In China the mass-production principle, swept into the hinterland from the coastal cities by the forced migration of industries during the Japanese invasion, is destroying the world's oldest and hitherto its stablest institution: the Chinese family. In India, industrialization has begun to corrode the Hindu caste system: ritual restrictions on proximity and intercourse between castes simply cannot be maintained under factory conditions. Russia uses the new mass-production principle to try again where Byzantium failed: to mate Europa and the Bull, the technological fruits of Western thought with Oriental despotism, to produce a new world order which claims to be the legitimate heir to both East and West. In our own country the Old South, hitherto least touched by industry and still living in the ruins of its ante-bellum rural order, is speedily being "tractored off." Indeed, conversion of the Southern farm into a rural assembly line seems on the verge of "solving" the Southern race problem in a manner never dreamed of by either Southern Liberal or Southern Reactionary: by pushing the Negro off the land into the industrial cities.

At the time of World War I, only one generation ago, industry was, by and large, still confined to a narrow belt on either side of the North

Atlantic. The only exception, the only successful transplantation of the machine to new soil, was in Japan. The representative unit of industry, even in the most heavily industrialized countries, was the family-owned or family-managed medium-size factory employing fewer than five hundred workers and differing from the workshop of pre-industrial days mainly in its use of mechanical power.

Today the situation is reversed. The areas not undergoing rapid industrialization are few and isolated; the representative, the decisive, industrial unit anywhere is the large, mass-production plant, managed by professionals without a stake in ownership, employing thousands of people, and altogether organized on entirely different technological, social, and economic principles. The change has been so great that, in retrospect, the typical factory of 1910 seems to have been closer to its great-grandfather, the artisan's workshop of pre-steam-engine days, than to its own son: the modern mass-production plant. The new industrial territories, only yesterday rural and largely innocent of machine and factory, are jumping directly into the mass-production age without going through the first "Industrial Revolution."

The geographic spread of the mass-production principle, its sweep in width, is accompanied by a sweep in depth: the penetration of the traditional pre-industrial and nonindustrial occupations. This aspect of the industrial world revolution is fully as important as the industrialization of the raw-material-producing countries.

The great bulk of productive work a generation ago was done in forms antedating industry by hundreds, if not thousands, of years. Even in the most highly industrialized country, it was completely non-industrial in character. Only a minority of the people, though in some countries an important minority, lived and worked in an industrial world. Even in the most highly industrialized country, the mass-production principle was still regarded generally as a mere technique, such as the assembly line, and largely confined to the automobile industry.

Two World Wars showed that the principle which underlay Henry Ford's first plant forty years ago is completely independent of specific tools or techniques, and that it is a basic principle for the organization of all manufacturing activities. Today it has become abundantly clear that the mass-production principle is not even confined to manufacturing, but is a *general principle for organizing people to work together.*

The Russian collective farm was the first application of the principle to agriculture. Its labor organization which uses the individual as a highly specialized tool performing essentially one simple job repetitiously, its control through the state-owned tractor station, its system of compensation—all are applications of mass-production technology. Yet the Russian collective farm is already technologically as obsolete as an automobile plant of forty years ago. The fully mechanized cotton plantation in the Mississippi Delta, or the vegetable co-operative on the irrigated land of California's Central Valley, have gone much further in breaking with the pre-industrial traditions of agriculture. And in their grandiose scheme for raising peanuts in tropical Africa, the British proposed to reorganize a whole colonial empire on the mass-production basis. Yet agriculture has traditionally been regarded as opposite to, and incompatible with, industrialization, if not as the very symbol of the pre-industrial tradition.

Without assembly line or conveyor belt, clerical operations in large-scale business enterprises are today increasingly organized the same way in which Henry Ford organized the production of the Model T. The typists' pool of a large insurance company, check-sorting and check-clearing operations in a big bank, the sorting and filling of orders in a mail-order house, and thousands of other operations in business and government offices do not differ in substance from the automobile assembly line, however much they may differ in appearance.

Similarly, scientific research has been organized on mass-production lines. This has been true for many years in the engineering and chemical research carried on by American industry. The mass-production method is now being carried into medical and biological research. In the new Sloan-Kettering Institute for Cancer Research in New York—significantly founded by two of the pioneers of the automobile industry—concepts and methods of work are those of the assembly line. During the War the application of this mass-production principle to scientific research resulted in the atomic bomb, which could not have been produced by any other method. Even pure research, unconcerned with application, has been organized on the mass-production pattern in some of our most productive laboratories, such as those of the Bell Telephone System or of the General Electric Company.

The principle has even been applied successfully to work that has always been considered to be essentially personal in character. The efficiency and effectiveness of the Mayo Clinic, for instance, rests largely on its organizing diagnosis and examination into a production line. Henry Luce's "group journalism," by means of which *Time*, *Life* and *Fortune* are being produced, is largely assembly-line work.

Most startling, however, is the application of the principle to military organization. Of all pre-industrial types of organization, the army was the most highly formalized and apparently the most rigid. But the great Allied invasions of World War II were prepared and carried out as mass-production processes, with each officer doing only one highly specialized and largely mechanical task. He was seldom shifted from operation to operation, not did he usually know where his piece fitted into the total. This application of the mass-production principle to the conduct of war was one of the most important contributions this country made to victory. It represented a greater change in the organization of warfare than anything that had been developed since Spain's "*Gran Capitan*" first created the concept of the modern army almost five hundred years ago.

"Industry" once meant any organization for human work. It was only during the eighteenth and the early nineteenth centuries, the era of the first "Industrial Revolution," that the term was narrowed to mean "manufacturing." With the second industrial revolution, the revolution of mass production, "industry" again reverts to its earlier meaning. The industrial principle of today, the mass-production principle, promises to put all major organizations for group work, no matter where or of what kind, on the same basis, and to organize them according to the same concept. It is not only the most revolutionary principle of production man has ever found but also the most general.

The mass-production principle is not a mechanical principle. If it were, it could never have been applied beyond manufacturing, and independently of assembly line, conveyor belt and interchangeable parts. It is a *social* principle—a principle of *human* organization. What was new in Ford's plant was not the organization of mechanical forces, but the organization of human beings performing a common task. And this explains the shattering impact of the new principle on traditional cultures, on the relationship between man and society, and on the family.

Of these impacts, *the divorce of the worker from the product and the means of production* is the most visible.

This separation has long been recognized. In the past it has always been blamed on the legal or economic "superstructure." It has been considered an accident, rather than an essential, of the industrial system. That was, for instance, Marx's premise and on it rest almost all his major conclusions. It was the premise of Marx's enemies, the Guild Socialists and the Syndicalists. It was shared by all other critical students of the effects of the first Industrial Revolution. It underlies the two famous Papal Encyclicals on the industrial order, "*Rerum Novarum*" and "*Quadragesimo Anno*." There was a general belief that the worker would have control of production if only he were given legal control over the means of production.

In the mass-production system, this belief can no longer be maintained. The divorce of the worker from product and means of production is essential and absolute. It has nothing to do with legal control or political institutions. The worker by himself cannot produce. He must have access to that highly complex organization of men, machines and tools we call a plant. As we shall see, even the collective of the workers, such as a co-operative, a union or a syndicate cannot control this organization—except in a purely formal and entirely fictitious sense—let alone the individual worker.

In fact, the worker no longer produces, even in the plant; he works. But the product is not being turned out by any one worker or any one group of workers. It is being turned out by the plant. It is a *collective* product. The individual worker usually is not even capable of defining his own contribution to the productive organization and to the product. Often he cannot even point to a part or a process and say: this is *my* work.

This applies wherever the mass-production principle has been applied. The most striking examples are indeed to be found outside of manufacturing. There are apparently no "means of production" in a clerical organization; but when a bookkeeper, a comptometer operator, a shipping clerk, is cut off from the organization he is completely helpless and unproductive. Similarly, an engineer or an industrial chemist is not productive unless integrated into the organization, no matter how highly trained he may be. Here it is clear that the productive unit, the "means of production," is the organization itself rather than any material tool.

There have always been trades and occupations where access to the organization was necessary if the individual was to be effective and productive. It has been a long time, for instance, since the individual soldier armed with his own equipment could go out and gain a kingdom all by himself as he does in the fairy tales. It is also true that, for his subsistence, the individual in all but a few societies is dependent on an exchange of products with his neighbor—that is, on co-operation of some sort. But while not able to *subsist* independently, the overwhelming majority of the people living in any traditional society has always been able to *produce* independently, commanding not much more than the equipment they were born with or that they could make themselves. This applies not only to the hunter, the husbandman and the farmer, but to the craftsman and to the professional in a traditional society. The tailor, the wheelwright or the baker, the priest, the medicine man and the scribe—they all could function productively as individuals.

In an industrial society the situation is reversed. It is only a very small minority of artists and professional men who can produce at all by themselves. All the others are dependent upon access to an organization to be productive. *It is the organization rather than the individual which is productive in an industrial system.*

This divorce of worker and means of production threatens the status and prestige system of any traditional society, whether of the West or of the East; it dissolves the traditional community and uproots the individual.

It also makes unemployment and the threat of unemployment unbearable—not because of their economic, but because of their social, consequences. This in turn imposes on government the new and unprecedented task of preventing and curing depressions, a job far beyond the ability of any government yet devised by man.

Finally, the divorce of worker and means of production makes the old problem of the concentration of power infinitely more urgent because it makes possible an altogether new total tyranny.

If it is the organization rather than the worker which produces, then social status, social prestige and social power cannot attach to the individual's *work*. They can only attach to the individual's *job*. They can flow only from his membership, status, prestige and power within the organization.

As we shall see, it is not true that mass-production technology destroys skill and eliminates satisfaction in workmanship. On the contrary, it would be more nearly correct to say that it tends to eliminate unskilled work. Certainly, it requires an altogether unprecedented supply of very highly skilled men; both the number of skilled men needed and the skill required of them is steadily increasing. But the skills of the new mass-production society are different from those of traditional society. They are social and intellectual skills, rather than skill in handling tools and materials.

Industrialization, therefore, destroys the social prestige of traditional occupations and skills, and with it the satisfaction of the individual in his traditional work. It uproots—quite literally—the individual from the social soil in which he has grown. It devaluates his traditional values, and paralyzes his traditional behavior.

An industrial system is clearly incompatible with the structure, the status and class system of pre-industrial society. Industrialization explodes the rigidities of such a society. It will also block its opportunities. Witness the pressure, economic as well as social, on the old middle class of the "free" professions which, in the West, have traditionally been the main channel of social advancement.

Even in the West the destructive social impact of the divorce of worker from production and product can easily be seen, for instance, in the Southern White or the Southern Negro in Detroit. The much-publicized problem of the "second-generation American" in our big industrial cities reflects in most cases the impact of the industrial revolution on the culture and values in which that generation had grown up at home. But it is outside of the West that the divorce of worker and means of production has the most shattering impact on social structure, social values and social satisfactions.

Unemployment as a Social Threat

The divorce of worker and production which is inherent in thè mass-production technology explains the central importance which depression and unemployment have attained in our industrialized society. It is not primarily the economic impact that makes unemployment the nightmare it has become for every industrialized country. In this country we were able during the Depression of the thirties to keep the great majority of the chronically unemployed and their families on an economic level well above physical subsistence, and probably well above the level any but the very rich could have lived on only a century ago. We managed to do this even in the first chaotic years of the Great Depression when we had neither plans nor organization to cope with the disaster. Yet it is in this country that the Depression had the most profound psychological, social and political effects, which is simply another way of saying that the United States is today the most industrialized country in the world.

The main effect of long-term unemployment is not physical but psychological: loss of self-respect; loss of initiative; finally, in extreme cases, loss of sanity. Denied access to the organization without which, in an industrial society, nobody can be productive, the unemployed becomes an outcast whose very membership in society has been suspended. It is no accident that the "depression shock" was by no means confined to those who actually suffered long-term unemployment, but hit fully as hard the men who never, during the Depression, were out of a job, and who may never have been in real danger of losing their job. For a decade they lived in the constant fear of being fired the next payday; to become actually unemployed may well have been more bearable than to go on living in constant terror.

Precisely because the industrial system permanently divorces man and production, prevention of depression and chronic unemployment has become an absolute necessity for any industrialized country. The citizen can neither control nor understand the forces that threaten to cast him out from society and deprive him of his effective citizenship. Unless modern industrial society can banish these forces, it will not be acceptable or rational to its members. It must become instead meaningless, insane and demon-ridden, and turn into an obsessive nightmare. Depression and depression unemployment are indeed economic problems, in the sense that the solution will have to be found through economic tools and economic policies. But in their origin and in their larger impact they are not economic but social and psychological—the effect of a profound cultural disturbance.

The divorce of man from production makes impossible reliance on "natural adjustment." The patient may have a better chance of fast economic recovery if left alone; but he is likely to die of social shock and exposure just when he should be ready for recovery.

To say that the threat of depression and unemployment makes inevitable the abandonment of *"laissez faire"* misses the point however. *Laissez faire* means the absence of restrictive regulations. There is nothing in the threat of depression and unemployment that would demand restrictive regulations. They require the very opposite: positive economic action.

This is something radically different from an "abandonment of *laissez faire*." It is also infinitely more difficult. Few governments have ever even tried it on any considerable scale. And even fewer governments have been successful in their attempts at positive economic action.

In the first place, positive government action in the economic sphere requires extraordinarily reliable and complete information, extraordinary competence and experience in the making of policy decisions and equally extraordinary administrative skill. The government official would have to combine the best qualities of the economic scholar, of the political leader and of the trained administrator; and not merely one such paragon possessing all these qualifications—and personal integrity into the bargain—would be needed, but a good many.

It also demands either an extremely well-informed, not to say wise, citizenry, or a dictatorship that is completely independent of public opinion and pressure. To prevent or to overcome depressions, it is necessary to stop booms. But no government dependent on votes for its existence has been able so far to convince its constituents that it should "shoot Santa Claus." Even governments as independent of votes as those of Nazi Germany or Soviet Russia have never been able to take effective anti-inflationary action in the face of public opinion and pressure.

Finally, positive government action in a depression means giving orders for capital goods. And no government so far has been able to give large enough orders for capital goods other than armaments.

An effective depression policy calls for an entirely new concept of the government in economic life, that is neither *"laissez faire"* nor collectivism, but one of joint responsibility. No government can refuse to accept responsibility for such a policy; yet the demands of this new responsibility may well go beyond anything of which the institution of government is inherently capable.

The New Leviathan

The fact that the individual can now be denied access to the means of production, that he is not capable of producing by himself, also makes concentration of power infinitely more dangerous than it has ever been before.

The main problem is the power that has to be vested in government. The individual's dependence on access to the means of production makes possible a regime that totally controls the individual—it makes possible totalitarianism. Control of access to the productive organization, if concentrated in one hand, can easily be used to establish control over the livelihood, the social and political status, if not the very life, of the individual. Only in the primitive tribe, in which the member cowers in dread of the dark forces of the unknown, do we find equally absolute and complete domination. The industrial world revolution tends to do away with the traditional inability of government to exercise complete control, which alone has enabled the individual in most societies to enjoy some liberty and privacy.

The absolute dependence of the citizen on access to the productive organization endows tyranny at the same time with a new attraction. If freedom carries the risk of the social disfranchisement of chronic unemployment, freedom becomes unbearable and tyranny appears as the liberator. The mass-production society must have a government strong enough and powerful enough to cope with the unbearable menace of chronic unemployment. It must have a government weak enough and limited enough not to menace the freedom, the happiness and the private life of every citizen.

We have had many despotisms, many police states and many tyrannies in the history of man; but beyond the primitive level of the tribe, in which magic, taboo and ritual control the totality of human existence, we have never had a totalitarianism—that is, a regime in which the individual is completely and in all his activities submerged in the state. That it is a tyranny is not the essence of totalitarianism. What makes it "total" is that it completely denies the person. This could never be done in a culture in which the individual by himself can become productive, that is, socially effective. Any tyranny, however brutal and arbitrary, has limitations if it cannot make the whole of man's social life subject to its commands.

In addition, as long as the individual by himself can become productive, he can arm himself against unbearable tyranny and terror. To consider the "right to revolution" the last and ultimate safeguard of freedom was a profound insight of traditional political thought. In a thoroughly industrialized society it is impossible for the citizen to resist a government in control of the means of production. The "right to revolution" becomes an empty abstraction against tanks and bombing planes. Even the *"mystique"* of the "General Strike" is entirely powerless against the totalitarian dictatorship. All that is possible for the citizen is to conform outwardly and to hope to be able to salve his conscience through mental reservations. But though a totalitarian government may not be able to control the souls of its citizens, it can control all their actions; and how long will a faith persist if it cannot come to life in works?

In the past it appeared sufficient to curb power by legal provisions and legal limitations. As a last resort a government violating the constitution could be resisted and overthrown by force. But in an industrialized society, there can be no resistance against a government which makes itself absolute and total. *The best constitution in the world with the most carefully worked-out balance of power would not have prevented Hitler from assuming power, let alone have stopped him once he had assumed power.* He could not be resisted; his control of the access to the means of production made it possible for him to make his power total and to control every social activity in his, an industrial, society.

Industrial society must decentralize power in autonomous hands. But at the same time it cannot afford, in doing so, to turn itself into an anarchic society, comparable to the society of the fifteenth century, with its amorphous mass of petty principalities, free cities, exempt bishoprics and noble highwaymen. On the contrary, it must have the power and unity for effective action against a depression.

Unless industrial society can *decentralize* the power of giving or denying access to the means of production, it will not remain a free society; it will be in permanent danger of becoming totalitarian. But if it loses the power to act, it will fail to remain a society altogether.

In the West the problems arising from the divorce of worker and production have been the most disturbing. At least, they are the ones of which we are most conscious. Outside the old industrial territory of the North Atlantic community, however, the most truly revolutionary effect of the industrial world revolution is its impact on the one institution on which all others are founded: the family.

All society, from the most primitive to the most highly developed, has been based on the coincidence of biological, psychological and productive unit of human life. The family, however much it may have its origin in the biological necessities of human survival, has been always and everywhere the carrier of emotional cohesion. It has also been the unit of production. With few exceptions, man and wife have always been a necessary partnership biologically, psychologically and socially; and with but few exceptions, children have always been integrated as much into the social as into the psychological unit. Once out of their infancy, they were as much members of the productive unit as they were, by birth, members of the emotional and ritual communion.

In primitive civilization the wife gathers root crops, berries and small game while the husband goes on his hunting expeditions; the children help the mother until the sons are old enough to accompany their father. In the civilizations of the husbandman, the woman tends the gardens or the small animals, spins and weaves, and cooks for the husband and his shepherds, while the men are out tending the beasts; the children grow up spinning and weaving until they are old enough to go out with the herdsmen. In an agricultural society the coincidence of biological, emotional and productive unit is even stronger—perhaps the major reason for the amazing strength and resistance of the family-farm society. The craftsman and artisan of highly developed civilizations also depends upon his wife who presides over the store and over the house, who looks after the journeymen and apprentices as well as after customers; the children are junior members of the unit, sharing in the life and the work of the family as apprentices, or at least as close observers.

This coincidence of biological and psychological with socially productive unit disappears under industrialization. *Industrialization divorces the family from society.* The place of business moves away from the place of residence: the father goes to work in the plant or in the office, miles away from the home. Wife and children are no longer integrated into the productive work. They may, indeed, have their own jobs and go to work themselves; but even if they should work in the same plant or the same office as the man of the family, they do not work as a family unit.

The widespread child labor in the nineteenth-century English cotton industry has always been considered the result of industrialization. Yet when children of five and six were employed in cotton mills to card or spin, they did not really do any work children of that age had not always done, including the children of the relatively well-to-do. The horror and degradation did not lie in the work's being given to children, but in its being industrial work. When transferred from the weaver's home to the factory, it was no longer the same work. Those children worked, indeed, next to their mothers. But they did not work as children within the family. They worked *next* to, but not *with*, their mothers; even though the mother sat next to them, there was no family left. They worked as stunted adults rather than as children.

Our reaction to the child labor of early industry was the right reaction, even though it was based on fallacious reasoning. It is immaterial whether, as the Factory Commissions wrongly believed, child labor was an innovation, or whether the traditional labor of the family unit becomes vicious, brutal and corrupted when transposed to the factory. The important fact is that child labor in the industrial system is destructive and vicious, and that the employment of children in industry has to be forbidden. But this does not solve the problem of the child in industrial society.

In any traditional society, the mother of adolescent children is the very symbol of strength, fulfillment and social power. In an industrial society the mother of adolescent children is apt to be a problem to herself and to society, even if she has something better to do with her time than to play bridge. In a pre-industrial society the problem of the "equality of women" hardly exists. The man may appear to hold the power legally and ritually; but outside of a very small ruling class relieved of the necessity to work for its living, the mother holds the power socially. Economically, man and wife are necessarily equals because the production is a joint effort. In an industrial society, however, the wife and mother is outside production, outside society.

This is brought out strikingly by the disrupting effect on the unity of the family which going to work on the part of wife or dependent children is likely to have. The length to which the unemployed worker went during the Depression, the sacrifices he was willing to make in order to escape this extremity, shows very clearly that in the industrial age the family can maintain its unity only if divorced from production. That one's wife has to work is something for the man to be ashamed of; and it is very enlightening that this attitude is most prevalent in the working class.

The family is still as necessary as ever as a biological, and especially as an emotional, unit. Its very divorce from society makes it even more essential emotionally, and leads to glorification of motherhood, of children, of the family tie so extreme as to betray the increasing tension—especially as this emotional affirmation goes hand in hand with an increasing willingness to dissolve family ties in divorce. On the one hand, the family has become a luxury: children are no longer an economic asset but an economic liability. It is no accident that industrialization and a decline in the birth rate run parallel. At the same time, the emotional unit becomes increasingly precious. Disturbances of the emotional bond which in traditional societies are not much more than minor nuisances become severe crises and the cause of "maladjustments," "neuroses" or "complexes," destructive alike of individual and of family life.

The pre-industrial, non-Western societies have no resistance whatever against this attack on the traditional family. Their cultural cohesion collapses under it as under a new plague. But even in the West, where the weakening of the family has been a very gradual process, the divorce of family and society has had profound effects. It is this divorce which gives our industrial cities their frightening, unreal, oppressive look, the look of a built-up jungle. This has nothing to do with poverty—indeed, the brand-new car that stands outside so many of the neat five-room bungalows in Detroit's working-class districts, the new refrigerator or washing machine only add to the bleakness. That the home and the family are no longer the focal points of social life is the reason for this look of furtiveness and impermanence, and for the undertow of violence and lawlessness beneath the surface gentility, which contrast so strikingly with the beauty, the order and the clear, strong rhythm of the new industrial plant.

The industrial world revolution carried by mass-production technology will continue to spread irresistibly. Behind it are two of the most powerful agents of social change: the desire for a higher standard of living, and the need of defense—that is, the desire for a higher standard of warfare.

The agrarian's sermons against the evils of industrialization, as well as the intellectual's warnings against the dangers of materialism, are not only bound to remain ineffectual in the face of the wretchedness of existence in China or India, South America or Central Russia. They must seem mockery, if not sheer hypocrisy, and only a mask for the desire of a small privileged class to perpetuate its dominance. In the destitution of the pre-industrial countries—the destitution in which all economies lived prior to the Industrial Revolution—the promise of the slightest improvement in material conditions is bound to be irresistible.

This does not mean that industrialization will be a fast or a painless process. It does not mean that poverty will be abolished. Even in the United States, and even at the height of a boom, there is real stark poverty, though mainly in the nonindustrial sector. It also does not mean that any other country will reach the American standard of living, if only because America owes so much to special advantages of geography, raw material supply, low population density, etc. Certainly no other country can hope, at least for a long time, to enjoy simultaneously the highest standard of living and the highest standard of warfare as the United States did during the last war.

In other words, industrialization will not bring the economic millenium. But it promises to bring a greater rise in the standard of productivity and of living than any technological change since the shift from nomadic husbandry to settled farming.

The rise in the standard of warfare is an equally powerful incentive to mass-production industrialization. In most countries—Russia is the perfect example—industrialization for bigger and better warfare means that the people will not enjoy any of the benefits of a higher standard of living. The mass-production revolution will actually result in a sharp depression of the standard of living unless we can reduce the demands war and the preparation for war make in the age of the total weapons. Yet this will not slow down industrialization. On the contrary, the poorer and the more defenseless a country, the greater will be the pressure to build up the industrial defense against foreign conquest.

The social and political crisis brought about by this revolution will thus become more acute and more general. We have been talking a good deal of the "crisis of the West." But the "crisis of the East" threatens to be a much more profound crisis, one of the very foundations of society and culture.

The resolution of this crisis, the development of the new institutions of a functioning and free industrial society, is the most urgent task facing the West today. It is the pre-eminent responsibility of the United States. Ours is the most highly developed industrial country. Its wealth and productivity make it possible to work on problems which in other countries have become so inflamed by class war, poverty and tension that they are too sore to touch. We are also in a perhaps more critical situation than any other country, precisely because our industrial system is so highly developed. Indeed, all evidence indicates that we have only a very few years—perhaps a decade, perhaps a quarter-century, certainly no more—to tackle the job successfully.

Moreover, as the originator and prime mover of the mass-production revolution, this country has risen to world leadership and has become the greatest power. So far this leadership has been confined to the realm of technology. We have not developed the social and political institutions to go with this technology. But precisely because mass-production technology is a corrosive acid which no pre-industrial culture or social order can resist, the world requires a working model of the political and social institutions for an industrial age. Without such a model to imitate and learn from, the mass-production revolution can only produce decades of world war, chaos, despair and destruction. If the model is not furnished by the West, if it is not a model of a free industrial society, the model will be that of a slave industrial society.

The United States is in the best position to serve as such a model, if only because the world's technology is "made in Detroit." True, our leadership is no longer as generally accepted as it was thirty years ago, when the world believed that Henry Ford had found the answers, and when "Fordism" was a slogan of equal potency in India, in Germany or in Lenin's Russia. This naïve belief—reflecting Henry Ford's own belief in "Machinery, the new Messiah"—was rapidly destroyed and finally disappeared altogether in the great Depression.

But because of its technical leadership, because of its military and economic power, but also because the United States still stands for the basic ideals of the Western World, the leadership is ours if we can only exercise it.

If this country, however, fails to serve as a working model, if it does not succeed in developing at home a functioning and free industrial society, our very technological leadership will bring catastrophe to the world and to ourselves. It will lead to the acceptance, on a world-wide basis, of institutions and beliefs unacceptable and deeply hostile to the basic beliefs and institutions of the American tradition and to the tradition of the West. In such a world, the United States could not maintain its own institutions and perhaps not even its independence. No amount of military strength, no success of anti-Communist diplomacy, no Marshall Plan, could in the long run prevent this. These, however necessary and beneficial, are stopgaps and futile in the end unless they are followed up by that assertion of world leadership which only the successful development of a Constitution for a Free Industrial Society can provide.

CHAPTER I

THE NEW SOCIAL ORDER

IN 1928, at the peak of the boom following World War I, Henry Ford officially proclaimed the New Millenium of mass-production; his article bore the significant title: "Machinery, the New Messiah." Technology was also seen as the decisive element in "Fordism" by Lenin—one of Ford's greatest admirers in the early twenties. His slogan, that Communism is "Socialism plus Electrification," indicates a completely technological view of the new principle he was so eager to adopt.

The easy optimism of these pioneering days has long since evaporated; the collapse of 1929 marked its end. But the opponents and critics of mass-production who have held the center of the stage since, also see the essence of mass production in a mechanical principle. Technology is the villain in Aldous Huxley's *Brave New World*, which, published at the bottom of the Depression, expressed the disappointment of the earlier hopes. It was the villain in Karel Capek's *R.U.R.*, which gave us the word "robot." It was the enemy in Charlie Chaplin's *Our Times*. However much the Henry Ford of "Machinery, the New Messiah" and the Charlie Chaplin of *Our Times* may differ as to the effect of the new development on man and his society, they agree on its nature. The revolutionary principle is a new technique, a new machine or a new way to utilize machines, a new arrangement of physical, inanimate forces. The very slogan of most of our discussions is the "subordination of man to the machine."

But if we actually analyze this new so-called technology, we shall find that it is not a "technology" at all. It is not an arrangement of physical forces. It is a principle of social order. This was true of Ford's work. He made not one mechanical invention or discovery; everything mechanical he used was old and well known. Only his concept of human organization for work was new.

The mass-production revolution is the culmination of a major change in the social order that has been going on since the Industrial Revolution began two hundred years ago. In the mass-production revolution the basic principles of industrialism have come to full maturity. And through the mass-production revolution they have become universal—world-wide as well as all-embracing. What started out as a technology two hundred years ago, has in the mass-production revolution grown into a society. In the mass-production principle we have not only a solvent of the traditional social order of pre-industrial society. We have *a new principle of social organization.*

Specialization and Integration

The essence of mass production lies in two new concepts: "specialization" and "integration." Both refer to the relationship between men working together.

At first sight these may seem to be very old and familiar principles. "Specialization" appears to be nothing more than the familiar "division of labor" on which all human activity beyond the most primitive rests. Likewise any productive effort which depends on the work of more than one person—which means, any productive effort with the possible exception of the work of the artist—may be said to depend on "integration."

As used to describe the order of mass production both terms undergo a radical change of meaning. Traditionally, "specialization" meant confinement to one product. The shoemaker stuck to his last and made shoes, the cabinet maker turned out furniture and left beams and rooftrees to the carpenter. The classical example for the international division of labor, the example which the free-trade theorists used again and again to show its benefits, was the concentration of Portugal, with its warm and dry climate, on wines, while cold and rainy England specialized in the production of wool. In the traditional division of labor, an activity is specialized if it confines itself to turning out the one product an individual or a country is best equipped to produce.

It may be argued that this is far too formalized and simplified a picture. The shoemaker, after all, did not work by himself but with a journeyman and a few apprentices, each producing parts. But this only points up the difference between the new and the old concepts of specialization. The master shoemaker could easily have made the entire shoes from beginning to end by himself. The number of man-hours needed for him to do the entire job would not have been any greater than the total number of man-hours needed by his team to turn out the shoe. The journeyman too could have turned out an entire shoe, though perhaps not so good a one. And while the apprentices may not have been able to do the whole job, and certainly would have wasted a good deal of time to produce an inferior product, they were supposed to learn to make the whole shoe and all operations connected with it. It was simply more productive to have journeymen and apprentices do the easier work than to have the master shoemaker do the whole by himself. The point, however, is that he could have done it. Journeymen and apprentices were either learners or helpers to the master craftsman, subordinated to, rather than coordinated with, his work.

In the sharpest possible contrast nobody in the mass-production organization has a "specialized skill." A man may have worked all his life in a shoe factory; after a few days' training he will be a fully efficient worker in an electrical equipment plant. This applies even to top-management jobs. It is indeed an axiom of modern management thought that a production vice president is equally capable of running a shoe factory and a steel rolling mill, a general sales manager as skilled in selling automobiles as in selling chemicals.

In the organization of work on the mass-production principle, the unit of individual work is not the product. The unit of work is one operation, if not one single motion. The product is the result of thousands of such operations, each performed by one operator. No one operator could possibly turn out a product, no matter how much time he took. Only the organization, the plant, can turn out a product. Of course, there are few, if any, industries or processes in which this ideal of the mass-production engineer, the confinement of the individual operator to one motion, has actually been reached. But the new "specialization" which divides labor, not according to ability to turn out a product, but by individual operation or single motion, is the guiding principle for the organization of industrial work today.

What this means socially we can see at once if we try to express the new concept in symbolic terms. One of the oldest and most universal symbols of the fulfilled life has been the hermit turning out shoes or tending his beehives—in other words, the man who completely devotes himself to a "specialized activity," old-style. But nothing could be further from being a symbol of the fulfilled life than a hermit tending a punch-press or forever putting rear bumpers on imaginary cars alone in the wilderness. The picture of a man all by himself on the empty heath tending a high-speed lathe is perhaps the most screaming, the most bitter, satire of our civilization that could be imagined; it is a picture of utter frustration, utter emptiness and complete damnation.

What is important is not that the new concept of specialization takes skill out of the work. The "elimination of skill" is more a myth than a reality. Totally unskilled operations play a minor part in most industries. It is in the organization of very highly skilled workers that the mass-production method often produces the greatest increases in efficiency and productivity. On the other hand, the traditional system had a multitude of totally unskilled operations. There is no skill to weeding or to picking potato beetles off the plants, nor is there much skill to pushing a wheelbarrow.

But the old operations, however unskilled, were always directly related to the product. If the man who performed an unskilled operation did not himself produce a product—the farmer, for instance, though he weeds, also plants and harvests—he was a helper to the man who turned out the product. In the new specialization, however, no one turns out the product, everybody is confined to operations or motions.

Because nobody in the social order of modern industry makes a product, "integration" also assumes a new meaning. A product can only be made if the operations and motions of a great many individuals are put together and integrated into a pattern. *It is this pattern that is actually productive, not the individual.* Modern industry requires a group organization far exceeding in forethought, precision and cohesion anything we have ever witnessed.

It was Henry Ford who provided the original example of integration on which all later industry has modeled itself. The co-ordination of the labor of men with the flow of materials which he developed in the twenties at the new River Rouge plant, synchronized and integrated not only the work of the 80,000 men working there and the materials and parts with which they worked. It attempted to carry the same integration of work, rhythm and timing all the way back to the stage of raw-material production and procurement— the digging of iron ore in Northern Michigan, or the tapping of rubber trees in Brazil—and forward into the sales of new cars by the dealers. This plan would have embraced the work of millions of men within a time span of two or three years. Ford's attempt itself failed—being both too ambitious and premature. But the Russian Five-Year Plans are essentially modeled after Ford's concept. And in the great landings on the European Continent during World War II, Ford's concepts were applied to masses of men much larger and to operations much more complex than any he had ever tried to deal with.

Mass production is actually a considerably more skilled system of production than any previous one. Much more new skill is required for integration than has been eliminated by specialization. However, the new skill is not manual, it is not knowledge of tools or of materials. It is partly technical and theoretical: knowledge of principles and processes. Partly it is social: skill in the organization of men for work in a close group and in fitting together their operations, their speeds and their abilities. Above all, the new "skill" required is the ability to see, to understand and even to produce a pattern; and that is by definition imaginative ability of a high, almost of an artistic, order.

One example which shows this clearly is the story of the difficulties encountered during the last war with the production of a carrier-based plane for the Navy. When Pearl Harbor came, this plane was the only tested model suitable for warfare in the Pacific; yet only a dozen or so had actually been made—and by a small firm of airplane designers. At once the Navy needed not dozens but thousands of these planes. The original designers were quite incapable of producing such quantities; they did not even have the blueprints needed for mass production, as they had built each plane by hand in their small workshop. One of the large companies took over, converted hastily some of its best plants, put its best engineers, mechanics and skilled workers to work and began producing the plane. Yet not one plane could actually be turned out until the theoretical work—the analysis of the plane; its breakdown into the component parts; the breakdown of each part into subassemblies; the breakdown of the subassemblies into individual operations and motions; and the reintegration of operations into subassemblies, of subassemblies into parts, of parts into the plane—had been completed. It was work done entirely on paper—with some hundred tons of blueprints as the yield. It was done entirely on the basis of general principles. Airplane experts proved of no value whatsoever. The actual job had to be done by men who had never worked on plane production before. It was a slow job, taking almost a year during which nothing was produced. But once it had been done, the plant went almost immediately into full production; five weeks after the last blueprint had been completed, the plant turned out planes at the rate of 6,000 a year.

Without the integration there would not only be no product; there would be no work for anybody. For the individual as well as for society, the really productive element in modern industrial society is a concept—one is tempted to say a vision: the view of the whole, the vision of a pattern. In this pattern no one man is by himself productive. But the pattern would become disorder, the entire organization would cease to make sense, production would stop altogether, were the least operation left undone. There is no one "decisive" operation, but also no single "unnecessary" one.

In its interplay between "specialization" and "integration"— between the fundamentally unessential and replaceable, and the fundamentally essential and irreplaceable, character of each and every operation—the social order of the mass-production technology reveals itself as basically a hierarchical order. But it is a hierarchy of a very peculiar kind.

It is not altogether unique. The little we know about the men who built the great medieval cathedrals indicates that they worked in a pattern of specialization and integration strikingly similar to the modern mass-production factory. Another analogy would be a ritual dance put on by a tribe, or a theatrical performance: certainly a troup of actors producing a play work together on pretty much the same basis. Closer still would be the analogy to a symphony orchestra.

These parallels serve, however, only to point up the novel features of the mass-production order. The dancer in a tribal group may have only one small part. He may know that he can never get a big part if, for instance, the big parts are reserved for the chiefs. But if his operation is sufficiently similar to that of the leading man, he can understand the work of the star and also see the whole and his relation to it. The tympani player in the orchestra will never play the first violin, let alone conduct. But he can read the score—indeed, he has to know it fairly well to be able to come in at the right moment. The same relationship existed between apprentice or unskilled helper in a cathedral "production line" and the great craftsman and artist on the one hand, and the cathedral itself on the other.

In the social pattern of mass production, however, the difference between operation and operation, between job and job is so profound, the specialization carried so far, that the worker can have no immediate understanding, usually not even a superficial knowledge, of the next job. The relationship to the product is even less clear. The whole and the relationship of the individuals to it is visible only to the few people at the top—the conductors, to use the analogy of the orchestra. They see the pattern, understand the order, experience the vision. But the great many below do not unaided see anything but chaos, disorder and non-sense; and the further they are away from the top, the less able are they to see sense, order and purpose.

The integration on which the mass-production order depends for its cohesion and productivity demands a very high, an almost unprecedentedly high, degree of imaginative and intellectual ability. It demands a degree of understanding and support on the part of the individual member of the organization that goes far beyond anything traditional society requires. Citizenship is much more important in the mass-production order—if by citizenship we mean the intelligent participation of the individual member in the whole—but citizenship is much more difficult to attain.

Nor is the difficulty confined to the manual worker, as is often believed. The new industrial middle class—the responsible but employed and subordinate technicians, engineers, supervisors, accountants, statisticians and branch managers—finds it just as difficult to integrate its operations with the work of the whole as the manual worker. This class is the most rapidly growing class in any modern industrial society. As we shall see, it is this class which is decisive in such a society. As a disillusioned Soviet wit prophesied twenty-five years ago, the inevitable development of history has not been toward the victory of the proletariat but toward the victory of the secretariat. Yet this class is as much a stranger to its own work as the men on the machines.

This "lack of communication"—to use a technical term for what is definitely not a technical problem—is inherent in modern industry and the distinguishing problem of its social order. Certainly, it cannot be solved by mechanical means, by publicity, by good intentions or by speeches—let alone by that magic abacadabra of modern management, the "Organization Chart." It requires new institutions. The mass-production principle will never be a functioning principle of the social order without the establishment of "communications." Industrial society itself will not be able to function or even to survive unless it appears to its members as rational—that is, unless the members see the relationship between their own work and purpose and the purpose and pattern of their society.

CHAPTER 2

THE ENTERPRISE IN MODERN SOCIETY

TO HENRY FORD the machine was the new and the important element of modern society. But in reality the new factor is not a mechanism but an institution: the modern large enterprise.

In every industrial country the enterprise has emerged as the *decisive*, the *representative* and the *constitutive* institution. It is very much the same institution whether it takes the form of the privately owned and independently managed corporation in the United States, of the government corporation of Britain's nationalized industries or of the Soviet "Trust" in a completely government-owned and government-controlled economy. Whether industrial society is organized under Capitalism, Socialism, Fascism, or Communism, the enterprise is its central institution, looks alike, behaves alike, and faces similar decisions and difficulties.

The industrial enterprise is an autonomous institution. It has its own law and rationale in its function. It is not a creature of the State. It does not rest its power on delegation from its shareholders or from any other owner; in fact, the divorce of control over the enterprise from ownership is everywhere all but complete. Its function is essentially beyond the control of the State and largely unaffected by even the most radical changes in political system or in political beliefs. It is the first autonomous local institution that has come into existence in our society in five hundred years. Its emergence brings back problems of political organization and national unity with which we have become quite unfamiliar.

Despite its importance and prominence, the enterprise is so very new a phenomenon that we do not even have a generally agreed or generally understood term for it. "Big business," though a literal description, is an emotional slogan, breathing resentment and bitterness. Also it is practically always used to describe privately owned enterprises; to apply it, for instance, to the Tennessee Valley Authority or the British Coal Board—both very big businesses indeed—would seem forced. "Corporation," which I used in my last book,[1] is understandable only in the United States; even here it has a narrow legal meaning that excludes for instance the huge monopoly enterprise of the Atomic Energy Commission.

"Industrial Enterprise" is obviously also unsatisfactory. It is not a term in common usage. It is not usually understood to comprise the labor union, which however (as we shall see) is part of the enterprise structure. But it is the best term we have so far and it will therefore have to do despite its shortcomings.

We not only lack a name for the new phenomenon. We lack an understanding of it. Everyone in an industrial country, certainly everyone in the United States takes the enterprise for granted and believes himself well acquainted with it. Actually, hardly anybody has ever taken a good long look at it, let alone analyzed and studied it. In the vast literature on the ills of our age, it is barely even mentioned.

We still think and talk of the basic problems of an industrial society as problems that can be solved by changing the "system," that is the superstructure of political organization. Yet the real problems lie within the enterprise. It is not the solution of the problems of the "system" that will set the structure of the enterprise. On the contrary, it is the solution of the problems of the enterprise that will shape the system under which we shall live.

This does not mean that there is no real difference between the ideologies whose battle rends our world—the thesis Mr. James Burnham put forth in his *Managerial Revolution* ten years ago. It means, on the contrary, that the differences are so great and so decisive precisely because they are at bottom differences over the ordering of the new institution. The great question of our time is: on what basis of values and beliefs and to what purpose are the problems of the enterprise to be solved? The task of those who believe in the values of the West and want to preserve them, is to build the enterprise on the beliefs and values of a free society. And while much of the analysis

---

[1] *Concept of the Corporation* (New York: The John Day Company, 1946). The English edition was called *Big Business*.

of the enterprise in this book is equally applicable to free-enterprise America, Socialist Britain, Communist Russia or Hitler Germany, the author very definitely and very strongly himself believes in a free society and demands therefore that the enterprise be a local self-government, neither swallowed up by, nor dependent upon, the central government.

It will be argued at once that the large industrial enterprise could not possibly have the decisive importance I ascribe to it because it constitutes a numerical minority. Certainly quantitatively it holds a small sector of the economy. In the United States it probably carries no more than a quarter of the total economic activity. Even in Russia, where even farming has been generally organized in large industrial enterprises, the majority of the people is likely to live outside of, and seemingly little touched by, the enterprise system.

But the quantitative is never decisive in a social structure—the great difference between the City of Man and the communities of the social insects such as ants or bees. What distinguishes American from Russian society—and both from that of the Zulu—cannot be found by statistical analysis.[2] What gives essence and form to a society is not the static mass but the dynamic leavening; not the multitude of facts but the symbol through which these facts are organized in a social pattern; not the preponderant nor the average, but the representative. The values, the beliefs, the social satisfaction, the image of society—even the livelihood and the mode of living—of the majority are actually determined by the representative institution of its society, however remote it might appear to be from their daily lives. We do not, therefore, have to be concerned because the big enterprise comprises only a small sector of society and economy, as long as we can show that it gives our society its quality.

The *decisive* character of the enterprise is displayed in its role in the economic process. The great majority of the people do not work for one of the large industrial enterprises. Yet their livelihood is directly dependent upon them. Any analysis of our economy shows that it is the big enterprises which occupy the strategic centers. The little businesses, the independents, the professionals, even the

[2] For a fuller discussion, see my *Concept of the Corporation*, Page 6.

farmers, gain their livelihood largely either as suppliers or as distributors for the big enterprise.

The enterprise determines economic policies and makes the economic decisions. A small number of big enterprises sets the wage pattern and establishes the "going wage" of the economy. The small businesses may, and very often do, deviate from this "going wage," but it is a deviation, that is, something which is measured by everyone against the norm set by the big enterprise.

The same applies to price policy. It applies to the decisions on capital expenditure and capital expansion programs, which, in the last analysis, decide the level of business activity and of employment. It applies even to the mood and outlook of the economy, its temper, its confidence, and its thinking.

The last war showed the technological leadership of the big enterprise. The greatest expansion of employment during the War took place in small business. But the burden of the conversion to war production was carried by the big enterprise. The big enterprise did the research and engineering. It developed the new products, the new methods, the new tools. It laid out the work, established the standards and organized production. It also took the orders and with them the risks. The small businesses came in as subcontractors to carry out work completely organized for them by the big enterprise. They were primarily fabricators, suppliers and assemblers.

It is the big enterprise which establishes the pattern of union-management relations. It is the big enterprise at which government control and government regulation of industry aim. Finally the big enterprise establishes the social pattern of the plant community for the entire society.

That the major expansion in profits during the boom after World War II occurred in small business and in farming was well known. Yet, when a Joint Congressional Committee was established in the fall of 1948 to consider whether profits were too high, every single one of the twenty-one industrialists heard represented a big enterprise—with the smallest employing about six thousand men. Neither the union representatives nor any of the other witnesses, such as economists or government officials, ever mentioned small business. Every one simply assumed that the profits of small business—though much larger in the aggregate than those of the big enterprises—had no decisive influence on the economy.

The Enterprise as Society's Mirror

The large industrial enterprise is also the *representative* institution of an industrial society. It determines the individual's view of his society. A man employed in a small shop, even a man employed in the corner cigar store, apparently far removed from the world of the big enterprise, still judges society by the extent to which its basic promises and beliefs are fulfilled in the big enterprise. He does not consider his own store typical; he considers U. S. Steel typical. His own relations with his employer may be excellent. Yet he will think of labor relations as poor and of the worker as exploited if the relations between the big enterprise and its workers are poor or poisoned. He will consider his society to give a high standard of living if the employee of the big enterprise enjoys a high standard. He will believe that his society fulfills its promise of equal opportunities if the enterprise gives adequate chances for advancement. In other words, the big enterprise is representative because it is accepted as such by the people in an industrial society.

This may be a sort of optical illusion. The large industrial enterprise—General Motors for instance, or United States Steel—is so much more visible than the corner cigar store. But the large enterprise is representative also in another way. It actually represents the new organizing principle of an industrial society in the purest and clearest form. Just as the crystal in the mineralogical cabinet only presents in perfect form the principle which the mineral always tends to follow in whatever shape it is found, so the enterprise only brings out, makes visible and realizes the crystalline structure which, though hidden and imperfectly realized, is the organizing principle of our entire society. To use another metaphor, the enterprise is the mirror in which we look when we want to see ourselves.

As an example, let me use the State in which I live: Vermont, thinly settled, poor, without one sizable city. Large-scale industry is totally absent. Nine out of ten factories employ fewer than fifty men; companies employing more than a thousand men can be counted on the ten fingers. Much of the industry—especially wood-working which is the biggest employer—is also marginal, producing goods for which there is not enough of a market to attract one of the big manufacturers elsewhere. In this State a determined effort is being made, through a State-founded and industry-supported Bureau of Industrial Research, to introduce into the very small units the production and marketing methods, and the principles of organization of the big enterprise.

Clearly these methods and principles can be used in the small business only to a very limited extent; small business can embody the organizing principle of the big enterprise only roughly, never in the pure crystal form. Yet, the Bureau of Industrial Research has successfully introduced the "production line" into a wood-working shop of five employees, and has used time-motion studies, scientific plant lay-out and assembly-line techniques in a furniture plant employing forty men. The important thing is not that these mass-production concepts and techniques could be applied to the small and unstandardized production of these tiny units. In fact, their application was most limited. What is important is that even this rudimentary use yielded very substantial results. It increased workers' output by a fifth, and cut costs and waste about the same. The efficiency and productivity of the small business and its ability to survive thus improve in direct proportion to its ability to copy the large enterprise. The structure, organization and principles of the big enterprise have become the norm against which even the small workshop with five employees has to measure itself. To use a term of the metaphysician, the big enterprise is the "entelechy," the developed realization of the inner, underlying principle of form and structure of our society.

Perhaps an even better illustration is the development of the Vermont family farm. The Vermont farmer, with his small holding, his poor, rocky soil and his very short growing season, has been specializing in dairy farming ever since the refrigerated railroad car made possible the long-distance shipment of milk. During the last twenty-five years the character of his specialization has been changing profoundly. Whereas previously he specialized in a product, he can now —with little exaggeration—be said to specialize in one process. He no longer grows his own fodder. In many cases he no longer raises his own calves. He feeds fodder grown in the Midwest and South to cows bought from a breeder. He also no longer processes the milk. He delivers the raw milk to a creamery which processes it and delivers it to a distributor. The distribution of this apparently so simple product is actually a most complicated job—organized entirely on mass-production principles, such as the breakdown of the operation into simple, component operations, the synchronization of the flow of materials and subassemblies, or the interchangeability of component parts. The farmer does not make his own butter; the butter he buys comes from Wisconsin or Iowa fifteen hundred miles away. Sometimes it is not even economical for him to keep his own milk for his own consumption, but cheaper to buy his supply in the store.

Outwardly little seems to have changed. Actually the Vermont dairy farmer—or the Iowa corn-hog farmer, the Minnesota wheat farmer, the citrus grower in California—has become a link in an agricultural assembly line. It would be difficult to say who his "management" is and where it is. But he is surely being managed. His processes, his policies, very largely even his actual operations are laid out for him by an organization over which he has very little control, even though it be a co-operative. His only freedom of action is to go on a "milk strike" (the very term is significant). The farmer's relationship to economy and society has become increasingly remote as well as increasingly complex. Integration has become as much a problem for him as it is a problem for the worker in the big mass-production plant. Almost as much as the man on the automobile assembly line, he needs to understand what he is doing and why; and he finds it almost as hard to obtain a view of the whole as does the unskilled worker in Detroit.

The big enterprise is the true symbol of our social order. Its internal order and its internal problems are considered the distinctive order and the pressing problems of an industrial society even by those who are not, apparently, affected directly. It is also the place where the real principles of our social order become clearly visible. Above all, in the industrial enterprise alone can the problems of our industrial society be tackled. The structure that we shall build in the industrial enterprise, the solutions we shall find—or fail to find—for its problems will thus decide the structure and the solutions of industrial society altogether.

The Divorce of Control from Ownership

The enterprise exists in essentially the same form in every industrial society no matter how organized; it is thus the *constitutive* institution. The industrial enterprise arises from the needs of industrial life rather than from the beliefs or principles underlying political organization.

One symptom of the autonomy of the enterprise is the process known in this country as the "divorce of control from ownership." With but few exceptions, all the very large enterprises in this country are no longer controlled by the stockholders. The stockholder is neither interested in controlling "his" business nor able to do so. Even in those few big corporations where ownership is still concentrated, the actual control is increasingly exercised by professional managements. The legal owners are represented on the Board of Directors but they take less and less part in the running of the business. Management considers them "outsiders" and resents any "interference" from them.

One of the best illustrations is that of America's foremost chemical company, Du Pont de Nemours. Stock control has always remained firmly in the hands of the founding family and is exercised through a family trust. Until twenty years ago management too was firmly in the hands of the family. But since then the top management positions have increasingly gone to professionals who came up through the ranks. Only the fiction of family control has been maintained; every one of the professional managers who actually run the company has been "adopted" into the family through marriage to a Du Pont daughter which followed—not preceded—his admission into the top group.[3] While this device has prevented managerial power from slipping out of the family altogether, it also shows that the large enterprise cannot do without the professional outside manager—even where the owners are an unusually close-knit, unusually numerous, unusually able family group with a long and highly successful record of family management.

Very similar was the development in the equally "dynastic" German steel industry in the twenty years between the First and the Second World Wars. Being originally the creation of an individual tycoon, every large German steel company was firmly controlled by one family. When the largest of these family enterprises were forced

---

[3] As a result the Department of Justice in the antitrust action begun in 1949 found it necessary to ask that all Du Ponts and *all their in-laws* be prohibited from holding General Motors stock!

to merge in the German Steel Trust during the middle twenties, the founding families retained both share-control and the desire to run the enterprises. But while the Thyssens, Krupp, Kloeckners, et al. grew still richer, while they increased their social prestige under the Republic as well as under Hitler, they increasingly lost managerial control of their own companies to their "hired hands," the professional managers. Their own considerable surprise and bafflement at this development comes out strongly in Fritz Thyssen's book on his relations with Hitler. The same thing happened during the same period in Britain's largest industrial company, Imperial Chemicals, as well as in the British steel industry.

In this country the "divorce of control from ownership" has been regarded widely as both undesirable and unnatural. Undoubtedly, it poses serious problems—though the one that is discussed most generally, that of the "legitimacy" of management power, has actually nothing to do with the divorce but arises in exactly the same form where the management of a big enterprise is still based on property. But the divorce is not only natural. It is also in the social interest. It expresses clearly the idea that the enterprise cannot and must not be operated in the interest of any one group: stockholders, workers or consumers, but in the interest of society, that is, as we shall see, in the interest of economic performance. Without the divorce we could neither isolate nor resolve the basic political and social problems of an industrial society.

The Marxist will assert that the divorce of control from ownership can happen only in a capitalist country; indeed, he may interpret it as a symptom of the internal dissolution of capitalism. But exactly the same process goes on no matter who holds the legal title of ownership. The most conspicuous examples of autonomous management in Britain are to be found in the nationalized enterprises—precisely because they are the largest enterprises in the country. In the few years of their existence, the managements of the British Coal Board and of British Transport have proven themselves quite as independent of the control of their legal owner, the State, as the management of the large privately-owned American corporation is of its shareholders. Their policies, their decisions, their mode of operations have by necessity been "enterprise-oriented." They behave like managements.

The same thing has been happening in Russia, as is shown by the emergence of the management group as a major organized center of power in Russian politics—side by side with Communist Party, Red Army and Secret Police. It shows even better in the frantic attempts of the political powers to keep the management group under the control of the "legal owners," the government, through police terror, close supervision by Party officials and increasing centralization of all decisions. All this bespeaks growing uneasiness and concern over the tendency of the managements of the large industrial enterprises to slip out of control.

Industrial Society Is a Pluralist Society

The enterprise is an *autonomous institution*. It does not derive its power and function from the motives, purposes or rights of its owners, whoever they may be. It does not derive its structure, aims and purposes from the political or legal organization of society. It has a "nature" of its own and follows the laws of its own being. Historically, the enterprise of today is the successor to the firm of yesterday. Legally, the enterprise is a creature of the State and nothing but a legal fiction. In nature and function, however, the enterprise is *sui generis*.

This does not mean that it is impossible for the State to exercise any control over the enterprise. Nor need industrial society degenerate into an industrial feudalism in which effective authority will pass to the enterprise, with the State reduced to the empty dignity of a figurehead. On the contrary, industrial society requires a very strong and powerful central government. The enterprise is not an equal to the central government of the State. The power of both management and union has to be limited and their conduct regulated. Great care has to be taken that the seat of sovereignty not be usurped by the big business enterprise or the big labor union, and that they remain properly subordinate to the national policy and the national welfare.

Both the State and the enterprise have, however, to be organized on the same basic beliefs and principles. An industrial society cannot survive if the social beliefs and values which the enterprise fulfills, contradict the beliefs and values which society professes. Such a clash would cause constant friction and conflict. The citizen demands of the representative institution that it fulfill sufficiently the promises on which society rests. Society will lose its rationality and cohesion if the enterprise denies the social beliefs or if it fails to give them adequate fulfillment. Either the beliefs themselves will become meaningless, or society will become a failure and will lose the allegiance of its citizens.

But society too must be organized so that the enterprise can function. Economic policy and political control must of course always focus on the common weal. But if the basic requirements of the enterprise have to be denied for the sake of the common welfare, society will become split against itself. We will not be able to maintain a free and functioning society if we fail in either task. We will, for the sake of function, have to sacrifice freedom and become totalitarian. Or we will, for the sake of freedom, sacrifice function and tumble into anarchy.

The emergence of the industrial enterprise may herald a basic reversal of the trend that has prevailed in Western history ever since the collapse of the medieval order. The totalitarian State of our days marks the reduction to absurdity—criminal, wicked, insane absurdity—of the trend toward the State as the sole center, the sole focus and the sole power that began in the fifteenth century. Certainly, the enterprise is the first autonomous institution to emerge since then. The modern political party and the modern army are both institutions of the modern world, and highly important ones. But they are by and of the State—even though the party started out as an illegitimate and unwanted child which the parent had tried hard to abort. The enterprise, however, is independent of the State in its origin as well as in its function. It is an organ of society rather than one of the State.

The problems of industrial society are thus *problems in pluralist organization.* There is not one prime mover in our society but at least two: State and enterprise. These two have to live in harmony, or they will not live at all.

CHAPTER 3

THE ANATOMY OF ENTERPRISE

THIS new institution, the industrial enterprise, presents itself in three major aspects:

(1) Its physical aspect: the enterprise is of necessity big.

(2) Its impact on the social structure of society: the enterprise has brought into being two new classes—a ruling group of industrial executives and union leaders; and a new industrial middle class of technicians, professionals, foremen, accountants, middle-managers, etc., a class enjoying both considerable power and great social prestige, yet employed, dependent and subordinate.

(3) The functions which it discharges: at one and the same time it is an economic, a governmental and a social institution.

The "curse of bigness" has been a familiar theme in American political discussion for fifty years or so. That bigness is neither necessary nor efficient—let alone desirable—has been a standard argument.

Certainly, there are definite limitations on the size of an enterprise economically, socially and managerially. But the "small business" which today's enemies of bigness have in mind as their ideal is actually a very big business measured by any earlier standard. The question is no longer, do we want big or small business? It is how big can the big enterprise become before it is too big?

The shift in our usage of the term "big business" is a striking commentary on the impact of the mass-production revolution. Fifty or sixty years ago "the big business," "the octopus," was a unit employing between two and five thousand men; the "small business" was a workshop owned and run by one or two men, and employing one hundred men or less. Today "small business" in the important American industries is an enterprise employing five to ten thousand people and run by a managerial group of two hundred men. Today we can only talk about degrees of bigness. In an industrial society there is no possibility of a return to the "family-size business." The industrial enterprise by necessity represents a large concentration of power, of capital investment and of people.

The same change in size has occurred in the labor union. The nation-wide industrial union of today compares to the "chapel" in which skilled craftsmen organized seventy-five or a hundred years ago, as does the large corporation to the machine shop of the Victorian Age. Even the local unit of the large union is in many cases very large. The Ford Local of the United Automobile Workers, with its 65,000 members, is as unique as Ford's River Rouge plant where these men all work. But in extreme form it represents the pattern.

We called the bigness of the enterprise its physical aspect. But the change has been so great as to be qualitative in its effect on both enterprise and society. It is like the change from the grain of sand to the sand pile which, though but a heap of grains, is yet something entirely different.

The bigness of enterprise and union creates problems of social control which never existed before. A measure of their newness as well as of their complexity is given by the struggle to adapt the old concept of monopoly with its focus on deliberate action in restraint of trade to the new situation in which mere size—without any monopolistic action or intention—is accused of producing all the effects of market domination. The bigness of the unit and the amount of capital required to produce effectively under modern industrial conditions shift the focus of the monopoly problem from the economic to the social sphere. The problem is now one of entrance into an industry for the individual or for the small and young business, rather than of high prices and low production.

The very bigness of the modern enterprise makes its stability and preservation a concern of society. The big enterprise cannot be allowed to collapse. The effect of such a collapse on the economic stability of society in the form of unemployment, financial shock and disruption of established trade routes would be much too great. The economic loss to society from a dispersal of the resources of the big enterprise would also be tremendous. The machines, the plants, and the human organization are only productive together; torn asunder, they lose much if not all of their productivity. The great industrial empires which collapsed during the Depression, those of Insull or Kreuger, for instance, had to be preserved—right through their bankruptcy—in basically unchanged form, even though they had been jerry-built in the first place. Changes in the bankruptcy laws of every major industrial country during the last twenty years have come to give priority to the maintenance of the "going concern," that is, of the organization of mechanical and human resources, over the claims of any one group, whether creditors, workers or stockholders.

As regards the internal structure of the enterprise, bigness has produced profound qualitative changes. The enterprise must have a management whose responsibility is to the enterprise rather than to any one group: owners, workers or consumers. The emergence of a "professional" management is perhaps the best proof that the enterprise is an institution. The organization of management, its proper functioning, the selection, development and training of properly qualified executives, and the code and ethos of management have become major problems, in which society has as much of an interest as the business enterprise itself.

The leader of a big union similarly exercises managerial functions. His responsibility too is primarily to the union rather than to its members. That the union leader is capable of discharging his duties is as much the concern of society as is the problem of a functioning management.

Bigness has also profoundly changed the relationship between enterprise and employee from one that was predominantly economic to one that is primarily political and social. To discharge its responsibility for the enterprise, management has had to assume governmental authority over the members of the enterprise.

The New Classes

The emergence of the enterprise has radically altered the pattern of society by creating two new classes: the new ruling group of executives and union leaders, and the new middle class; neither existed sixty or seventy years ago.

Numerically, the new ruling group is not very large, though it may be larger than any previous ruling group in history. But it is as powerful, as much in the limelight and as characteristic of our society as any earlier ruling group.

It is, however, the emergence of the new middle class which may turn out to be the decisive social development of mass-production society. This group has been growing the most rapidly and will continue to grow rapidly. In the United States, for instance, the employed middle class accounted for less than ten per cent of the working population in the census of 1880. By 1940 it had risen to more than twenty-five per cent; and it is likely to number almost one-third in the 1950 census. In absolute numbers, this means a rise from five to forty-five or fifty million men and their families.

All the older classes have lost ground meanwhile. The mass-production revolution has completed the destruction of the power and position of the land-owning aristocracy of the *"ancien régime"* which began two-hundred years ago. But it has also dethroned the ruling groups of bourgeois society itself: the merchants, bankers, capitalists. Symbolic of this is the slow but steady decay of the great merchant oligarchies: the "City" in London, "Wall Street" in New York, "State Street" in Boston, etc. Where only twenty years ago the bright graduate of the Harvard Business School aimed at a job with a New York Stock Exchange house, he now seeks employment with a steel, oil or automobile company. It is not only that credit has become less important than industrial capacity to produce. The old money powers have lost control over money and credit, as witness the shift of the financial headquarters from Wall Street to the government agencies in Washington and from the City to the British Treasury.

Economically, the nationalization of the Bank of England was quite unimportant and not much more than a polite bow to a popular, but sadly outdated, slogan of the Labor Party. Long before, the banks, including the Bank of England, had become fully subservient to the government, so much so that they had become little more than repositories for government bonds. There is very little room in an industrial economy for the international banking, international capital movements, and international commodity-trading on which the power and position of the "capitalist" ruling groups rested primarily—in London, in New York and Boston, in Amsterdam, Paris, Berlin, Frankfort and Vienna. But as a political symbol the nationalization of the Bank of England was of major importance—and so, in its way, was the conversion of the House of Morgan into a deposit bank divorced entirely from the securities business. These two events marked the disappearance of "finance capitalism."

Likewise, the old middle class has declined in importance. Seventy years ago this old pre-industrial class of independent and small businessmen, independent professionals and family-farmers was practically the only middle class in existence. It offered the main channel for social advancement. It has not declined much in numbers; but it has sharply declined in proportionate importance—from thirty-seven per cent of the U. S. population in 1880 to eighteen per cent in 1940, with the downward trend accelerated since. Thus it is no longer the only or even the main avenue of social advancement. The young men who graduated from the American colleges in 1949 overwhelmingly pinned their hopes on a career in management. And the nominally independent small businessman has, in very many cases, become a part of the enterprise structure in all but name; the "independent" who sells only the gasoline of one company at a price established by the company and in a gas station built by the company, or the "independent" who sells only the cars of one company at the price set by the company and on the basis of a franchise freely revocable by the company, are only two—and two not very extreme —examples.

The most important phenomenon in the long run is, however, that the industrial working class—that first child of the Industrial Revolution—has passed its peak both in absolute numbers and in its proportionate weight. In this country in 1940 it accounted for roughly the same percentage of the population as it did seventy years ago— just under forty per cent. All indications are that the percentage will decline in the future, if the decline has not already begun. In the new industries the ratio of manual workers is much smaller, that of the industrial middle class much higher than in the older industries. As the older industries are modernizing—and the process is running along at high speed—they too will employ proportionately fewer wage earners and more salaried middle-class men.

Also within the working class a new shift from unskilled to skilled labor has begun—reversing the trend of the last fifty years.[1]

[1] See the analysis of the trends from 1910 to 1948 in "Industrial and Occupational Trends in National Employment" Research Report No. 11, (Philadelphia: University of Pennsylvania Press, 1949).

The unskilled worker is actually an engineering imperfection, as unskilled work, at least in theory, can always be done better, faster and cheaper by machines. But the more machines replace the unskilled man, the more men are needed to design these machines, to build them, to arrange them for production, to service them and to repair them. The new skills are not manual skills, though their practitioner may be called a mechanic. They are basically intellectual skills: knowledge of engineering principles, draftsmanship, shop mathematics, metallurgy, production engineering, etc. Increasingly the worker is being converted into a member of the new industrial middle class, into a new petty bourgeois.

In the glass industry, for instance, manual labor has been eliminated almost completely. The only "workers" on the floor are a handful of highly trained and highly paid specialists who know what to do if things go wrong. But the number of people needed to design, set up, service and repair the machines which do the work formerly done by unskilled or semiskilled men, is probably larger—it certainly is not smaller—than the number of manual workers displaced by the machine. Another example of this trend is the chemical industry. There are practically no manual workers in the newer fields, such as petroleum chemistry or plastics; but the number of trained, skilled and educated men to keep the plants working is prodigious and steadily on the increase.

To call our society "laboristic," as one of our prominent economists[2] has recently called it, may be an adequate summing up of the last, rather than an apt description of the next, fifty years. We may doubt the replacement of the working class by the new middle class, which Georges Friedmann,[3] Europe's most distinguished student of the social problems of mass production, predicts. But in the already industrialized countries there certainly will be no further increase in the proportionate strength of the working class—there has been none for seventy years anyhow. The trend toward greater prominence of the new industrial middle class—numerically as well as proportionately— will continue.

[2] Sumner Slichter of Harvard.
[3] Cf. his *Automatisme et Travail Industriel, Cahiers Internationaux de Sociologie*, Vol. I (Paris, 1946).

The Triple Personality of the Enterprise

The enterprise may finally be analyzed from the point of view of its function. It is an institution, but what kind of institution?

It is an *economic* institution, designed to perform vital economic functions. It is the major economic tool of an industrial society.

Viewed as an economic institution, the important fact about the enterprise is that it is a collective. The producer is actually the organization of large groups of men standing in a definite relationship to each other as well as to the mechanical tools. By himself, the human being, whether worker or manager, is incapable of producing.

The enterprise by necessity requires a large, long-term capital investment. The investment made today will not be productive for a long time. After it has started to be productive, it must continue to produce for a considerable time before the investment is repaid. This is obvious in respect to the mechanical equipment, the buildings, machines, etc. We have also learned that it is true for a supply organization or for a sales organization, as well as for the product itself. It applies just as well, however, to the human organization, which also requires both a huge capital investment and a long period of time to become productive.

The time unit of industrial economics must therefore be different from the time unit of pre-industrial economics. The "present" of industrial production is not a moment, a day or a year, but a long period, either that of the business cycle or that of the physical life of the equipment. Moreover, the future is as important an element in industrial production as the present. In industrial economics the present must always be focused on the future. This, as we shall see, gives an entirely new meaning to such traditional terms as "profit," "income," "cost," etc.

But the enterprise is also a *governmental* institution, inevitably and necessarily discharging political functions.

The enterprise controls the access to the productive organization, without which the individual is unable to produce. The enterprise thus controls access to the citizen's livelihood. And there has never been any doubt that whoever controls access to the citizen's livelihood exercises political control.

Access to the productive organization determines the citizen's social effectiveness, if not indeed his very citizenship. The purpose of production may vary: it may be subsistence or economic betterment, worship of the gods, or war. But the social organization of the community's productive effort is the frame within which the member becomes effective, obtains standing and prestige, acquires social identity. The very name by which he is known has, in the West, been largely derived from his trade and occupation.

But even if it should not be a general law that social effectiveness depends on access to the productive organization, it is certainly true of industrial society. If we learned anything from the Great Depression, it was that the unemployed is cut off from social effectiveness, that he loses standing, social identity and self-respect, and that he is in effect cut off from any but the most nominal citizenship.[4] Long-term unemployment disfranchises.

In its internal organization too the enterprise is a government. The organization of industrial production requires an internal order based on authority and subordination, that is, on power relationships.

The authority in the enterprise exercises regular governmental functions. It is a law-making body, laying down rules for the individual's behavior and for the settlement of conflicts. It establishes and inflicts the penalties for the infraction of these rules. With separation from the enterprise through dismissal carrying the threat of unemployment —that is, of denial of access to effectiveness—the penal power of the enterprise is great indeed. To use traditional terms, the enterprise has considerably more than the "low jurisdiction." Only in a totalitarian state will it ever have the "high jurisdiction" of capital punishment. But it has what the lawyer has always considered almost an alternative to the "high jurisdiction," namely the power of banishment and of suspending a man's civic rights.

The enterprise also has considerable executive powers over its members. It makes decisions and sets policies that affect the individual's livelihood, his future and his social and economic standing. It tells him what to do, when and where. It organizes an amorphous mass into a functioning and productive group.

The governmental nature of the enterprise shows in the conflict be-

[4] On this we have a wealth of documentary material, especially the studies made by E. W. Bakke in this country and in England.

tween management and union, which is primarily a conflict over power. The union demands a share in the power to give or to deny access to the organization: in demanding that employment be made dependent upon union membership; in demanding that disciplinary action, including dismissal, be based on contractual rules agreed to by the union and carried out through a formal process in which the union participates; finally, through the strike, by means of which the union attempts to turn the tables and to *deny the enterprise* access to the productive organization.

Above all, the conflict between management and the union is one over the allegiance of the members of the enterprise. Wherever we speak of allegiance, we deal with a governmental institution. Allegiance is the basis of governmental authority. The origin of the term in the relationship between lord and vassal shows this very clearly. We are lax in the use of most of our political and social terms. But we have always been precise and careful in the use of the word "allegiance" to describe only that relationship between an authority and its subjects which we call a political relationship, and which endows the authority with governmental power.

The first demand on any governmental organ is that it be able to function. Machiavelli taught us that before we can demand a "good" government we must make sure that we have a government capable of governing, that is, a functioning government. This raises questions regarding the management function, the management organization, the qualification and training of management personnel, and the orderly and rational succession within management. These seemingly internal problems of the enterprise are thus endowed with considerable public interest.

Also raised is the question of management's responsibility to its subjects, the members of the enterprise. Like any other government, management must be legitimate, that is it must exercise its authority in the interest of those it governs. But the first responsibility of management is the responsibility for economic performance. Here is a basic split between the enterprise's economic function and its governmental authority. This conflict underlies the emergence of the trade union and defines the union's functions.

But the union itself stands in a position of conflict. Its function is to be in opposition; it can discharge its function, survive, and maintain its cohesion only as an *antibody*. At the same time it must accept responsibility, both toward society and toward the enterprise, for the survival and prosperity of the enterprise. It must be a "loyal opposition" even though it can never become itself the government. And the coexistence of management and union in conflict puts the individual member of the enterprise into a perpetual conflict of loyalties, into a "split allegiance," which is bearable for neither enterprise, union nor individual.

It will be readily admitted by everyone that the enterprise is an economic institution. In the last quarter-century we have come to accept the enterprise as a social institution. But that it functions as a government is likely to be disputed vehemently both on the Right and on the Left.

This refusal to accept the consequences of the enterprise's governmental character is not only shortsighted; it is dangerous. It is especially dangerous to a "free-enterprise" society. Refusal on the part of the enterprise to accept its government responsibility and to work on the solution of the problems of political structure and government within the enterprise will almost certainly destroy a "free-enterprise" system. The political problems have to be solved. If the enterprise itself does not solve them by developing a functioning and legitimate government, the national government will inevitably be brought in by public pressure; and collectivism will take over by default. One look at the history of the West in the last fifty years shows how far the process has already gone.

The Plant Community

The enterprise, finally, discharges social functions. It contains the plant community, which in an industrial society is the distinctive and representative social unit.

Every study of workers shows that they consider the social function of the enterprise the most important one. They place the fulfillment of their demands for social status and function before and above even the fulfillment of their economic demands. In survey after survey the major demands of industrial workers appear as demands for good and close group relationships with their fellow workers, for good relations with their supervisors, for advancement, and above all, for recognition as human beings, for social and prestige satisfactions, for status and function. Wages, while undoubtedly important, rank well down the list.

That the enterprise is a social institution is a most flagrant denial of the dominant beliefs of the late nineteenth century. Thirty, perhaps only twenty-five, years ago it would have been ridiculed as rank nonsense, or condemned as a subversive and revolutionary slogan by industrialists and businessmen as well as by union leaders. Today the same industrialists have accepted the new doctrine and are busily attempting to translate it into action in the form of "modern personnel administration" and "modern human-relations policies."

Actually, the thesis that the enterprise is a social institution is very old. It antedates even the industrial system. It was first put by the French "Romantic Socialists," particularly by Fourier and Saint-Simon, in the opening years of the nineteenth century, when the industrial enterprise as we know it today was still far in the future. But it is only during the last generation that we have rediscovered this old insight.

So many people have contributed to this rediscovery that only a few studies can be mentioned here. Best known in this country is the *Hawthorne Study* made at the Western Electric Company in Chicago under the leadership of Elton Mayo during the late twenties and early thirties. Mayo himself summarized the work in two short books, *The Human Problems of an Industrial Civilization* and *The Social Problems of an Industrial Civilization.* Fuller presentations are *Management and the Worker* by Roethlisberger and Dickson, and T. N. Whitehead's *The Industrial Worker.*

Entirely different in approach and emphasis, but equally productive, were the studies made by E. W. Bakke of the unemployed worker in England and in the United States. Yet another approach was taken in the investigation conducted by A. W. Jones in Akron, Ohio in the mid-thirties and published under the title of *Life, Liberty and Property.*

One of the most comprehensive studies is the "Contest" which General Motors conducted among its employees in 1947, and which yielded 175,000 individual essays for *My Job and Why I Like It* written by the men themselves. There has been no time yet to publish more than the very first results, which appeared during 1949 in *Personnel Psychology.*

Of work outside the United States, I would only mention the studies of· the effects of unemployment on the individual, his family and his community, made by Paul F. Lazarsfeld and Marie Jahoda in the early twenties in Austria; the pioneer work of the English industrial psychologists around Professor Myers; and the brilliant and original researches of Georges Friedmann in France, especially his *La Crise du Progrès*, published in 1936.

These studies—and many others—differ in their purposes, their methods and their focus. But they all show conclusively that the plant community is a real community, indeed that it is the community which appears to the member of the enterprise as the representative and decisive one for the fulfillment of his social aspirations and beliefs.

Nothing stands out more emphatically in all our research than the individual's demand for social status and social function. Lack of this fulfillment creates profound individual and social dissatisfactions, tensions and frustrations, and poisons the entire social organizations of the enterprise.

Yet the industrial enterprise must give the individual social status and social function not only to propitiate him but to satisfy its own basic requirements. For the proper functioning of the industrial enterprise, its members, down to the last sweeper and wheelbarrow-pusher, must have a "managerial attitude" toward their own work and toward the enterprise; they must look upon it as their own and upon themselves as "citizens" rather than as "subjects." To be productive and efficient, the enterprise needs the abilities, initiative and co-operation of every member more than any other previous system of production. Its human resources are its greatest asset—and the one least used. The more the member of the enterprise regards himself as a "citizen," the more he acquires the "managerial attitude," the more productive and efficient will he be. The major incentives to productivity and efficiency are social and moral rather than financial.

As a social institution, the industrial enterprise is the carrier of a specific principle of social organization, the principle of mass-production technology. This social organization poses problems of its own, and requires for its functioning specific relationships between the individual member and the enterprise.

Finally, the industrial enterprise is definitely regarded by its members as the *representative* social institution of an industrial society. It must fulfill the beliefs and promises of its society by giving social status and function in the plant community. Otherwise the ethos of society and the order of society's representative institution will be at cross purposes, which can only result in the moral disintegration of society or in the functional disintegration of the enterprise.

The enterprise is an economic, a governmental, and a social institution, and it is all three at one and the same time.

It is easy enough to develop economic or governmental or social solutions for the specific problems of the enterprise. But no solution can possibly be accepted by the enterprise unless it satisfies at one and the same time all three aspects. A solution which does violence to the requirements of the enterprise as a governmental institution or as a social institution in order to resolve a conflict in the economic sphere, is unacceptable and impractical. It can only aggravate the very difficulty it attempts to solve.

In this book an attempt will be made to look upon the enterprise as a whole, that is as an institution discharging all three different functions at the same time. In our *analysis* we have to separate the functions to come to grips with the problems. But in developing an *approach towards the principles* of *industrial order* we will always have to be conscious of the three-fold function of the enterprise, and will talk of the enterprise as a whole.

The Primacy of Economic Performance

The governmental and the social functions must be most important to the member of the enterprise. But to the enterprise itself, as well as to society, its function as our central economic institution must always be the most important one and take priority over the other functions. It must be the most important function for the enterprise because the enterprise's survival is dependent on the efficient performance of its economic responsibility. It must be most important for society because, from society's point of view, economic performance is the purpose of the enterprise and its justification.

We have never, in recorded history, known a governmental and social institution that was subordinated to economic performance. The feudal manor had to feed its members. Yet food production was not its main purpose, which was governmental and social. The market—insofar as it ever was a reality—put economic performance first. But by definition it did not discharge governmental or social functions. Indeed the sharp separation of the economic sphere from the governmental sphere in *laissez-faire* theory was meant to establish the complete independence of the two functions.[5] In the enterprise, however, no such separation is possible. The functions are discharged in and through the same institution and carried by the same organs. At the same time, the decisive function of the enterprise, the criterion of its decisions and the yardstick of its success, is economic performance.

This accounts for some of the most difficult problems of the enterprise. It underlies the economic conflicts within the enterprise: the wage issue, the workers' resistance to technological progress, and the workers' rejection of profitability and profit. It also underlies the political problem of the enterprise, the problem of management as a legitimate government, which in turn has led to the emergence of the union as a permanent opposition to management and enterprise.

Altogether the primacy of the economic performance over governmental and social functions is so unprecedented as to require extended analysis. Before we can go on to the problems of an industrial order, therefore, we will have to discuss why profitability is the law of the enterprise.

[5] That this separation was untenable and that the resulting conflict between the economic rationale of the market and the survival of society explains the collapse of the market system has been cogently argued by Karl Polanyi in *The Great Transformation* (New York: Farrar & Rinehart, Inc., 1944; published in England in 1946 under the title of *Origins of Our Time*).

CHAPTER 4

THE LAW OF AVOIDING LOSS

NOTHING shows more clearly how deeply we are still entrapped in pre-industrial thinking than our preoccupation with "profit." The central fact of industrial economics is not "profit" but "loss"—not the expectation of ending up with a surplus, its justification, and the legitimacy of the claims to a share in it; but the inevitable and real risk of ending up with an impoverishing deficit, and the need, the absolute need, to avoid this loss by providing against the risks.

The central importance of loss is the one thing that sets modern industrial economy apart from pre-industrial economics. It expresses the two basic innovations: The economic unit of an industrial economy is not an individual but an enterprise, which means an organization of a great many people and a heavy fixed investment of capital. The economic activity of an industrial economy is not the "trade" taking place in the almost timeless instant of exchange, but production over a very long period. Neither the organization (the human resources) nor the capital investment (the material resources) are productive in the "here-and-now" of the present. It will be years before the organization or the investment will begin to produce, and many more years before they will have paid for themselves.

An industrial system therefore has two kinds of costs: current costs—the "costs of doing business"; and future costs—the "costs of staying in business." When we ordinarily speak of cost we rarely include any but "current costs": payments for raw materials, wages, salaries, etc. The cost concept of the accountant is confined mainly to the visible and tangible costs of the present, the costs of resources such as material and labor actually used up in the productive process. It does not include, on the whole, the cost of the capital resources, material but also human, needed in the future to keep the enterprise productive. *But in an industrial system the future costs, the "costs of staying in business," are the decisive ones.*

This is in the sharpest possible contrast to the model of the "trading economy" as it was developed by Ricardo who gave to nineteenth-century economics its basic concepts and terms, its major tools, and above all its attitude and mood. Ricardo was a stockjobber, and he constructed his model of economic activity in his own image. No other business could have furnished so good a model of a trading economy as the stockjobber, who is the perfect "economic man in the market." But none seems as ill-suited to serve as the model for an industrial economy. The stockjobber works without employees and without organization. The time element does not enter into his activity. He turns over his entire capital immediately, for he has to clear the books and liquidate all positions every day. Every morning the stockjobber starts business anew, as it were from scratch. Every evening he liquidates his business completely. His is a timeless world very much like the universe of the classical physicists. Indeed, the time concept of classical as well as Marxist economics is very much like the ether of the classical physicists—everything is placed in time but nothing ever happens in time.

Ricardo still dominates our economic thought—orthodox or heterodox, Marxist, Liberal or Conservative. There are indeed signs of a shift. There is, for instance, the revival of pre-Ricardian ways of economic thinking. The very idea of a war economy, with its emphasis on "flow" and "bottlenecks," as well as the whole theory of national-income analysis on which our financial and fiscal policies are increasingly based, hark back to the eighteenth-century economists whom Adam Smith and Ricardo were supposed to have refuted forever. The resemblance between the once celebrated *"Tableau Economique"* of Quesnay—the masterpiece of the Physiocrats—and a national-income table is much more than superficial; war production and allocation charts are *"Tableau Economique"* pure and simple. Antedating the Physiocrats were the Mercantilists and the Cameralists of the seventeenth-century, whom Keynes and others have revived because they thought in terms of an economic institution, the State, rather than in terms of the "isolated individual in the market."

But by and large we have not yet developed an adequate theory of industrial economics—even though the two pioneering studies: Frank

H. Knight's *Risk, Uncertainty and Profit* and Joseph Schumpeter's *Theory of Economic Development* were both written more than thirty years ago. And no mere revival of seventeenth- or eighteenth-century thinking will give us the concepts, the methods and the tools to analyze, to understand and to control our industrial economy.

Yet we know the central facts:

(1) Whereas a trading economy focuses on the past, an industrial economy focuses on the future. A trading economy consisted of an infinite number of individual and unconnected transactions; an industrial economy consists of a steady and long-term process of production carried on by large organizations of human and mechanical resources.

(2) In a trading economy all costs are in the past. The surplus of current income over past costs is "profit." It is measured by comparing the present income with the past outlay; it is a projection of the present on the past. Its explanation must, therefore, lie in the past. Since "functioning" always entails a projection of the present on the future, the "profit" of traditional economics cannot have a function. All it can have is a justification and an explanation.

(3) But in an industrial economy the costs are as much in the future as they are in the present—and they are never in the past. The future, however, is always unknown, unpredictable and uncertain. Future costs are risks. The difference between current costs and current production—the "surplus" of a trading economy—constitutes, in an industrial economy, the "premium" for these risks of the future, for these "costs of staying in business." While this surplus is called "profit" in both cases, its nature is entirely different in the two economies. In a trading economy the problem of "profit" is primarily a moral one—not to say a theological one: Who is entitled to the profit, what justifies it? In an industrial economy the problem is primarily one of function: What are the risks, how large are they, is today's apparent profit large enough to cover them?

(4) Finally, it is clear that the problem of the adequate coverage of these risks must be the central problem of an industrial economy; its solution determines economic performance. "Loss," to use the standard definition, is a decrease in the ability to produce economically useful goods; it is a shrinkage of productive potential. Popularly this is expressed—and correctly—in the saying that continued loss can be

met only by eating up productive resources. An individual who operates at a loss becomes poorer; and so does an enterprise, or an economy. The risk of future loss, therefore, endangers the ability for future economic performance. And the only way to prevent future loss from eating into productive resources, impoverishing the economy and cutting economic performance, is by setting aside today adequate reserves against the risks of tomorrow—reserves which obviously can only come out of the difference between current costs and current production.

The Future Costs of Industrial Production

There are four major "costs of staying in business": *replacement, obsolescence, risk proper* and *uncertainty*. All four have to be covered out of current costs for the enterprise to survive and to be able to perform its social function.

Replacement and obsolescence concern the productive equipment, risk and uncertainty the product. The first two affect the ability to turn out the goods desired by society. The last two affect the desir-ability of the goods which the enterprise is equipped to produce.

Obsolescence and uncertainty are entirely unknown in a pre-industrial society. They are the specific risks of an industrial system. Risk and uncertainty, while not totally absent under pre-industrial conditions, become both so much larger and so much more difficult to assess the further an economy industrializes, as to change character altogether.

Replacement is the only one of the four risks that can be calculated by fairly strict methods. It is the only one, therefore, that can be treated in the same fashion as current costs: as "depreciation" of existing equipment by so much every year, or as "amortization" of past investment at a fixed annual rate. The problems of replacement, while very difficult, are therefore mainly technical. That no enterprise and no economy will remain able to produce unless they replace old and outworn equipment is obvious. Even so, our replacement concept today takes into account only the mechanical equipment. But the human resources of production wear out just as much as the machines. They too have to be replaced; and their replacement cost is an inevitable charge against current production, no matter how it is defrayed.

Obsolescence is, by and large, neither considered a genuine cost of staying in business nor properly provided for. Yet it is a much more serious risk than that of ordinary replacement.

In an industrial economy we cannot assume that the economic life and the physical life of equipment are of the same duration. Equipment may still be fully productive; it may even be brand-new. And yet it may have become economically unproductive through an advance in the art, or through a new process. The *rate of change* is in itself a major risk which has to be provided for out of current income.

What makes obsolescence so dangerous is its unpredictability. Major changes in techniques and equipment do not come gradually; they arrive quite suddenly. Also they follow no clear pattern. An industry may go without any major change for years, even for decades, and then suddenly be revolutionized—virtually overnight—only to settle back, perhaps, into another long period of static techniques. A good example is the steel industry. For almost fifty years there was no major change in the techniques of steel-processing. Raw steel was worked on equipment dating back to the second half of the nineteenth-century. All of this equipment had to be scrapped overnight when the automatic rolling mill came in, in the early years of the Depression. A similar development seems to be about to occur in the making of raw steel itself—a process little changed since the days of Andrew Carnegie and largely carried on today with equipment built before or during the First World War. Within the next decade most, if not all, of this equipment may well become obsolete. That major technological changes like these are likely to become effective during a depression —when more economical methods have to be adopted no matter what effect they have on existing equipment—does not lessen the seriousness of the risk.

If replacement and obsolescence concern the ability to produce, *risk proper* and *uncertainty* concern the marketability of the product.

Risk proper is the result of the inability to foresee the economic future of a product or service. It has always been an important element in production. But in pre-industrial economies the main proper risks were physical. The husbandman ran the risk of an epidemic among his sheep, the farmer the risk of a hailstorm. What was produced was always marketable; the only question was whether there would be anything to market. One of the greatest achievements of the mercantile age was the conversion of many of these physical risks into something that could be predicted and provided against. It is no exaggeration to say that without insurance an industrial economy could not function at all.

But in the place of physical risks which have been tamed by the laws of probability, the industrial system faces genuine economic risks, risks of acceptability and marketability of the product. Nobody can say whether a new product or a new service will succeed economically; nobody can say how long an old product or an old service will continue to be economically acceptable. The speed with which that apparently most stable and secure industry, the interurban streetcar, disappeared when the automobile appeared, is only one example of the reality of risk.

The advocates of planning claim that in their economy there will be no risk proper because there will be no free, competitive market. There is some validity to this claim, though no more probably than there is to the claim that a monopoly eliminates risk. In the first place the control of risk, even in the most rigidly planned economy, is likely to be successful only as long as the economy operates under conditions of extreme scarcity when any product is eagerly bought at any price. There was, for instance, little risk involved in production during the inflationary postwar period when everything, however shoddy, could be sold. It is no accident that the Soviet economists consider a permanent inflationary situation necessary to successful planning. But this means that in order to avoid risk the economy has to operate permanently under the threat of a boiler explosion.

It is also likely that the risk can be controlled only so long as the planned economy is backward; for then it will confine itself to imitating, by and large, products and services successfully developed and tested in a more advanced economy. If ever a planned economy reaches the stage where it is ahead, technologically and productively, it is likely to run the same risk in the development of new products and services and in the continuation of old products and services under which a market economy operates.

Uncertainty, finally, is the economists' expression of the time factor itself. It is altogether new. The farmer knew that if he did not have a corn crop by the time the frost came, he would not have a corn crop at all that year. The husbandman knew that if the ewes failed to lamb in the spring, he would not be able to restock his herd. But in industrial production it cannot be predicted with any certainty when a product or a service will be successful. Whether it will be successful is the risk we call "risk proper"; but whether it will be successful in one year, five years or in twenty years, is "uncertainty."

It is characteristic of industrial production that every single increase in efficiency and productivity increases the uncertainty of industrial production. (This is just a reformulation of Boehm-Bawerk's famous principle of the "Productivity of the Long Way Round.") The more highly developed an economy, the greater becomes the uncertainty against which the enterprise has to protect society and itself. It is obvious that this protection, like the provision for all other risks of the future, can only come out of current production.

How important "uncertainty" is can be seen from the fact that our research engineers now estimate ten years as the minimum period for the successful development of a new product or a new process; and this does not take into account the period of research laboratory work itself, which may easily take another ten years. Companies like General Electric or the American Telephone Company, as well as the major chemical companies, even concentrate on "pure research" and expect the marketable process to come out as a by-product. They consider the time factor to be so unpredictable and incalculable that it is more productive not to try to predict or calculate it at all.

An example is the development of synthetic rubber. The basic work in chemistry was done during or shortly after the First World War. Since the mid-twenties it was known how to make rubber synthetically. But for twenty years it was doubtful whether a synthetic rubber could ever be produced economically; except for the impetus of the rubber shortage of World War II it might well have taken another twenty years to develop a usable product. It required new developments in low-temperature and carbon chemistry, and new metallurgical discoveries which were entirely unpredictable twenty years ago, and which grew out of work entirely unconnected with the work on synthetic rubber. Yet every major rubber company and every major chemical company had to invest large sums in synthetic rubber research all along, or risk sudden extinction.

It is in the planned economy, however, that uncertainty assumes nightmarish proportions. The essence of planning is to take extremely long odds on timing. Not just one development has to be predicted —and predicted correctly. The planner must be right in his timing of ten or twenty separate developments, all of which must arrive at the same point at the same moment lest the whole plan collapse. The uncertainty of the competitive market is like a gamble that seven will come up at the next roll of the dice. But the planner stakes all on an unbroken series of twenty rolls of seven. The very high profit margin on which Russian industry operates—by all indications, very much higher than that of American industry—reflects in large part the uncertainty of planning.

The Dry Holes

For the economics of the "isolated enterprise" it would indeed be sufficient to say that it must provide out of current production against the four risks of major future loss: replacement, obsolescence, risk proper and uncertainty. However, the enterprise is not isolated, but a particle in an economy composed of a great many enterprises.

Society must demand of the *successful* enterprise not only that it provide for its own future costs, but that it contribute toward the risks of the less successful enterprises; in other words, that *it carry a share of the losses other enterprises will sustain in the future.*

From the point of view of the individual oil company, it is sufficient for one well to produce enough oil to cover the costs and the risks of digging a new, equally productive well. But the economy must demand that the productive oil well also provide for the steel pipe and the human labor that is going to be sunk into an unsuccessful dry well by another competing oil company. *Society must demand from the successful enterprise a surplus of current production over and above what is needed to provide for the risks of the enterprise itself.* This "surplus" is not a "profit" but a premium against the risks of the other enterprises. In the balance sheet of an individual enterprise, this "surplus" will appear as a profit. Economically, however, it is a genuine cost; for if not provided against, the economy would be bound to shrink.

If we assumed that all enterprises were successful, that is, able to cover the risks of future losses out of current production, there would be no need for an additional risk premium on the part of the successful enterprise. But such an assumption would be totally untenable. In 1941—the most prosperous year of the American economy between 1929 and the war boom—almost half of all American business enterprises operated either at a loss or barely broke even. And the Russians, despite planning and complete control of prices, base their economy on the assumption that about half of their enterprises will operate at a cost exceeding the price which they receive for their goods, that is, at a loss.

Socially and economically it would also be most undesirable if there were no "dry holes." It would mean that no enterprise would take a risk. It would also mean complete rigidity. As the existing enterprises would all manage to stay alive, new enterprises, new industries, new men could hardly get started. Just as a society needs social mobility to stay alive—with new men rising into the ruling groups, while the descendants of former leaders drop out—an economy needs economic mobility and a turnover of the "economic elite." Such economic mobility is only possible if the successful enterprises produce enough of a surplus of current production over current cost to offset the costs of the "dry holes."

In addition, the enterprise has to bear, out of its current production, the *social burden* of society—all the services, whether supplied by government or carried by the individual himself, which do not pertain to the economic process. What these services are in particular is not our concern here. The extent to which, for instance, a good school system or decent medical services contribute directly to productive capacity is entirely beyond the scope of this discussion. Nor are we concerned with the question how much of a social burden a given economy can afford or should afford. Today, when the military burden—historically the biggest of all the social burdens—threatens to cripple the economy of even the richest countries, this is a most important question of economic and social policy. Here we are interested only in stating that there is a social burden, that it cannot be borne except out of current production, and that therefore it has to come out of a surplus of current production over the enterprise's own replacement costs and risks.

To summarize: the current production of the enterprise must provide for:

(1) The *current costs* of the enterprise, the "costs of doing business."
(2) The *future costs* of the enterprise, the "costs of staying in business":

> replacement,
> obsolescence,
> risk proper,
> uncertainty.

(3) The enterprise's *contribution to society* in respect to the future costs of the less successful enterprises—their replacement, their obsolescence, their risk proper and their uncertainty.
(4) The enterprise's share in the *social burden of noneconomic services*.

Only if the enterprise can provide adequate coverage against all these costs and risks can it preserve its own and society's productive resources intact.

The Avoidance of Loss and the Social Interest

Certainly the law of loss avoidance must be the first law of the enterprise. For on its economic performance depends the very survival of the enterprise; and like every other institution the enterprise must put first its self-preservation.

The avoidance of loss is also the enterprise's first social duty. The enterprise is not an end in itself but a tool of society. It discharges, as we shall see, governmental and social functions of great importance. But first and foremost it is society's *economic* tool. We have only accepted industrialization because the economic purpose—cheap and efficient production—is best realized in the modern industrial enterprise. If the establishment of local government or of a community had been the first purpose, we would not have accepted the industrial enterprise at all, as it raises extremely difficult social and political problems. The political and social functions of the enterprise, however important they are and however vital their discharge is to society, are only incidental to the primary economic purpose.

Of course, we will often find it advisable to sacrifice some economic performance to achieve other things of social importance. Certainly only in extreme emergencies—total war or a major depression—would we be willing to accept the principle of "economic performance at any price." But this is extraneous to our discussion. We cannot even raise the question whether we ought to sacrifice economic performance unless we know what it is we are sacrificing. We cannot discuss the political and social problems of an industrial society—and that is our aim rather than the development of economic theory—without first understanding the objective rationale of the enterprise, the rationale of its economic performance.

The enterprise is the steward for society's always limited productive resources. Some of these resources are tangible: machinery and equipment. Others are intangible: skills, experience, "know-how." Some are human: labor; some material: capital. The organization of men, materials and machines into a productive unit is in itself a major resource. The minimum responsibility the enterprise has to society is the preservation of these resources at the same productive strength they had when they were entrusted to the enterprise. Failure to do so would make the whole society poorer by wasting a part of the national patrimony. To run at a loss is to default on the first *social* duty of the enterprise.

It has become almost axiomatic to regard the internal and the social rationale and responsibility of the enterprise as incompatible and as in conflict with each other. This "conflict" provides the theme for the bulk of the discussions on the subject—as a conflict between the "profit motive and abundance," between "pecuniary and social accounting," between "private greed and the public interest"—or as a "conflict between demagoguery and thrift," though this theme and its variations have not been so popular of late.

If there were indeed such a conflict between industrial society and its constitutive institution, industrial society as we know it simply could not survive—neither as a free enterprise nor as a collectivist society. We would either have to adopt the "managerial society" which Mr. Burnham prophesied ten years ago, in which social and individual purpose are entirely subordinated to the self-interest of the enterprise; or we would have to find an entirely new society which manages to do away with the enterprise. A change of "system" alone will not change the enterprise; "pecuniary accounting," for instance, is nowhere more firmly entrenched than in the Soviet Union, with the "control by the ruble" the final and absolute yardstick of economic decisions.

There are indeed major conflicts of aim, purpose and rationale in every industrial society. But the much-publicized conflict between the self-interest of the enterprise and its social function is not one of them. There is no such conflict. We do not even have to discuss whether "profit motive," "pecuniary accounting," and "social accounting" exist or what they might be; they are irrelevant to the real problem.

In any society, whether Capitalist, Socialist, Communist, Fascist or cave man, the first and overriding social function and responsibility of the enterprise is economic performance. Similarly, the enterprise's survival in any society depends on economic performance.

The demands of economic performance which society makes on the enterprise are identical with the demand of the enterprise's self-interest: the avoidance of loss—that is, operation at a surplus of current production over current cost adequate to cover the risks of the future. There is no conflict between the social purpose and the survival interest of the enterprise. Both are in harmony; both stand under the same rationale; both are measured at one and the same time by the same yardstick.

CHAPTER 5

THE LAW OF HIGHER OUTPUT

EVERY economic system is subject to change. But in a nonindustrial economy change comes from the outside. The economy itself desires to remain changeless. Changelessness is its norm; change is disturbing and upsetting. In the industrial economy change is "built in." It generates itself the forces of change. It has no static equilibrium. If it does not expand, it contracts. Change is indeed the very purpose of economic activity and economic institutions in an industrial system.

In a pre-industrial economy the major change is *dislocation*: the shutting off or the opening up of a market or of a source of supply, resulting in a shift in the use and usefulness of resources. Dislocation is not unknown in an industrial economy. The crisis from which Western Europe has been suffering since 1914 is a dislocation crisis. But the typical change in an industrial economy is *expansion*: the development of new resources, new products and new markets from within the economy.

Pre-industrial change is apt to be abrupt if not catastrophic. The specific industrial change is gradual and evolutionary. Pre-industrial change could be directed and influenced only in a very small degree; there was practically no way to predict it, to prepare for it or to provide against its risks. Expansion, however, can be directed, controlled and prepared. That expansion is possible was the great discovery of the Industrial Revolution.

From this follows the second basic law of the enterprise: *the law of higher output*. Because expansion is both the purpose of an industrial economy and its imperative need, society must demand of the industrial enterprise that it prevent contraction and provide expansion. The enterprise must increase its productivity; for increased productivity is the only basis for expansion. At the same time, increased productivity is a necessity for the enterprise. It is its main protection against the threat of dislocation to its own survival and stability—even in a noncompetitive economy.

Change in a Pre-Industrial Economy

Historically, economic change has largely been the result of outside forces acting on the economy: war, conquest, geographic discoveries, religious movements, etc. The great and dramatic changes in pre-industrial economies have all been the result of dislocation. The shift in economic activity and outlook resulting from the Crusades and the reopening of the Mediterranean to Western trade; the economic revolution caused by the shift of the trade routes to the Atlantic in the sixteenth and seventeenth centuries; and, in our own day, the collectivization of Russian agriculture, which bodily lifted millions of peasants off the farms and dumped them into industrial factories—all were dislocations of productive resources. In these great dislocations the economic result was often a by-product and purely incidental; they brought economic destruction and impoverishment as often as they brought expansion and wealth.

As long as catastrophic dislocation was the only form of economic change, economics as a discipline and a field of study could not exist. All that could be said on the subject of economic life was said by Aristotle in a few brilliant sentences at the beginning of the *Politics*, where he contrasts "oeconomia," the productive activity of the basically self-sufficient household, with "money-making," that is trading.

But even the pre-industrial economists of the trading economy did not see the possibility of expansion. The first examples of modern technology, that is, of the deliberate attempt to create new productive resources through the rearrangement of old ones, antedate the discipline of economics by several centuries. The earliest systematic attempt was made in mining and metallurgy in the fifteenth century—an attempt that marks the beginning of both the science of mechanics and the science of chemistry. The state factories which Richelieu established in France in the first half of the seventeenth century, and which were instantly copied all over Europe, were based upon the belief in the possibility of expansion and dedicated to the development of new and better production methods. Yet Adam Smith, writing one hundred and fifty years after Richelieu, knew of only one way to increase production: the husbanding of existing resources. How to bring this about was the great problem to which the whole classical tradition, from Adam Smith to John Stuart Mill, addressed itself. But productive capacity itself was considered God-given and unchangeable. Only on this assumption can the major concepts and doctrines of the classics be understood or upheld, above all the free-trade doctrine and the concept of an automatic, self-adjusting gold standard.

Marx, unlike the classical economists, understood that expansion was necessary to the new economy that was coming into being in his lifetime. But he saw only one possibility of expansion: expansion into new territory. Out of this grew the Marxist theory of "imperialism" as developed by Hobson, Luxemburg and Hilferding and adopted by Lenin, according to which capitalism in order to expand must enslave. Out of it grew also Henry George's theory of new land as the source of all enrichment, and Franz Oppenheimer's theory of conquest as the dynamic principle in history. But clearly Marx and the Marxists did not believe that expansion was possible; indeed, they based their prediction of the inevitable collapse of capitalism on the conviction that expansion, while necessary to the capitalist system, was inherently impossible beyond narrow limits.

Expansion in the Industrial Economy

Expansion through increased productivity is thus quite new. We take it for granted today. We take it as a matter of course, for instance, that the rayon industry increased its productive efficiency fifteen to twenty times since it emerged into commercial operations thirty years ago—not through major new inventions, but through thousands of small and unspectacular changes in techniques, processes and equipment. Yet to any earlier age this would have seemed miraculous, if not devil's work. It would also have been totally unexpected and unpredictable, whereas every engineer or chemist in the rayon industry a generation ago would have predicted just such a development even though he could not have said where exactly the improvements would come from.

In expansion a new combination of resources resulting from the application of technology results in an actual transformation of old and fully utilized resources into bigger and more productive resources. *Resources thus are actually made more productive.* No new resources, hitherto idle, are acquired or appropriated. No old resources, hitherto employed on a wasteful activity, are now used to better advantage. Nor—as in the case of dislocation—is one activity eliminated or cut down to free resources for something new. The same resources employed in the same activity are made capable of producing more of the same goods. Or without any cut in existing production and hence without dislocation, the economy can shift resources to produce a new product that could not be made formerly.

Increased productivity releases productive resources. It operates not as a "return *on* capital." The agent of expansion is not the "capitalist" but the "innovator";[1] and the marriage between the constitutionally timid "capitalist" and the "innovator" was not only very recent but a "shotgun marriage" as well. Increased productivity is a return *of* capital. It is a genuine surplus.

It can become economically effective in four ways. The enterprise can use the released capital to turn out more of the same commodity. The enterprise can lower the price—with or without an increase in output. It can raise real wages. Finally, it can show the released resources as if they were a profit and distribute them.

All four methods redistribute capital resources. But in the enterprise's accounts the four ways are recorded differently. The first method is purely internal. It will be reflected in the cost accounting of the enterprise; but as far as the income statement is concerned, the increase in productivity will show up only as an increase in future earnings capacity. The second way shows itself as a decrease in the enterprise's profit per unit. The third way shows as an increase in current costs. Only in the fourth method, where what is actually a capital repayment is presented as a current profit, do increased productivity and expansion operate through the profit figures. Only for this method could it be said that profit—or what is normally known as such—has anything to do with expansion. And, historically, lower prices and higher real wages have always been at least as important as the means to make the benefits of increased productivity available to the economy, as capital repayment through the profit mechanism. The one major exception to this rule is, probably, Soviet Russia where practically all capital resources released by increased productivity are transferred to the State in the form of profits.

---

[1] This was first worked out by Joseph Schumpeter in his *Theory of Economic Development*, (Cambridge: Harvard University Press, 1934) published in the original German in 1911.

CHAPTER 6

PROFITABILITY AND PERFORMANCE

WHILE increased productivity creates a surplus of resources, it does not create a "profit" in the strict sense of the word—even though it may appear as such in the financial accounts. And while the provisions for the risks of the future are normally shown as if they were profit, they are actually true costs. What is customarily shown as "profit" is a mixture of risk premiums against the future costs of "staying in business" and of capital repayments made possible by increased productivity—confused even further, as a rule, by items which reflect nothing but changes in the purchasing power of money.

But "profitability" is a meaningful concept in an industrial economy. Indeed it is *its central concept. For profitability is the only yardstick of economic performance we possess.* It measures both the size and adequacy of the provisions against future costs and increased productivity. It is not the purpose of the industrial enterprise to make a profit. Its purpose is to turn out goods or services. It is not the social duty of the industrial enterprise to operate at a profit. Its social duty is first to avoid loss, and, second, to increase the productivity of the resources entrusted to it. But only profitability can measure the performance of these two duties. And since the ability of the enterprise to turn out goods or services depends, in the last analysis, on the discharge of its twin duties to society, only profitability can measure how well the enterprise fulfills its purpose.

There are seven areas in each of which we need a tremendous amount of study, research and thinking before we will have an adequate economics for an industrial age.

(1) *The relationship between "profitability" and the profit figures of the bookkeepers and accountants.* These profit figures are the only

thing a management has to go by when it makes its decisions—in a collectivist and planned as well as in a free-enterprise economy. They are inevitably the first yardstick and gauge of performance. The figures should, therefore, be as close an approximation of profitability as possible. But today's "profit" is at best a crude indication of profitability—if only because our accounting is still largely pre-industrial and designed to make an inventory of the past rather than to chart the future.

(2) *The proper time unit of industrial production.* The calendar year is certainly not the proper time-unit of industrial production. It is not what we mean by "current" in the terms "current production" and "current costs," the difference between which is the only available reservoir for the provisions against future costs. Yet the profit figure on which practically all enterprises base their decisions is the annual profit.

Industrial production neither begins nor ends with the production of a given unit or the performance of a given task. For the farmer the time-unit of economic activity is the cycle of the seasons from sowing to reaping. The husbandman has a longer time-unit, the reproduction cycle of the herd ranging from one to three years or so. Is the time unit of industrial production the life period of the mechanical equipment—a long period, extending to twelve or fifteen years, but still a definite period? Or must we throw out all concepts of a definite time span and, following Keynes, use instead the concept of a "rhythm" such as the "business cycle"?

This question is particularly important, as any attempt to fight the mass unemployment of a serious depression must be based on a long-term time-unit of industrial production.

(3) *The relationship between the "real" economy of goods, labor and services and the "symbol" economy of money.* The "symbol" economy has largely become autonomous, with money having social and prestige functions quite independent of its purchasing power.

(4) *The application of the theoretical concepts of future costs to the concrete enterprise and the concrete economy.*

(5) *The specific future costs peculiar to a market economy, a monopolistic economy and a collectivist economy.* I have indicated the preponderance of certain risks in a market economy or under planning.

But the job to be done here is a difficult one and at the same time very important.

(6) *The decision how large the profit margin has to be in a concrete economy and for a concrete enterprise to cover the future costs of the economy adequately.* So far we have only "hunches" on this all-important question. My own hunch is that today none of the larger industrial economies operates on adequate profitability with the one exception of Soviet Russia. The Russian profit margin, according to the best figures and reports, is three to five times what it is in the United States—a discrepancy not entirely explainable with the much greater uncertainty of a planned economy, nor with the need for much greater productivity increases in an economy expanding as rapidly as the Russian.

(7) At the last would come the questions which have been in the foreground of the discussion for a century or more: *How should the reserves against the future risks be accumulated and by whom? How should the resources released by increased productivity be transferred and to whom?*

The furious discussion of these questions in the past has been almost entirely in terms of morality: justification of profits, fair return on capital, rights and just deserts of labor, etc. They are bound to assume an entirely different complexion if we do not talk of profit on past investment, whether of labor or of capital, but of future costs and increased productivity; if, in other words, the problem is not moral justification but economic function.

It is, for instance, fairly obvious on any basis that the contribution the individual enterprise makes to the future costs of the economy, that is to the future costs of the unsuccessful enterprises, must not be retained within the enterprise but must be distributed. Otherwise the economy would soon become dominated by a few very successful enterprises. Equally, the resources released by increasing productivity must be distributed lest new enterprises be cut off from access to productive resources. But is distribution to shareholders the best way to create the contingency reserves of the economy? Are higher wages, lower prices or the mechanism of capital accumulation in a competitive capital market the most satisfactory way to make released resources available?

It is not to be expected that such questions, which intimately concern the economic standing of powerful groups, and which touch upon their basic beliefs regarding the structure of society, could or should be answered on purely functional grounds. But if based on economic function, the discussion might at least cease to be a mere rationalization of preconceived moral and political convictions in economic terminology, as most of our arguments on the nature, function, justification and distribution of "profit" have always been.

Every single one of these areas is of real importance. Together they offer work for a generation of economists—work which goes far beyond the "economic revolution" of the Keynesians, and which might lead to a revival of a genuine discipline of "political economy." But our purpose is not to develop a theory of industrial economics but to study the industrial enterprise as a social and political institution. Our purpose is served if we establish the rationale of the enterprise's actions and behavior.

It is, therefore, sufficient to state:

(1) *The rationale, behavior, policies and decisions of the enterprise have nothing whatsoever to do with the "profit motive."*

Archangels in command of an industrial enterprise would have to make profitability as much the first law of their actions and policies as the greediest "capitalist." And so must the most faithful Commissar who not even in his dreams ever strays from the Party Line. Indeed, it is Communist theory which—so far alone—has recognized profitability as the decisive element and as the dominant consideration in an industrial economy. To raise Cinderella Profitability out of the gutter into which Marx flung her and to put her on the throne as the prince's forever beloved, is the essence of the "Stalinist revision" of Marxist economic theory.

That profitability is the final and decisive criterion of industrial production has nothing to do with the entrepreneur's desire for profit. Indeed it has nothing to do with any individual motive. We do not even have to discuss whether the "profit motive" exists and where it might be found. Profitability is founded in the objective necessity and purpose of industrial production and industrial economy.

What applies to the "profit motive" applies with equal force to all other theories that explain the enterprise's concern with profitability in terms of individual motivation, such as Veblen's juxtaposition of "business" to the "instinct of workmanship," or the popular contrast between "pecuniary accounting" and "social accounting."

Altogether, the behavior, policies, concerns and actions of the industrial enterprise are entirely independent of subjective motive or drive and of individual purpose. Whether man be "economic man" or "moral man," the enterprise would have to function just the same. Nor could its behavior and rationale be changed or influenced by changing or influencing human nature or human behavior, by psychological adjustment, moral reform or religious conversion. Subjective behavior, rationale and purpose are irrelevant to the enterprise's behavior, rationale and purpose, which are given objectively by institutional structure and function.

(2) *The rationale, behavior, policies and decisions of the enterprise are the same regardless of the legal or political structure of industrial society.*

Profitability operates as much under collectivism as under individualism, under government control and government ownership as in a free-enterprise system. And it works exactly the same way. Nor does it make any difference what goods are being produced, how they are being priced, whether they are sold in a competitive market, etc.

From this follows that the only structural or constitutional changes that could affect the basic policies and the basic behavior of the enterprise, are changes in the structure or constitution of the enterprise itself. Changes in the legal or political "system," however much they may affect the livelihood or the life of the individual, cannot affect the structure or behavior of the enterprise.

(3) *The rationale, behavior, policies and decisions of the enterprise are completely independent of the mode of distribution of profits.*

Who is entitled to receive what share in the profits is a very important question, socially and economically. But as far as the actions and behavior of the enterprise are concerned the distribution of profit is irrelevant.

The enterprise would have to act and to behave exactly the same way if profit were a mere bookkeeper's fiction invented to account for the costs not capable of being accounted for under traditional pre-industrial bookkeeping methods.

Indeed, the enterprise must act on the assumption that there is no profit, that is, no surplus of income over cost. It must act on the as-

sumption that there are only costs—current and future—and the capital repayment resulting from increased productivity. Monopoly profit, windfall profit, inventory profit, eating up of capital, speculative gains and other such apparent profits may indeed exist; and while they are clearly not "profit" from the point of view of the whole economy, they may be very important to the individual enterprise. But in its actual decisions and behavior the enterprise must always assume that whatever part is not needed to cover costs, represents increased productivity. A "surplus of earnings"—even if it actually should exist—cannot be assumed or accepted in the enterprise's policies and decisions. Stated differently, the enterprise must always approach its operations with the question whether its current income is adequate to cover current and future costs. If this question can be answered in the affirmative, the enterprise must ask whether the increase in productivity is large enough to maintain the enterprise efficiently, and able to withstand dislocation and competition.

(4) *Finally, profitability must be the sovereign criterion and rationale of the enterprise. It is the expression of both its responsibility to itself and its responsibility to society.*

Industrial production is focused on the future. The risk of future losses is its first problem, the prevention of such losses is first law. *Current production* must always be projected on *future costs*; and to prevent future losses, the surplus of current income over current costs —that is, the profit margin—must at least balance the risks. The second law of the enterprise is the *law of increased productivity*. Both future costs and increased productivity can be measured only with the yardstick of profitability. The industrial enterprise must therefore base itself on profitability and must accept profitability as the guide for its policies and as the governor of its performance. And society must measure the performance of the enterprise by the same yardstick of profitability.

CHAPTER 7

THE REAL ISSUE IN THE WAGE CONFLICT

OUR discussion of the economic needs and requirements of the enterprise and of its social responsibility for economic performance may have tasted like an old dish not too much improved by being smothered in an abstract terminology. It may have sounded like one of those full-page advertisements of "economic truths" that emanate from the National Association of Manufacturers to prove the divine institution of the "free-enterprise system." Or those familiar with Communist Party-Line economics may have been reminded instead of the official arguments in favor of Soviet State capitalism with its extremely high profit margin and its exclusive concern with profitability and increased productivity. The reader might even expect our discussion of the necessity and function of profitability and increased productivity to lead straight into a flag-waving glorification of the beauty and benefits of the existing economic system—though with the question left open whether I shall wave the flag of free enterprise or of collectivism.

Profitability and increased productivity are requirements of the enterprise. But they are not requirements or purposes of the member of the enterprise. At best they are irrelevant to his economic needs and purposes, if not in apparent or real opposition to them. To impose on him the yardstick of profitability and increased productivity must therefore appear to the member as arbitrary, if not hostile, making profitability and increased productivity themselves appear alien and harmful.

The very fact that profitability must be the law of the enterprise thus underlies the economic conflicts of industrial society. It underlies the conflict over wages. It underlies the worker's resistance to increased productivity, of which "featherbedding" rules and union restrictions on output or on the use of new tools are only a very small part. It underlies, finally, the worker's opposition to the principle of profitability itself, which threatens the very survival of the "free-enterprise" system and—to an even greater extent—the experiments in "Democratic Socialism" now going on in Europe.

It would be a rare day without a wage conflict in the headlines. Conflicts over wage rates are the core of most industrial disputes, and the stated reason for most strikes. But is there really a wage issue? Or is the wage conflict a mock conflict staged to hide completely different issues, issues of power and of citizenship? Every study of industrial workers has shown that wage rates are not uppermost in their minds. Differences in wage rates between various jobs are very close to the workers' hearts because they establish prestige. But absolute wage rates are only rarely very important. They matter a great deal—they may indeed be the most important thing—in an economy very close to subsistence, that is, in the very early stages of industrialization. They also count in an inflation, when incomes never quite catch up with prices. But otherwise wage rates do not rank very high among the workers' concerns.

The key to this riddle is that the wage rate is the traditional symbol for the real conflict rather than the issue itself. The basic problem is a conflict between the enterprise's view of wage as cost, and the employee's view of wage as income. The real issue is not, properly speaking, an economic one but one over the nature and function of wage: shall the need of the enterprise or the need of the employee be the basis for determining the function of wage? Is wage to be considered primarily a current cost incurred in payment for a commodity consumed in the productive process? Or is it primarily a future cost of conserving and increasing the human resources of production?

Wage as Current Cost

From the point of view of the enterprise, "wage" is necessarily a part of the unit cost of production. It is the $1.60 of wage in each pair of shoes or the $400 of direct wage costs in the new car. Whether the wage is paid by the piece, by the hour, or by the week, the enterprise must always figure it as piece-work wage. It follows that the enterprise must demand *flexible labor costs*. For the enterprise to survive, let alone to be profitable, wage costs per unit must move with the selling price of the goods the enterprise makes. The more important wages are in total costs, the more "labor intensive" an operation, the greater, of course, this need for a flexible wage rate.

But labor costs must also move with the ups and downs of production. The elasticity of the total wage bill is a key factor in the enterprise's ability to survive a business setback. The larger the decline in production that an enterprise can stand without having to operate at a loss, the greater, obviously, its economic power of resistance and its chance to survive. Labor costs are of course not the only costs. But they are the only ones that are not either entirely flexible and self-adjusting like raw material costs, or entirely rigid and fixed like capital costs. They are the only costs that can be either flexible or fixed, depending upon the policy of the enterprise. Hence they are the crucial costs. They may come down either by a cut in the wage rate or by a cut in the number of men employed. Which way is more economical and more likely to help the enterprise weather a storm, depends on the industry. But a *flexible labor burden* is vital to all industries and to all enterprises.

This does not mean that the enterprise needs a low wage rate or low employment. On the contrary, a high wage rate may in effect constitute a very much lower wage cost per unit of production; it may bring forth much greater productive effort and efficiency—the argument on which Henry Ford based his five-dollar-a-day wage policy of 1914, and which underlies all incentive wage plans. The enterprise must only be opposed to anything that will result in greater rigidity of wage costs, to anything that will push up either the minimum wage cost per unit or the minimum labor force necessary to operate the enterprise. But the real point is that *the enterprise must regard "labor" as a commodity which is bought according to the current level of production and priced according to the current price level.*

Wage as Income

The wage earner, however, cannot consider wage part of unit costs. It is his income, the basis of his family budget, of his own livelihood and of that of his wife and children. He cannot accept labor—that is, himself—as a commodity. He cannot even understand this view. It contradicts every single fact within his own experience and denies every single one of his needs. From the point of view of the enterprise the worker's contribution enters the product and is consumed in the process of production. Wages are "current cost." But the expenses of the worker which he has to cover out of the wage are payments on account of the "future costs" of the economy, that is, payments necessary to maintain and to replace the human resources of production: himself, his wife and his children. The worker must therefore demand a reasonably stable as well as a reasonably secure income. He needs above all a predictable income on which he can plan and budget. *Hence the worker's own insistence on "security" as his first need and as vastly more important than the wage rate.*

The conflict between wage as cost and wage as income is only one facet of the issue. For the enterprise wage is indeed purely economic. But for the worker "wage" is synonymous with "work" and with "job." Job and work are much more than sources of income in an industrial society. A man out of work is a man disfranchised. He loses social standing and prestige. He is in danger of losing his self-respect as well as the respect of his family. The insistence on a flexible wage burden must therefore appear to the worker as a denial of his full citizenship and of his human dignity.

To lay off a worker in slack times implies no personal criticism but is forced upon the enterprise by impersonal, economic forces over which it has no control. But it is precisely this subordination of the worker's citizenship and personality to an impersonal force which is the trouble. To be discharged for misconduct or incompetence—or because the boss wants to give the job to his brother-in-law—may well be a sentence of economic death. It may be deserved or purely arbitrary and unjust. But it does not establish the *principle* that the worker's access to social effectiveness and social satisfaction is marginal. To consider labor a commodity goes, therefore, against the economic needs of the worker as well as against his social and political needs.

The crucial fact is that both the views of the enterprise and the views of the worker are right, and indeed necessary. Both claims are well founded. We must, therefore, find a solution which satisfies both the enterprise's demands for flexible wage costs based on the function of wage as unit cost, and the worker's demand for wage as income and as a basis of citizenship. We must find a wage basis which is at one and the same time "enterprise-oriented" and "worker-oriented."

One of the main reasons why the conflict is so hot and bitter is precisely because it centers on wage rates. Wage rates as the focus make little sense to either party. Traditional wage policy has indeed been "enterprise-oriented." But it is very doubtful whether that has worked out to the satisfaction of the enterprise. The enterprise may have carried its point in principle; but in the process it has given up almost all the substance.

Today's wage structure, though focused on wage rate, does not give the enterprise the flexibility of the wage burden which it—and the economy—require. Our wage rates have become frozen at the high point. They have pushed the level of business at which an enterprise can still operate without a loss—the so-called "break-even point"—well above the rate of operations many enterprises can hope to maintain over the business cycle. This is a threat to economic stability; a slight setback in business or in the price level may make even a stable enterprise run at a loss, and may result in mass lay-offs and shut-downs that could easily lead to panic.

This does not benefit the workers. On the contrary, their insecurity becomes greater than ever. They will, however, have to press for the highest and most rigid wages as long as wage rates are the center of wage determination and wage policy. At the same time they will also demand guarantees of full employment from enterprise or government to offset the increasing insecurity. The emphasis on the wage-rate focus thus threatens to deprive the enterprise of both flexibility of wage rates and flexibility of labor force, and to freeze the wage burden at the peak level—something neither the enterprise nor the economy can survive.

The wage-rate focus makes it also very difficult for any union to accept responsibility for a rational wage policy. Because of the wage-rate convention the highest wage rate—rather than maximum employment or maximum income for the members—has become the symbol of union strength and the test of union leadership. To admit that wage rates could go down is as impossible for the union leader as it is for a statesman to admit in the middle of a war that his country could be wrong. To accept a flexible wage structure—let alone to accept a cut in wages—would not only be accepting defeat, it would be the "stab in the back" and considered high treason.[1] This forces the union not only into permanent war against the enterprise. It creates an internal conflict between the interest of the members in the largest possible and the most secure income, and the interest of union and union leader in the highest wage rate for the moment.

A very good example was furnished by the American building-trades unions during the last depression. The unions refused to agree to any cut in the official wage rate, though they looked the other way when their members took work below union scale. But the very building projects that would have given the most employment—the large projects—could of course not be allowed to pay below-scale wages. Therefore many of them could not be undertaken at all.

There is, of course, nothing wrong with collective bargaining over wages. Indeed, as the conflict is over the purposes and needs of the two parties, it can only be handled successfully by bargaining and negotiation between the representatives of the enterprise and those of the workers. Also, the true issues are both economic and social, so the blend of economic arguments and power pressure that is collective bargaining seems appropriate.

But if collective bargaining focuses on the wage rate, it can never lead to any resolution. The two parties are always sparring with a straw man expressly set up to be knocked down. Instead of attacking a common problem through group conflict and compromise, collective bargaining degenerates into a hair-pulling and name-calling contest or into an armaments race for bigger and better industrial warfare in which no one can win.

Finally, the wage-rate convention tends to focus all problems and issues of the plant on an insoluble and irreconcilable conflict. This must make a conflict out of every issue in the relationship between management and union, between the enterprise and its workers. Even areas where the interests and purposes of the two are in essential harmony —as in almost everything relating to the social structure and organization of the plant community—become battlegrounds instead of com-

[1] As Arthur M. Ross, in *Trade Union Wage Policy* (Berkeley: University of California Press, 1948), has pointed out, this political and symbolic meaning of wage rate renders futile any attempt to explain union wage policy in economically rational terms. Altogether, Ross's book is the best analysis of the actual behavior of union and union leader under traditional wage determination.

mon grounds. The wage-rate focus embitters the entire relationship and poisons the very atmosphere of industrial life.

To change the focus would be very much in the interest of the enterprise. It would definitely be in the interest of society. Most of all, it would be in the interest of the union.

The present practice puts the union ultimately in opposition to society, which must insist both on flexibility of wage costs and on priority for maximum employment over maximum wage rate. And no union movement can afford to be in opposition to society.

Also, the present practice must eventually lead to wage-fixing by government decree—even though this too would fail to come to grips with the real issues. Government fixing of the wage rate would strengthen monopolistic tendencies and would seriously weaken the small and medium-sized enterprise. The government is bound to set one national wage pattern for an entire industry—and such a pattern will be cut to fit the financial ability of the largest and strongest units. As control of government and of public policy would at once become weapons in the wage conflict, free government would be threatened. But to the labor union, government dictation of wages would be absolutely fatal. It would undermine the union to the point where it might lose all genuine support from the rank and file of the members. It might also mobilize public opinion—including that of the union members—against the union as a selfish and self-seeking pressure group subordinating the common good to shortsighted greed.

Theoretically, the union has therefore the greatest stake in a change. Practically, it will be extremely difficult for the union to accept such a change, let alone to start it. "Bargaining over wage rates" has become a sacred cow of the labor movement, a slogan fraught with emotions far beyond its carrying capacity. Union leadership has acquired a vested interest in the wage-rate convention. The qualification for labor leadership is largely skill in fighting the wage-rate war. To defy the convention and to abandon the myth of the wage conflict as one over wage rates will, therefore, require high integrity and courage of both managements and union leaders.

CHAPTER 8

THE WORKER'S RESISTANCE TO
HIGHER OUTPUT

THE desire for "security" also underlies the worker's resistance to increased productivity and technological progress. Other factors undoubtedly enter. The line between increasing productivity through an improvement in tools and methods and increasing output through the "speed-up" is easily blurred. The popular argument, "Why should I break my neck so that the boss' wife can have a second fur coat?" indicates a close link between opposition to increased productivity and opposition to profit. What we are concerned with here, however, is the more general and infinitely more important resistance to new methods, new tools and processes, in short, to technological changes.

Opposition to technological improvement is as old as the machine. But it has become overshadowed by the wage issue and by the opposition to profit, neither of which achieved importance until much later, at least not in an organized form. At first sight, it might even appear that today the opposition to technological progress has become a minor matter. The worker's attitude toward the machine and toward technology in general has certainly changed fundamentally since the days of the Luddite "machine wreckers" a century ago. That technological progress is beneficial, that it raises the worker's standard of living, and that it creates jobs rather than destroys them, are accepted by the great majority of the workers.

But these arguments are accepted as general statements. When it comes to the particular and concrete, that is, to the worker's own operation, technological improvement is still regarded as an enemy, and still resisted with all means at the worker's command. There is very good reason to believe that this resistance is growing. As good an observer as the London *Economist* seems to consider it by itself the major threat to the performance of the British industrial system.

The resistance shows in "featherbedding" and other restrictive union rules, which are prevalent particularly in the older and tradition-bound industries such as railroading and building. But these open restrictions on efficiency and productivity are only the part of the iceberg that is above water. Much more important are the invisible, unwritten, informal restrictions decreed by the custom and common law of every plant. Every study of an industrial operation—whether manufacturing or clerical—has brought to light unwritten but ironclad arrangements to restrict productivity and output. In some cases they simply consist of a tacit setting of production quotas which a worker would be ill-advised to exceed. Often the workers have developed ways to do the job better and faster, a new gadget, a special arrangement of tools or of material, sometimes even a new process. These inventions are, however, hidden carefully from the engineers and production men; they are not used to increase productivity but, instead, to produce the official output with less work.

Attempts to overcome these informal restrictions may not only strengthen them; they may even be used by the workers to enforce their own production code. In a large Midwestern candy plant, for instance, the packers are being paid on a sharply rising scale for any day's output above the standard. Each team of packers in this plant manages to turn out a truly phenomenal number of filled candy boxes one day each week, thus earning the highest bonus. On all other days it turns out just enough boxes not to get docked. Each worker manages to earn a good deal more than if he were to exceed his quota each day by a small amount. Yet he also prevents any increase in the production quota! In fact, during the day allotted to a team for record production—always the same day each week—all the other teams in the packing room are expected to help the day's "Stakhanovites."

Clearly, an arrangement as complicated and as obvious as this—and there as many others similar to it—could not work without the knowledge of foreman and plant superintendent. The bosses have learned, however, that an attempt to break the production code of their department will bring nothing but serious trouble. They also sympathize as a rule with the men's attitude—they themselves may well share the workers' fear that increased productivity may cost them their job.

Even the production engineers, who for a long time were apt to brush aside the worker's resistance as "reactionary" or as plain loafing, seem lately to have learned their lesson. This, I think, explains the new popularity of incentive pay plans. But experience with such plans has proven that they may easily do more harm than good. They only increase production where increased productivity is certain not to cut the number of jobs.

The problem is not that the worker is opposed to new and better ways of doing the job. On the contrary, all our experience—with "suggestion systems" for instance—shows that the American worker is profoundly interested in technical improvement and able by himself to find better ways of doing the job. But he cannot afford to indulge this interest or to employ this ability.

The problem is also not one of ignorance of the benefits of technological progress and increased productivity. The worker may know the arguments of the economist and be convinced by them. But he cannot apply the logic of these arguments to his own job. They are sound "in the great mass" and "over the long run" rather than for one individual worker and immediately. And the promise of greater abundance and of more employment twenty years hence is not an adequate substitute for unemployment or downgrading today. Also the traditional arguments assume both transferability of skill and geographic mobility of labor. In reality, both are extremely limited even for "unskilled" labor and even in as mobile—I almost said, as semi-nomadic—a country as the United States.

It is not only the fear of the worker for his own job that leads to resistance against increased productivity. It is also the fear of the worker for the job of the man next to him, his concern for the future of his community and for the social, economic and prestige system of his entire society. The most constructive habits and values of group-life and group-order, the habits and values on which the very cohesion of any society depend, are thus mobilized against increased productivity.

The resistance to technological progress is not entirely the result of economic insecurity. The psychological insecurity of the worker in the mass-production plant, the fear of the new, the failure to understand it, the need to change what has become familiar, are all powerful factors. But at the root of the worker's resistance to technological change is the conflict between labor as a commodity and labor as a resource. Increased productivity imposes upon the worker a risk of obsolescence strikingly similar to the one which technological change imposes on the enterprise. The enterprise can guard itself against this risk, partly by setting aside a risk premium out of its current production, partly by assuming leadership in technological change. The individual worker, by and large, has no way of protecting himself. He cannot, as a rule, lay up reserves or even assess the risk. It does not help him at all to improve his efficiency or productivity. A man can be the best steel-roller in the country. But if the rolling of steel changes from a manual to an automatic process, or if the one rolling mill in his community is moved five hundred miles away, his job is gone, no matter how good he is at it.

The only possible solution, therefore, is to consider the risk of technological unemployment as a genuine risk of the enterprise, and to provide against the risk either out of the savings which will result from new methods and new tools, or out of current production.

This might read like an argument for severance pay such as a good many industries have adopted. But severance pay is usually too low to be more than a consolation to the worker. At the same time it imposes far too heavy a burden upon the enterprise to be generally practical. Above all, it puts the emphasis where it does not belong. It penalizes the enterprise for increased productivity; yet it does not remove the worker's fear of it. A practical program to overcome the resistance to increased productivity would have to try to prevent technological displacement through careful planning of innovations, close co-operation with the workers, their retraining and placing. Severance pay should be the last recourse to be used only in a few cases.

An approach to such a program was the plan worked out by Philip Murray, now President of the CIO.[1] The aim of this plan was to "re-absorb workers displaced by technological changes in the regular labor turn-over of the companies installing them." To this end the worker should be informed six months in advance, should be retrained for a new job, and should be given priority on jobs that become vacant within the company. If he cannot be re-employed right away, he

[1] Philip Murray, "Technological Unemployment," Steel Workers Organizing Committee Publication No. 3, (Pittsburgh, 1940).

should be kept temporarily on the payroll and used for work especially set aside for such a purpose. Severance pay would have to be paid only rarely—and more often as stand-by pay for a short period between jobs than as a compensation for dismissal. The program would be financed by setting aside each year a small amount for "social costs" out of the savings resulting from technological improvements. "The objective, of course, primarily is not to provide dismissal wages to displaced workers, but to compel industry to keep workers on the payroll by planning the introduction of technology, so that industry will not have to pay dismissal wages and workers are not displaced."

Such a plan would not be a panacea. I do not share Mr. Murray's belief that it could prevent technological unemployment in a major and industry-wide technological upheaval, such as the shift from manual to automatic rolling mills in the steel industry which he mentions. The displacement caused by such a change in the structure of an entire industry is likely to be far too large to be taken care of out of the fund for "social costs"—no matter how much planning goes into the change. A technological revolution threatens the survival of even the strong enterprises, and would even in good times strain their resources beyond the point where much planning or much preparation could be done. How could any plan have prevented—to change our illustration—the displacement of the musicians in the movie theaters when the sound film came in, or how could any fund have provided adequate severance pay when every movie house suddenly had to find the capital for the expensive new equipment or else go under?

Mr. Murray's plan would also do very little to prevent the resistance against innovations that threaten to abolish whole crafts, a resistance that underlies most "featherbedding" practices, most restrictive union rules on the use of new tools or new methods, and many of the jurisdictional restrictions such as plague the building industries. It would be totally inapplicable to developments that threaten to close an entire plant and to displace an entire community living off it. Yet this dislocation—in the literal sense of the word—works the greatest hardship. That it is not even mentioned by Philip Murray is all the more amazing as the dislocation of a whole community has been historically one of the major hazards of the steel worker.

But that Murray's plan has limited aims is in its favor rather than against it—however impractical some details of his plan may be. The

Bell Telephone System has used successfully a very similar plan in shifting from the manual to the dial telephone, which cuts out the jobs of almost all the switchboard operators in central offices. To be sure, the Bell plan would not work except for the high normal turnover rate of telephone operators. But it would certainly seem to prove the approach a practicable one in handling day-to-day changes and improvements. The worker fears these small but frequent changes much more than the much bigger, but also much rarer, basic changes. Also under the Murray plan the psychological obstacles to change would be largely overcome as the worker would have some time to accustom himself to the new. For the enterprise too these changes present the major problem of worker resistance. The major changes are usually too spectacular to be resisted short of wrecking machines. The small improvements and changes, however, can be successfully sabotaged by the informal code of the plant.

Basically, the problem of resistance to increased productivity is very similar to the wage conflict. Its root is the opposition between wage as current cost and wage as income, between labor as a commodity and the worker as a capital resource. The approach to a solution in both cases is to consider wage both as current cost and as future cost, that is, as an investment in the major productive resource of any enterprise, its labor force.

CHAPTER 9

THE HOSTILITY TO PROFIT

IN REJECTING profitability the worker rejects the very principle on which every industrial economy must be based. It is therefore a most serious matter that the rejection of profitability is far more general and far more deeply rooted in all industrial countries than opposition to the enterprise over wages or over technological improvements. It is also by no means confined to the worker but pervades our society. Altogether it is the central *economic* issue an industrial society—whether free-enterprise or Socialist—has to resolve if it wants to survive.

It has become fashionable in the United States during the last few years to attribute this rejection to ignorance of the true facts. To be sure, an almost unbelievable ignorance exists. Observer after observer has found the great majority of American workers convinced that business profits are at least twenty-five per cent of sales—the correct figure is five per cent in a good year. Even more amazing, the great majority of the workers—and apparently the great majority of the population —is convinced that profits are many times as large as wages, whereas actually profits are rarely more than one-tenth of wages.

The conviction that business profits are tremendous showed in a recent wage dispute in one of the plants of the Atomic Energy Commission. The workers flatly refused to believe that the company which operates the plant for the Commission, works for a fixed fee and is thus disinterested either in profits or in wages. There is a general belief that business must profit from a depression, that indeed, a depression is the time when business profits must be largest. This follows "logically" from the "axiom" that wages and profits are in conflict; hence profits must be highest when wages tend to be lowest, that is, in the slough of a depression. The evidence to the contrary, the businesses that go bankrupt and close shop in a depression, can hardly fail to be visible. But it is not perceived—the belief in the axiom is much too strong.

Ignorance undoubtedly contributes to the opposition to profitability. Business, particularly in the past, has often been guilty of making a secret of its operations, and of refusing to give the worker or the public reliable information in easily accessible form. Equally important perhaps is the difficulty the average layman has in piercing the accounting fog and in making any sense of the figures and terms used in a balance sheet or on the financial page.

Also, the figures are much too large to convey anything to the average reader. Two million dollars, twenty million, two hundred million, two hundred billion are all the same to a man who budgets on a fifty dollar weekly pay check. They are beyond his experience and imagination and simply mean "infinitely large." To the man on the street it makes no sense that a twenty-million-dollar profit is actually only a profit of a few cents on each dollar of sales or a profit of a few cents for each dollar of wages; the infinitely large remains infinitely large, no matter how many times it is divided.

In a recent survey people were asked what profit they would consider "fair" for an electric power company with an investment of forty million dollars. The great majority said, "eight to ten per cent." Later in the interview the same people were asked whether a profit of two million—the actual figure—would be low, fair or excessive. An even greater majority—including practically all the people who had declared eight to ten per cent a "fair return"—considered two millions an excessive profit.

But ignorance plays only a small part. It is not that the worker does not know the true facts. He lacks the willingness to listen and to believe the facts. The facts contradict everything in his experience and cannot therefore be believed.

When the worker and the American public choose a profit of ten per cent "fair and equitable," they do so because to them the figure seems absurdly low. It does not mean that they look upon profit as something the economy needs in its own interest and in that of its members. The most that can be said about the attitude of the American man in the street, is that he is willing to put up with profit provided it is kept at a minimum. He is deeply convinced that the profit rate on which the American economy operates must be slashed drastically before that tolerable minimum is reached or even approached. And he certainly shows no sign of accepting profit as fulfilling any function whatsoever.

The American worker is, indeed, more tolerant of profit than the European worker to whom the very word has become anathema and the symbol of all evil. But basically the difference is one of degree rather than one of kind. Unlike the European, the American worker has not formulated and crystallized his attitude in a doctrine. But his approach is almost the same.

The attempt made at present by American management to tell workers and public how very low profits are, and how little they amount to in the economic scheme of things, may well have an effect exactly opposite to that desired. Emphasis on the smallness of profit may lead the public to conclude that profits can be done away with altogether. In the long run even the popular misconceptions about profits might be more to industry's interest. At least the worker is convinced that profits are important. His only mistake is his belief that it must be large because it is important—and that is a mistake most of us are apt to make.

Profit as Exploitation

That the opposition to profits cannot be overcome by providing information should have been obvious from the slogan in which it has been voiced for over a century: the slogan of "exploitation."

We are not at all concerned here whether there is such a thing as "exploitation." Even the orthodox Marxists have now admitted that "profit" is not synonymous with "exploitation." But the question whether or not profit is "exploitation" does not touch the real issue. The battle cry of "exploitation" is not a rational argument but an emotional slogan. It does not reflect the conclusions of a statistical or of an analytical study but the direct and immediate experience of the worker.

This experience is one of conflict between profit and his interests, needs and purposes. Being an experience, it cannot be shaken by logical arguments. It is impervious to information; information which contradicts everyday, obvious experience simply cannot be accepted. The only way to shake experience is through experience, not through argument.

In rejecting profitability the worker rejects the rationale of the economic system itself. The rationales of the enterprise—profitability and increased productivity—have very little to do with the needs or purposes of the worker. There is no direct, clear and understandable link between the economic responsibility of the enterprise as measured by profitability, and the economic and social needs of the members of the enterprise: the need for a predictable income and employment, the need for a functioning and legitimate government of the enterprise, the need for social status and function in the enterprise. Of course, the worker benefits eventually from profit; in an industrial society in which the bulk of the population is employed and works for wages, the worker is indeed the major beneficiary.[1] But this is a long-range connection visible to the statistician who plots a twenty-five year curve, but not to the wage earner and indeed not even to management. It is an abstraction, not something alive and tangible.

Even if the worker were convinced that he benefits from profit, he would be equally convinced that he has had to fight for every penny of benefit he ever received. Far from having been automatic, the connection between profitability and the workers' own welfare has been one of conflict. The workers' demands have been opposed both with the assertion that a higher wage, shorter hours or higher social benefits were not economically possible, and with the claim that they would cut into profits. There has been only one important exception to this rule: Henry Ford's action in 1914 when he set the daily minimum wage at his plants at the then unheard-of figure of $5.00 a day. But Ford found few imitators; nor did he himself continue with the pattern of his early days. The worker's experience—no matter how far off the truth—is thus one of conflict between his needs and demands and the enterprise's desire for profit. Compared to this immediate experience, the argument that he would not have a job, let alone a good wage but for profitability, is gray theory.

Yet the enterprise must inevitably base its policies, decisions and actions on profitability, whatever the constitution of society or economy. The policies, decisions and actions of the enterprise, however, decide the worker's livelihood and that of his family, his future and

---

[1] He is not, however, the only beneficiary. Even in the most fully industrialized society, the nonworker groups represent at least half of the population; hence the fallacy of the argument advanced frequently by union leaders that increases in purchasing power in the form of higher wages have exactly the same effect as increases in purchasing power through lower prices. Of course, increasing wages is often the best way of distributing the fruits of productivity; but this is not true in every situation.

his standing in his own eyes as well as in those of the community. The worker and all that matters most to him is thus subjected to the rule of an alien if not a hostile principle.

The worker would probably be opposed to profitability even if it were not the governor of the enterprise. He might well consider it an unjustifiable "rake-off." But that profitability has to be the principle and purpose of *his* life, overriding his own needs and purposes at every turn, explains the intensity of his opposition to it. He sees himself not just "exploited"; he sees his right and dignity as a person denied by the primacy of profitability.

Executive Salaries and the Profit Issue

The rejection of profitability is greatly intensified by the all but universal resentment of the workers against the incomes of the top executives of the large enterprises.

When the United Automobile Workers in the spring of 1949 tried to get a higher wage at Ford's in the face of a business recession, they put all their emphasis on the high salaries of the automobile executives. I heard a broadcast by the Ford of Canada local of the union in Windsor, Ontario. The speakers were obviously from the shop, unfamiliar with radio and afraid of it. They shuffled awkwardly through their scripts. But their voices rose and became resonant with sincerity whenever they came to the "$500,000 C. E. Wilson of General Motors gets"—even though Mr. Wilson's income (actually half that amount) has no relationship whatsoever to wages at Ford.

Similarly, Philip Murray and the steel workers put all the emphasis in the deadlocked steel negotiations during the summer and fall of 1949 on the incomes of the steel executives rather than on the merits of their case. The pension guaranteed to Mr. Fairless, President of U. S. Steel—not the demands of the workers—became the big issue in the minds of public and workers.

Resentment against high executive salaries may appear to have nothing whatever to do with profitability. It may also appear as the pettiest of grudges. Yet it is the salaries of a few top executives as much as anything else that confirm the worker in his opposition to profit as "exploitation" and in his conviction that profits must be exorbitant. Every study shows that far from being petty, this resentment is a major factor in industrial conflict.

The worker is right in his appraisal of the importance of this factor. It is true, of course, that the top salaries are unimportant economically, that they amount to much less than one cent of every dollar of sales and to an equally negligible figure per dollar of wages. But the worker's resentment is not economical in its motivation. In this country it is not even predominantly based on envy—one of the major differences between the United States and Europe. He resents the big salaries as a sign of social injustice and as a denial of the promise of an equal society. It is significant that to the worker the reality of the "profit system" is represented perhaps more by these salaries than by dividends paid to the stockholder, who, after all, is remote and hardly more than a silk-hatted abstraction.

The resentment against the big salaries of the top executives poisons the political and social relations within the plant, aggravates the difficulty of communication between management and employees, and reduces management's chance to be accepted as the government of the plant. The mere mention of the "fat" salaries of the bosses is the one thing that never fails to arouse emotion in a union meeting—even in the most conservative "business union" of highly paid workers.

The reasons usually given for these top salaries are, frankly, nonsense. One argument is that the economic contribution of a good top executive is invaluable so that he cannot be paid enough. But the same could be said of a good nurse in a hospital or of anybody else in a crucial job.

Another argument is that top management personnel must be paid enough to compensate them for the fortunes they could make by going into business for themselves. But the qualifications of a good top executive are quite different from those of a successful, independent businessman. Also, the top executive enjoys a security the independent does not have; and the enterprise furnishes the capital which, as an independent, he would have to get for himself.

Then there is the argument that economically the top salaries do not mean anything; if fully distributed to all employees, each would only get a few dollars additional pay. But the resentment against the top salaries is not economic at all but social—they are felt to be a denial of justice and fairness. Finally, there is the absurd argument that the high salary is completely unreal since the income tax today takes most of it anyhow. This is true, of course; but why then pay it in the first place?

Yet there is a perfectly good reason for the top salaries. They are grounded in the structure of the big enterprise. We find the same high salaries for top executives in the nationalized industries of Great Britain. We find them in an extreme form in the Soviet Union, where none of the above arguments would make any sense. In relation to the worker's income, the top salaries of Soviet Russia's industrial managers are infinitely higher than the top salaries of American managers. They consist not only of money income that is relatively many times larger than American top salaries, but of incomes in the form of goods and services—a large house, a car, special vacations, special allotments of food, clothing, furniture, household equipment, above all priority on higher education for the children which money could not buy at all in the Soviet Union. There is evidence that the Russian worker resents these incomes of his top management fully as much as the American worker. Why then has the Soviet Union found it necessary to establish these salaries?

The answer lies in the hierarchical structure of the big enterprise operating, as it does, in a society in which authority and responsibility are primarily expressed by money income. A foreman must receive more money than the men working under him; a superintendent more money than the foreman; a plant manager more money than the superintendent; a divisional general manager more money than the plant manager; and so on to the executive vice president who must receive more money than the vice presidents reporting to him, and to the president who in turn must receive more money than the executive vice president. Since the bottom rung of the ladder must be a middle-class income, and since the steps must be fairly large, the top rung must be in the clouds. This explains why the top executive of a very big company—in Russia the general manager of a big plant or the Vice Commissar in charge of the Light Metals Trust—receives an astronomical income; and also why, despite an income tax that tends to become increasingly confiscatory once an income goes above $25,000 a year, executives in a large company will break their necks to get a little more money.[2]

[2] In sharp contrast, the income tax rates have had the effect of discouraging professional men, whose social position is not measured directly by their income, from trying to make more money and to work harder once they have reached a certain eminence. That this is the very opposite of the effect intended by the high tax rates—to penalize large business incomes and to encourage independent enter-

This argument, though perfectly valid, can obviously not make any sense to the worker, nor indeed to anybody except the management group in a big enterprise. It also certainly does not answer the charge that the high salaries are contrary to the spirit of our society. But it does show that the problem of the high salaries is not simply one of "greed" but is rooted in a need of the big enterprise. Actually, the problem of the big executive incomes—despite its seeming pettiness— is one of the very hardest to crack.

We Need More Profit—Not Less

An industrial system can function and survive only on a profit margin adequate to the demands of the future. The adequacy, if not the existence, of this profit margin is seriously threatened by the worker's rejection of profitability.

Over the next decades all Western countries will have to widen their profit margin considerably and will have to step up the rate of increase of productivity to prevent a decline in the standard of living. This is not primarily because of the destruction of World War II, and not even because of the added burden imposed by our demands for greater social services or for armaments.

We can no longer afford to use as if they were "current production" the capital reserves of nature: the fertility of the soil, the primeval forests of the unsettled American Continent, the deposits of coal, ores, petroleum and minerals, built up over millions and billions of years. The rapid depletion of these irreplaceable resources added a "surplus" to our income that carried risks and burdens which otherwise would have had to be borne by genuine profit. We can clearly no longer count on this "surplus." We cannot go on using up our natural heritage, at least not at the rate at which we have been destroying it.

The other reason, leading to a demand for a step-up in the face of technological improvement, is that we shall be less and less able to concentrate the benefits of increased productivity on the small minority living in the old industrial regions of the North Atlantic. By denying the inhabitants of the "colonial" areas more than the smallest share in these benefits, the population in the industrialized West—especially the European working class—used to get a considerably larger share for

---

prise—is only one more proof of the complete irrationality of our tax system and by no means its most irrational feature.

itself. If the political movements in the colonial areas will not set an end to this Western monopoly on a higher standard of living, the industrialization of the raw-material-producing countries certainly will. In fact, this development may be one of the major roots of Britain's economic troubles today.

In opposing profitability the worker opposes the basic rationale of economic performance. Since an industrial system can operate on no other rationale, the worker's opposition is bound to be equally strong under any system, whether free-enterprise capitalism, Socialism or Communism.

It is most dangerous for "Democratic Socialism"—and not only because the countries experimenting with it are the ones most in need of higher profitability and increased productivity. Under "Democratic Socialism" the government is a government of the workers. At the same time the government is the management of the industrial enterprises. Dependent for its votes on the workers, but dependent for its survival on the economic performance of its industry, "Democratic Socialism" can only operate if the members of the industrial enterprise, that is, the workers, abandon their opposition to profit and their demand for ever higher and fixed wage rates. Otherwise it must collapse both politically and economically.

The Socialist theoreticians—to the extent that they were willing to admit the necessity of profit—were convinced that the workers' opposition to profitability and productivity would disappear the moment the "capitalist" went, the moment the State took over. Nationalization has, however, had no such magical effects, nor could it have had them. Nationalization does not change the needs and purposes of either the enterprise or the worker. If they were in discord before nationalization, they will not be in harmony just because of nationalization. The experience with nationalized industry in all the countries of Western Europe amply bears this out. In fact, nationalization may very well strengthen the opposition. In the privately owned enterprise, the worker had at least a tangible enemy, a personal devil, who could be blamed. But under "Democratic Socialism" the only "bosses" he has to blame are his own leaders.

"Democratic Socialism" has to change the attitude of its own con-stituents practically overnight. The very sentiment, amounting almost to a religious conviction, on which "Democratic Socialism" has come to power everywhere—the conviction that "profit" is the enemy—is actually the greatest threat to its success and survival.

If "Democratic Socialism" does not succeed and succeed fast, it will have to turn into a totalitarian regime. Only a totalitarian State has the political power to break the opposition, to make wage rates flexible and to decree an adequate profit margin. Above all, if "Democratic Socialism" fails to overcome the opposition to profitability, it will become necessary to break by force the power of the labor movement; only a totalitarian government can do that in an industrial society.

But this is neither an excuse for inaction nor cause for self-congratulation for the "free-enterprise" system and those who believe in it. If the United States should go collectivist within the next twenty-five years, it will, in all probability, not be because the American people have turned Socialist. It will not even be because of another and more terrible war—unless we should be the losers. The most probable reason will have been inability of our industrial economy to operate on an adequate profit margin. This would seriously aggravate economic fluctuations. It would increasingly paralyze the economy to the point where the government would have to take over. It has been an old Socialist axiom attributed to no less than Lenin himself, that "the only thing that can be nationalized are losses." But it is equally true that an economy running at less than adequate profitability, that is, at a loss, must be subsidized by the State and ultimately be nationalized to keep alive.

Despite their seriousness the economic conflicts should be the ones that are most easily resolved. We shall even find that the principles for the solution of these conflicts are already operating within our economy and only have to be brought to the surface. These principles should satisfy the legitimate needs and wants of the worker. They should at the same time give substantial benefits to the enterprise in the form of greater productivity and lower costs. They should, in other words, establish a genuine harmony between the enterprise's demand for profitability and the worker's demand for security. The one exception, the one issue, which, so far, we can only hope to mitigate but cannot expect to resolve, is the problem of the high executive salaries.

Altogether, it is one of the outstanding features of an industrial economy that its wealth enables it to resolve economic conflicts to the satisfaction of both sides. Where a pre-industrial economy, clinging precariously to naked life, can fulfill the demands and needs of one interest only by denying all others, an industrial economy has something to distribute and can satisfy conflicting interests, at least in part. It does not have to strain every single resource of men and materials to stay alive today. Its economic conflicts are largely conflicts between the demands of today and the demands of tomorrow: in the wage conflict the issue is between the enterprise's today and the worker's tomorrow; in the resistance to productivity and in the rejection of profits the issue is between the worker's today and the tomorrow of enterprise and economy. But an industrial economy not only can take care of both, today and tomorrow, it *must* always take care of both simultaneously.

CHAPTER 10

CAN MANAGEMENT BE A LEGITIMATE GOVERNMENT?

THE enterprise is necessarily a governmental institution exercising vital authority over men. But the main function and purpose of the enterprise is the production of goods, not the governance of men. Its governmental authority over men must always be subordinated to its economic performance and responsibility. It can never be an autonomous function, a purpose in itself. *Hence it can never be discharged primarily in the interest of those over whom the enterprise rules.*

Political thought has agreed for almost 2,500 years that any government no matter how constituted must be legitimate. Otherwise it will not survive. A legitimate government is a government that rules in the interest of its subjects. But that the enterprise cannot possibly do. The first concern of the enterprise must be for profitability and productivity, not for the welfare of its members. The members are not the citizens for whose benefit the institution exists. They are a group of claimants—a very important group of claimants, but no more important than other groups such as consumers. They must be definitely subordinate to the claim of economic performance: profitability and productivity.

That the enterprise is not a legitimate government does not mean that it is an illegitimate one. Political thought has always assumed that the government that does not govern in the interests of the subjects will rule in its own interests—the classic definition of illegitimacy. But the governmental authority of the enterprise is neither to be discharged in the interest of its members nor in that of the management, but in the economic interest of the enterprise and of society.

From the point of view of the members subject to this authority, this distinction, however, is hardly relevant. All that matters to them is that the governmental authority under which they live and work is not an authority discharged for their benefit and in their interest. Even if discharged entirely in the social interest, it is still an alien authority. The problem is precisely that the worker's interest as a member of the enterprise and as subject to its governmental authority is not identical with society's interest in the economic performance of the enterprise.

The governmental authority of the enterprise does not result from legal, political or economic factors outside of the enterprise, but from the nature and the purpose of the enterprise itself. Management must exist and it must manage, no matter how control and ownership are organized politically, how profit and loss are distributed or how management is selected and appointed. Management has an objective function, grounded in the necessity of the enterprise, which makes it impossible for it to rule in the interests of the members, however "interest" is defined. It cannot be a "government for the people." Even if management were a "government of the people and by the people," if all legal power, ownership and control were, for instance, vested in the members of the plant community, management would still not be, could not possibly be, a "government for the people."

There is no way around the split. For one hundred years or more all attempts to find a way out have proven unsuccessful.

Fourier, the French "Utopian Socialist," proposed before 1820 to solve the problem through giving the ownership of the enterprise to the workers. Surely this would make the government of the enterprise responsible to them and legitimate. Almost a century and a half later, this solution still commands the widest popular support and has the most profound impact. For it applies to industry the very principle of political order which emerged victorious in nineteenth-century Liberalism: the principle of modern representative democracy.

Yet wherever tried worker ownership has failed miserably. It failed in those, by no means infrequent, privately owned companies that were given to the employees, such as the Zeiss Optical Works in Germany—worker-owned for a half century—or the even older worker-owned companies in France that go back all the way to Fourier. The elimination of the "alien" owner and the substitution of worker ownership does not result in a "withering away of management" or in any change in the behavior, the character or the attributes of management. Though the profits go to the workers, the government of the enterprise is as little a government for the worker as it had been before. As one old employee of the most successful worker-owned company in this country, the American Cast Iron Pipe Company in Birmingham, Alabama, said when the workers were trying to organize a union against their own company and against their own management some years ago:[1] "Sure this is my plant; but somebody has to protect my rights as a downtrodden working stiff against my privileges as a bloated capitalist stockholder."

Worker ownership fails equally in nationalized industries. The nationalization drives in Central Europe after World War I collapsed because the workers lost faith in them when they failed to change the basic nature of the enterprise and its governmental authority. Today the new Socialist regimes in Europe are already experiencing the beginning of the same disillusionment. While the rank and file of the trade union membership in England presses for more and "real" worker government to get rid of management, the Labor Government itself now fights this demand and insists on "professional" management. In Czechoslovakia trade union leaders are being told by the new Communist government that "now that capitalism has been conquered" there is no place for worker government and that trade unionists must assume the "managerial responsibility" for profitability and productivity. In the newly nationalized industries in France, government and worker have clashed head on in a fight between the demands of economic performance and security. The government's demand for sharp cuts in the labor force may well become the major issue of the Fourth Republic. In Germany the new managers of the Ruhr industries—nominated almost entirely by the trade unions and composed of their men—have barely taken over; but already the men complain that they are just like the old bosses.

The idea of worker ownership applies to the enterprise the concepts of a sovereign political body that is an end in itself. But only if the

---

[1] This is by no means an isolated example. Some very early examples showing exactly the same pattern can be found in Perlman's *History of Trade Unionism in the United States* (New York: The Macmillan Co., 1922).

enterprise supplied substantially all its members' wants would government *by* the members be government *for* the members. As Fourier
himself saw, worker ownership presupposes a utopian community
such as his "Phalanstery" which served as the model for so many of
the utopian attempts between 1820 and 1850 in the United States.

But what is the function of the industrial enterprise if it is not to
produce more and cheaper goods for the consumer, that is, for the
entire society? Why should any society burden itself with that complicated, delicate and problematical institution that is the enterprise,
but for the fact that it is the best means found so far to produce goods
for society and all its members?

The Divorce of Ownership and Control

Another confusion arises from the identification of "control" of the
enterprise, that is, management, with the legal ownership title of the
"capitalists." If "control" were indeed based on ownership, a shift in
the legal title from the "capitalist" to the "worker" would shift control
from "management" to the "worker." But ownership and control are
two separate things and are rapidly becoming divorced. One is grounded
in law, the other in function; the one is mobile and marketable, the
other tied to the enterprise. Ownership is primarily a right; control is
primarily a power and a responsibility. The two are so different that
their conjunction in one hand can be said to have been possible only
in a pre-industrial, a mercantile, society.

It is indeed not too difficult to imagine a different historical development under which the worker rather than the "capitalist" would have
been the legal owner and the recipient of the residuary profits. Under
such a system, "management" and "ownership" would have been
divorced all along. There would have been no problem of the "surplus
value" of Marxian economics, no "clash between human rights and
property rights" under such a system—which is, of course, why
Fourier's ablest disciples, the English Guild Socialists, dreamed of
something very much like it. But such a system would have needed a
management just the same. And it would be pretty much the same
management, as the management of Capitalism or that of Socialism and
Communism, acting the same way, concerned with the same problems,
following the same purposes. The political and social problems of
industrial society would be identical with those that face us now.

In actual development, the owner in non-Socialist countries, that is the shareholder, has largely abandoned control today. A growing number of our large enterprises is run on the model which Owen D. Young, then head of the General Electric Company, proposed twenty years ago, and in which the stockholders were to be confined to a maximum return equivalent to a risk premium. The remaining profit stays in the enterprise, is paid out in higher wages or is passed on in lower prices. Yet in none of these companies has the management function changed; in none has management become a "government for the workers" or is accepted by them as legitimate authority.

In other words: regardless where the profits go, regardless who owns the legal title, regardless how the management is selected and whom it is responsible to, the management-worker relationship is bound to be the same. As far as the worker is concerned, the management in the government-owned enterprise of a Socialist State is fully as much "management" as if the enterprise were personally owned by J. P. Morgan and operated for his exclusive benefit.

The Return to Enlightened Despotism

Neither can the problem be solved by the new paternalism so fashionable currently in this country. For its slogan, "Management has the worker's best interests at heart," implies that management can be legitimate if only it tries. This too applies to the political problems of the enterprise a traditional concept of the sovereign state: that of eighteenth-century Enlightened Despotism.

I shall not deal here with the desirability of Enlightened Despotism as a form of government. I am only concerned with the question whether the enterprise can be made a legitimate government on the paternalist basis. Management can never live up to the slogan. A management might be as solicitous of the worker's welfare, as genuinely concerned with his interests and purposes, as it can possibly be. It still must put the economic responsibility of the enterprise to society and the survival of the enterprise as an economic producer before anything else, including the interests of the worker. At best, the maxim that management always puts the worker's interests first can work in fair weather. As soon as hard times come management must reverse its policy. No matter how sincerely management believes in its paternalistic slogans, they must appear to the worker as hypocritical and as an insidious attempt on the part of the "bosses" to gain control over him.

That this is not theoretical speculation is proven by the one experience that is strictly comparable to modern industrial paternalism: modern colonial paternalism. Till well into the nineteenth century—the turning points are Macauley's Indian Education Act, the British North America Act of 1836, Raffles' administration of Singapore and the Indian Mutiny of 1859—colonies were regarded primarily as a source of raw materials and of trade—that is, purely economically. All emphasis was on the benefits to the home country. The old colonial system subordinated to its economic ends the fact that a colony is a political institution exercising governmental authority over people. It was this concept rather than any specific tax against which the American Colonists revolted, this concept that was under fire in the impeachment of Warren Hastings and in the attack of the Whigs against the whole idea of Colonialism. The point of attack was precisely that a colony was a government over people and that it, therefore, had to be a "government for the people," that is, a legitimate government.

The new Colonialism which accompanied the tremendous colonial expansion of the second half of the nineteenth century accepted the political responsibility its eighteenth-century predecessor had denied. But in attempting to give a "government for the people" it immediately ran up against the obligation to manage the colony in the economic, political or strategic interest of the home country. In this dilemma it resorted to Enlightened Despotism, to the assertion that colonial government has the natives' best interest at heart.

Formulated by Disraeli, sung by Kipling, the colonial system of the "White Man's Burden" was not insincere. It meant what it said, and it took its responsibilities a great deal more seriously than it is fashionable to believe today. Yet, it lost its empire as fast as the old colonialism. The split simply could not be resolved by good intentions, concern for the natives and paternalism. However much the new colonial administrators achieved, they could not achieve the one thing that mattered: acceptance by the natives as a legitimate government. The more they did to lift the natives economically, socially and culturally, the greater became the opposition. Indeed, it was the achievement which created the opposition; it made the colonial peoples conscious of the split between the ideals of colonial government and its responsibility toward the economic interests of the home country. Moreover this failure undermined among the colonial peoples the trust and belief in the very principles of responsible government in the name of which they were being subjected to an alien authority.

Similarly, Enlightened Paternalism in the industrial enterprise may drag down with it into failure and discard the principles on which it claims to be based: the principles of modern "human-relations" policies.

Such a development would be a major disaster. Human Relations is a tool that must not be blunted. It does not hold out the promise of overcoming the split in the political personality of the enterprise. But it is our major diagnostic tool in the whole area of the social life of the industrial society, of the enterprise as a social institution. On the intelligent use of this tool and on its acceptance by management and workers largely depend our chances to solve the difficulties in the social sphere of the plant-community.

CHAPTER 11

CAN UNIONISM SURVIVE?

THE answer, the only possible answer to the political duality of the industrial enterprise, is the labor union. Management with its political authority over the enterprise can neither be avoided nor be transformed, no matter what political, economic or legal arrangements are tried. At the same time this governmental authority can never put the welfare of its subjects first; it cannot be legitimate. Hence the split has to be institutionalized, has, so to speak, to be built into the very structure of the government of the enterprise. The only way to make the government of the enterprise legitimate is through a counterpower which represents the members against their government while at the same time itself forming a part of this government. The *union* is thus the institutional expression of the basic political tension of the enterprise. It is primarily a political organ. Even where the conflict is apparently over dollars and cents, the real fight is over power and control.

This contradicts the traditional concept of the union as an economic pressure group. This concept was not entirely unknown in Europe—the non-Socialist, white-collar unions of pre-Hitler Germany, for instance, subscribed to it. But up to a dozen years ago, it was the dominant American view. Inheriting it from Mark Hanna—who had developed the concept to integrate labor into the Republican party—Samuel Gompers built on it the American Federation of Labor.

The most consistent expression of this position we owe to John L. Lewis. In fact, his actions as the leader of the United Mine Workers Union during the past twenty-five years make no sense except as an expression of his conviction that unions are economic pressure groups exclusively concerned with the size of labor's share in the national income. They owe allegiance only to the members' economic interest and have neither political function nor social responsibility. John L. Lewis probably never said, when asked by the President of the United States to call off a coal strike because it endangered war production: "The President of the United States is paid to look after the national interest; I am only paid to look after the economic interest of the coal miners." But even if the statement is a reporter's invention, it expresses his basic position.

A good deal more can be said for this position than most contemporary critics admit. But it is nevertheless untenable—not only because of its social consequences but because it completely misinterprets the situation. Every single area of union activity is inevitably a management area, whether it be working hours or working conditions, job definitions, job assignments, hiring and firing policies, supervisory authority or seniority provisions. Even if a union were to abandon all these areas and confine itself entirely to the problems of cash income, it would have to set against profitability and productivity the needs of the worker for a predictable wage and predictable employment. And that is no longer a fight over the division of the economic pie, but one over the basic principles that should govern the enterprise. Every union has to insist on a grievance procedure, that is, on recognition of the union's demand both to participate in management decisions and to fight against them. Above all, every union has to demand the right to strike. But even where the ends of a strike are economic—and the real ends rarely are—the strike itself is the supreme political weapon, it is the "right to rebellion" of classic political theory.

Hence the union is always a part of the governmental structure of the enterprise. Whether it admits it or not, it is a governmental organ exercising, controlling, or vetoing vital governmental functions. It may make sense for a union to deny this, as the Gompers-John L. Lewis position does. But it is shortsighted to the point of folly for any management to deny that the union necessarily concerns itself with problems which are "properly management's prerogative." Any concern of the union is with matters which are properly management's prerogative; in fact, it is precisely because of this "prerogative" that the union exists.

The assertion that the union derives its function from the inability of management to be a legitimate government, grounds the union in the very structure of the enterprise. It therefore sharply contradicts the belief, so popular with American management today, that the union owes its existence to the sins of omission and commission of past "unenlightened" managements. In a way, even the Pope seems to have swung over to this belief when he recently (September, 1949) talked of the day when "capitalism" would have sufficiently reformed for unions to be unnecessary. This belief denies that there is any political problem in the relationship between enterprise and member. It leads directly to Enlightened Industrial Despotism. For its adherents conclude from this argument that the union would have no purpose and function in a properly managed industrial system, and would quietly wither away and leave complete control in the hands of an all-wise and benevolent management.

It is certainly true that the philosophy, policies, deeds and misdeeds of past managements account for the peculiar traits of union movements in particular countries or in particular industries. The unions are a *counterforce*, a *re*action against management. Past management characteristics have molded the personalities of present-day union leaders—and almost every major industry, certainly every country breeds distinct management types. The personality, philosophy and tactics—even the rhetoric—of that leader of the American coal industry who perorated that "the rights and interests of the laboring men will be protected and cared for, not by labor agitators but by the Christian men to whom God in His infinite wisdom has given control of the property interests of the country,"[1] has certainly had much to do with the personality, philosophy, tactics and rhetoric of John L. Lewis, who heads the coal miners today. Walter Reuther could not easily be imagined as a leader of railroad labor, whereas he fits in with a tradition of management in the early days of the American automobile industry. Ernest Bevin could not be imagined except in the British labor movement, etc.

In one important area management's sins of omission and commission are indeed the actual cause of unionism. This is the "twilight zone" of the industrial middle class, of supervision and middle management. On the one hand, these groups are employees like the rank and file, and stand in the same relationship to the enterprise. On the

[1] When government and public opinion demanded an end to the four-month lock-out of the miners in 1902.

other hand, they share in the managerial function to a considerable extent. They can identify themselves either with the rank and file against the governmental authority of the enterprise, or with the governmental authority of the enterprise. Which way they will go depends to a large extent on the willingness of top management to integrate them into the managerial group and to make their management functions real rather than nominal. It also depends on management's ability to establish a constructive relationship with the union representing the rank and file. Supervision—and probably also middle management—will be almost forced to unionize in self-defense if the management-union relationship remains one of latent or open civil war. They cannot survive in the no man's land between the front lines without the protection of a union of their own.

Yet in general the assertion that the "union is the result of management sins of omission and commission" is false. Management policies and behavior explain a good deal about the timing of the union development—though other factors such as economic conditions, labor supply and government policies are probably more important as releases or brakes on the growth of unionism. Management policies and personalities have a real influence on the attributes and accidents of any given union movement, any given union leadership. But the cause, the driving force, the purpose and function of unionism, are all independent of management policies and rooted in the one thing over which management has absolutely no control: the very existence and function of management itself.

The Limitations of Unionism

In all recorded history I know of only one parallel to the labor union. In Republican Rome there was a split—comparable to that in the enterprise—between the ritual and religious responsibilities of the chiefs of the old clans, the "senators," and the interests of their subjects, the "plebs," the new immigrant population which, though outside traditional rite and traditional culture, had to be governed by the senatorial class. When this conflict was brought to a head by the first general strike recorded in history, it was solved by building into the government of Rome a special organ, the Tribunate, representing the "plebs" against its own rulers.

But the emergence of the Tribunate created as many new problems as it solved old ones. Eventually the Tribunate was abolished; it was "nationalized" and the Emperor became the Tribune; but the Senate also lost all independence.

The emergence of the union also raises as many new, as it resolves old, problems. It is indeed the only way in which a resolution of the political dilemma of the enterprise can be obtained. But it is a precarious, troublesome and vexing solution. The problems of the union, its place and function in industrial society, its relationship with the enterprise, and its internal organization and cohesion are so difficult that the question must be asked whether the contribution which unionism makes is worth the price. The question is bound to come to the fore in every industrial country—and it is not going to be asked by "union busters" alone.

The temptation is great in every industrial country to solve the political problem of the enterprise by suppressing the union. This suppression will not take the form of outlawing the union; it is likely to be achieved by nationalizing the union—a much more subtle, but also a much greater, threat to unionism than outright and open suppression. And it would not be too difficult to do. While necessary to the enterprise, the union is not necessary in the same way that management is. An industrial system without unions is quite easy to imagine. The Nazis actually abolished them through nationalization, and in the Soviet system they are abolished in all but name. But an industrial system without management is unimaginable and impossible. The union is not the original, the dynamic, the moving, force of an industrial system. Just as the light of the moon is only a reflection, the union's function derives from management's function. Hence the industrial system will not stop if the union movement is suppressed—the way it would if any government tried to run industry without a management.

But the union fulfills a need that is essential. The tension which it expresses is inherent in the industrial system. The need to make the government of the industrial enterprise legitimate will persist no matter how society is organized. Neither tension, nor function, nor need can be eliminated by suppressing the union or by destroying its reality, as under the Soviet system. Suppressing the unions may give relief at a particular moment from what might appear to be unbearable pain; but the relief would be obtained at the price of making the disease incurable. The tension would only be driven underground, the need go unfulfilled, the function remain undischarged.

What is even more important, suppression of the union in an industrial society presupposes a totalitarian government: only such a government would have enough power to break the union movement. The only other way to provide relief from the tension caused by the "split personality" of the industrial enterprise, is through permanent mass hysteria, through keeping the masses continually excited and emotionally strained, in short, through the permanent emotional mobilization which only totalitarianism can provide and keep alive.

This is not to be misunderstood as an argument for complete union license. The problems of the union are such that they can only be solved by rather drastic changes in the policies and organization of the union. But the aim of these new policies must not be "anti-union"; on the contrary their purpose must be to make it possible for the union to function effectively and constructively—in its own interest, in the interest of the enterprise and in the interest of society. To make the union function is one of the biggest tasks confronting our society; on our success may depend our hopes of retaining our free institutions.

Can the union function so that society will function and survive; or must society in self-defense impose limitations on the union which will in effect destroy unionism?

Can the union function *within* the enterprise, as it must; or are the respective requirements of survival and function of enterprise and union mutually exclusive?

Finally, there is a big question whether a union can live with itself, whether it can survive the tensions and contradictions within its own structure.

The Structural Problems of the Union

The union is by definition and function an opposition. Its purpose is to assert the purposes of the employee *against* the purposes of the enterprise. It cannot abandon its opposition without also abandoning its function. It cannot hold the allegiance of its members except as an opposition. The greatest threat to a union leader's position is the accusation that he has "sold out to the bosses" and become a "management man."

At the same time, the union is an opposition which can never become the government. The moment a union or union leaders were to take over the management, they would be in management's political shoes and would have to act the "boss." They would lose their hold on their members and be confronted speedily by a union movement opposing them. This is what is today threatening the British unions who participate in the management of the nationalized industries.

The union is a political institution. Its purpose is power rather than economic production, income or profit. Because it is an institution, its behavior must be determined by its survival needs. Because it is a political institution, its survival depends upon political rather than upon economic performance: it must be able to hold the allegiance of its members. And for this reason union leadership is also a political office based upon the leader's ability to hold the members' loyalty rather than upon economic performance.

Because the function of the union is both negative and political, its cohesion depends in the last analysis on the "right to strike." The strike denies the enterprise access to the productive resources. The union, indeed, does not gain control of these resources through a strike. Nothing can make the union capable of producing—only the enterprise is productive. But the strike checkmates the enterprise. It is the Tribune's Veto. If the union cannot organize for production, it can at least prevent everybody else from producing. The strike is the most potent political weapon against the governmental power of the enterprise; it is also the only such weapon within reach of the union. A union movement without the "right to strike" would be unable to express its opposition.

Far beyond its importance as a political weapon, the strike is the emotional affirmation of union solidarity and of the common cause of the workers. This is what is meant by the old union adage that "No strike is ever lost."

The *"mystique"* of the General Strike, the belief in its magical, almost sacramental properties, which the Frenchman Georges Sorel preached at the beginning of our century, has been proven an illusion. A general strike can succeed only if there is no longer effective government. The threat of a general strike is bound to arouse public opinion to such an extent as to rouse even a cowardly and disorganized government to strong and effective action. But Sorel was right in emphasizing that the strike is both rationally and emotionally, as force and as symbol, the heart of unionism. On it, in the last analysis, rather than on ballots or benefits rests the power as well as the cohesion of any union movement.

Because it is an "anti" force, an opposition that can never rule, a union can never feel secure. However strong it may appear to be, however safe, however accepted, management will always be the dominant, the safe, and, above all, the dynamic and leading element. The union will always feel on the defensive if not on the brink of defeat. For a union leader to admit this is, of course, treason. But the very fact that a union must always grow stronger—must at least always claim that it grows stronger—shows the inherent insecurity and precariousness of the union's position—an insecurity no less haunting for being inward and psychological rather than outward and tangible.

In one respect, however, the insecurity is not just psychological. A union confined to one plant or to one enterprise cannot possibly be secure enough to discharge its function. It is forever in danger of becoming a "company union." Within any one individual enterprise management is bound to be dominant. A union operating in one company alone must be so concerned with the welfare and prosperity of its enterprise as to make it hesitate to stand in opposition.

Finally a union must demand the allegiance of the workers of the enterprise. It must demand that the workers look to the union for authority and leadership. It must even more demand negative allegiance—that the workers do not look to anybody else for authority and leadership. At the least, the union must demand that no one but its own members are employed by the enterprise—a demand reinforced doubly by the basic insecurity of the union and by the need for certainty that a strike call will be obeyed.

But every one of these "inner laws" brings the union into conflict with the requirements of society, the requirements of the enterprise, the requirements of the workers—indeed, into conflict with itself. Every one is likely to strengthen the demand that unionism be made "constructive" by being suppressed, or at the least by being bound and gagged.

CHAPTER 12

UNION NEEDS AND THE COMMON WEAL

AS LONG as unionism is weak and struggling it will be permitted by society to be opposition pure and simple. But once unionism becomes accepted and powerful, it must accept responsibility for the success of the enterprise, for its profitability and productivity, and for the stability, profitability and productivity of the economy. It cannot be allowed to remain the "spirit that always negates." It must become a "loyal opposition." But can an opposition be "loyal" unless it can hope to take over the government itself one day?

A Rational Wage Policy

This contradiction comes out in the demand for a rational wage policy. As long as the larger part of the economy is not unionized, the union movement can be allowed to operate on the assumption that wages should move only in one direction: upward, and to demand increasing rigidity of the wage structure. But as soon as unionization becomes the rule rather than the exception, society must demand of the union that it accept responsibility for the consequences of its wage policy. This means acceptance of the principle that the wage burden of the economy must be flexible and allowed to move down as well as up. It means even that the union will have to put the prevention of losses, that is, the maintenance of an adequate rate of profit, before the wage demands of its members. Above all, society must demand *that economically rational criteria be considered more important in the determination of the wage burden than the political requirements of the union.*

It is this last demand that causes the major difficulty.

Practically all discussions of labor economics assume that the wage conflict between enterprise and union is a conflict over dollars and cents, in which the enterprise fights for the lowest cost per unit and the union for the "maximization of labor income." At first sight, this would seem to be borne out by the language and terminology of both sides. The talk is about profits and costs, prices and real wages, etc. The arguments are couched in the language of economic theory; overproduction and underconsumption, insufficient capital accumulation and insufficient consumer purchasing power.

If the clash were really one of economic aims and the argument really one of economic theory, we would not have to concern ourselves with the problem of a rational wage policy. The problem would then be primarily a technical one to be solved largely by economic research.

The economic arguments and theories are, however, largely window dressing, at least as far as the union is concerned. They hide the real aims of the union just as they hide, for entirely different reasons, the real needs and demands of the member. If "maximization of wage income" were really the union goal, as the textbooks assert, union behavior would be completely incomprehensible and irrational.[1] The union stand is determined by the fact that the union is primarily not an economic but a political institution. Its survival does not depend upon economic performance but upon the allegiance of its members, for which it has to compete both with the enterprise and with a host of other unions. The union stand must be "union-centered," as Ross puts it, not enterprise-centered or even worker-centered.

The demand that the union adopt a "rational" wage policy beneficial to economy and enterprise does not necessarily conflict with the self-interest of the union. The members will increasingly measure the performance of a strong and established union movement by its success in preventing depression unemployment. Without an economically rational wage policy no country can hope to prevent or to overcome a serious depression. Prevention of a depression demands control of the boom that precedes it. It demands prevention of wage

[1] This has been brilliantly demonstrated by Arthur M. Ross in his above-mentioned *Trade Union Wage Policy* which should be required reading for every business executive. However, it hardly follows—as Ross seems to argue in his concluding chapter—that there is no need for an economically rational wage policy simply because the unions, as now constituted, cannot operate on economic rationality.

increases at a time of full employment; such wage increases are inflationary when everybody is at work and fully productive. Full employment is the one state of which it can be asserted dogmatically and beyond any shadow of doubt that increased production of goods must precede any increase in money income if the economy is to remain in equilibrium. And there is only one direction in which a full-employment economy can move if its equilibrium is disturbed: downward. Indeed, inflation is the one absolutely sure and infallible way to make maintenance of full employment impossible.

If the union movement is to preserve its strength when the boom comes to an end, it must have accepted responsibility for wage policy while the boom still lasts. If the union has not embraced the principle that wages have a rational connection with prices, costs, productivity, profitability, etc., in short, if it has not accepted the principle of a wage policy based on the national interest, it is bound to suffer severely during the downswing of the cycle. It will be unable to protect its members. The only protection, the security of a predictable employment and wage plan, presupposes flexibility of the wage burden. The union will at the same time be quite unable to prevent cuts in wages, which then will be defeats for the union and apt to undermine the allegiance of its members. This is what happened to the American labor movement after World War I, when the inability of the union to maintain wage rates during the 1921-22 depression led to the desertion of one-half or more of the members.

Today the American unions may very well face an even more severe setback. The great body of today's union membership has joined since 1933; the bulk of the major unions have come into existence since 1933. American union members and American union leadership have, therefore, by and large never known anything but the upswing of a business cycle. There was only one setback in 1938, and it lasted less than a year. Yet few union leaders in this country—and even fewer union members—have given any thought to the problems that will face them when the upswing will have passed its peak.

The refusal to accept a rational wage policy will inevitably lead to wage determination by the government. As far as the worker goes, this may not work to his detriment; after all, he has the voting power. It certainly will not work to the advantage of the enterprise.

But it must destroy unionism by undermining the allegiance of the worker and his dependence on the union.

Yet the political pressure against a rational wage policy within the union is greatest during a boom, that is, precisely when such a policy is most needed. With the labor shortage of full employment, with an apparently insatiable market and with high profits, at least on paper, management is in no position to resist wage demands. Since the boom phase is accompanied either by rapid increases in prices or by a rapid expansion in the standard of living and expenditure—usually by both —the union is under constant pressure from its membership to press its advantage, at least to the extent of keeping wages abreast of the increases in prices or of the rise of the "normal" standard of living. To demand of the union movement at precisely this moment that it accept responsibility for a rational wage policy means, in effect, to demand that it oppose the members just when the promised land seems to be within their reach.

More important, however, it the impact of the wage-rate convention on union behavior. Its effect can be likened to that of the injection of intense nationalist emotionalism—a cry of "revenge" or of "insult to the flag"—into an international crisis. It makes it almost impossible for a union to think or act in economically rational terms where wage is concerned. It subordinates union wage policy to considerations of "face" and of prestige. It converts the need for political cohesion and survival into a need for a great victory whatever its eventual cost. And to keep up the interest of its members, the union must always proclaim the wage rate, whatever it may be, grossly insufficient—just as an aggressor government must always make just one more conquest.

Finally, the competition between management and union, for the allegiance of the workers prevents acceptance of economic rationality by the union. Such acceptance would, in effect, be in an acceptance of management's authority. As long as the relationship between management and union is dominated by the claim of both sides for the absolute and exclusive allegiance of the workers, the union cannot even by implication acknowledge management's authority without surrendering some of its own.

Yet society must demand of the union movement that it subordinate its wage demands to the common weal, whether this means higher or lower wages at a given moment.

The Right to Strike

The strike weapon by itself—irrespective of the effects of any given strike—raises serious political questions. The strike is our contemporary version of the traditional "right to revolution." It may be argued that the strike is "nonviolent" and "peaceful," at least until a worker tries to cross the picket line or until the management tries to operate the plant with nonstrikers. But the fact that we have laid down the rules of civilized striking does not change its basic character. The strike is effective precisely because it is a violent break with the established order. Can society allow any group within the population a special "right to revolution"? Can society allow any group to enforce its demands, however legitimate, by threatening to paralyze the economy. It can be asserted flatly that no society can tolerate strikes that endanger the general welfare, such as a strike that shuts down an entire industry. Nor can any government tolerate a strike aimed at its authority.

But the "right to strike" is absolutely necessary to the cohesion, if not indeed to the survival, of the union; without it it cannot discharge its function.

Contrary to general belief, the strike is not likely to become less important with the recognition and acceptance of unionism.

All close students of trade unionism have noticed that economic disputes are very rarely the real cause of a strike. We do not have a strike because negotiations break down; negotiations break down because the situation is a strike situation. In this respect industrial war does not differ from any other war. In the early days of unionism the strike is characteristically a strike for union recognition. Its aim is to establish the union in a plant or in an area. It is thus a strike actually directed against an employer or a group of employers. Even if accompanied by violence, it is a private fight. Also, it is usually confined to one enterprise and does not endanger the whole economy.

But the major purpose of the strike in an accepted and recognized union movement is as an affirmation of union cohesion. The strike becomes a symbolic, almost a ritual, performance. It stages an emotional experience which the union member must have but cannot find in the humdrum routine of an established, successful, "fat" union. In effect, the strike in a union movement which no longer has to fight for recognition, is very much akin to the carefully arranged "spontaneous" demonstrations of a totalitarian regime which serve at one and the same time as a propaganda device to impress the outside world and as a means to rally the followers and to strengthen their allegiance. Union demands are increasingly the pretext for, rather than the cause of, the strike. The steel and automobile strikes of 1946, the coal strike from which the United States has suffered every spring these last ten years, the railroad strike of 1946, the strike in the meat-packing industry in 1946, the typographers' strike of 1947—in every one of these the apparent issues could have been settled without a strike. The real purpose of the strikes was to display the power of the union to its own members and to the public, to overcome strife and conflicts within the union, or to beat a rival union. The strike as "symbolic violence" becomes an end in itself.

This "ritual" strike becomes increasingly difficult to control. Early union tradition maintained that a strike is not to be called lightly but is the last, extreme recourse. It also laid down the rule that strikes must never be fought over minor issues. The utter disregard of these rules in this country during the last decade may have been due to the boom, which seemed to make a strike relatively riskless for union and workers alike. When economic conditions become less easy, the old rules will again be remembered, no doubt. But the increase in the propensity to strike, and especially to strike over petty differences, has been too great to be explained entirely by the boom psychology.

Also, strikes become increasingly difficult to settle. It may even be said that the increasing willingness to strike over petty differences (in the four months General Motors strike of 1946 for instance, the difference between union demand and company offer was one cent an hour) reflects a growing unwillingness of union leaders to call a strike over big differences. They know that they cannot afford to "settle" a strike; they must win a complete victory. If the strike were really over its apparent economic issue, this would make no sense. But if the purpose of the strike is to affirm the solidarity of the union, compromise becomes very difficult. Emotionally, the effect of a compromise settlement is likely to be worse than that of a "defeat with honor," which creates the bond of common heroism and leaves the legacy of a great legend. In such a situation the intelligent leader does not start world wars but sticks to petty issues. Indeed, one American union leader—and a very conservative one at that—pointedly drew a parallel between his situation and that of the German Army in the First World War. "The mistake of the German generals," he said, "was that they did not realize before 1914 that they could not compromise, and that therefore they had to play for small stakes. A negotiated peace would have meant the end of the social and political power and position of the Army. But when they came to understand this, around 1917, it was too late to change the war to one they could win. Hence they had to fight to the bitter end to create at least the chance for a revival of militarism in the bitterness of defeat and the heroic legend of sacrifice."

Increasingly the real target of the strike is society rather than the employer. I do not mean by this that the strike becomes increasingly revolutionary or an instrument in the class war. Obviously the more established, the more recognized a union movement, the less revolutionary, the more conservative will it be. This applies even to the Communist-dominated trade unions of France or Italy, who are very potent tools of Russian foreign policy but very poor tools of class warfare. What I mean is simply that the union more and more expects to win by putting pressure on society rather than on one employer or one industry. Union action increasingly aims at forcing the government to intervene on its side, to bring about a change in public policy, or to hold up the consumer. In the two-week strike of the American coal miners in the Spring of 1949, the real object was to prevent price cuts in coal. The real purpose of the strike threat in the steel industry in early 1946 was to force the government to lift the wartime ceiling on steel prices so as to enable the industry to pass on to the consumer the cost of higher wages.

Finally, strikes tend to become industry-wide rather than directed against one plant or one company. An established and accepted union will inevitably have to operate on a craft-wide or industry-wide basis. It does not even need a formal strike call against all the companies in the industry, to make a strike industry-wide. In every industry there are a few key operations the shutdown of which stops the entire industry in a matter of hours or days. The decision whether to call out the workers in the entire industry or whether to close down the key operations is a tactical one and depends on the internal political needs of the union at the moment. But the economic effect is the same.

The impact of an industry-wide strike on the economy is radically different from that of a strike against one plant or one company. Whereas the local strike puts the individual enterprise under the threat of losing its market to its competitors, the industry-wide strike puts no pressure on the enterprise at all as a rule. The whole pressure is on society and government. It is effective exactly in proportion to the social and economic damage it inflicts and to its threat of paralyzing the economic life of the country.

Where the earlier strike for recognition served a socially rational and clearly defined purpose, the ritual strike is socially irrational, undefinable and, basically, limitless. It is not a "private fight" between two economic interests but an affirmation of the "right to rebellion" and thus a direct challenge to the authority of government. In addition, it is likely to endanger the economy. Indeed, pressure on the economy becomes the major weapon, if not the real aim, of the strike.

But can any society tolerate such a strike? Can it permit any one group, no matter how deserving, to paralyze the economy? Can it even permit any group, no matter how loyal, to possess such a weapon? Private armies are rightly regarded as incompatible with functioning government no matter whom they serve. Is the problem of the strike so different from that of the private army just because the weapons are economic? We definitely would not allow the enterprise to use the economic weapon of the lock-out if it thereby endangered the economy. An industry-wide "lock-out" would probably be considered a criminal conspiracy. But the cohesion and function of the enterprise does not rest on the right to lock out its workers. The cohesion and function of the union, however, do most assuredly rest on the "right to strike."

The only attempt made so far to protect both society and the union's "right to strike" is the recent proposal to distinguish between "essential" industries, in which strikes would be forbidden, and "unessential" industries, in which strikes could be allowed. That this proposal has the support of men friendly to the union movement and thoroughly aware of its structure and function, shows how critical the problem of the union has become.

But in effect this means forbidding strikes altogether. The ban on strikes in essential industries would outlaw practically all industry-wide strikes and all strikes which, while ostensibly directed against one enterprise, would shut down a whole industry. It would also outlaw all local strikes in industries essential to the life of the community: public utilities, transportation, distribution.

Altogether, the "essential" industries employ the bulk of our industrial workers and are organized by the strongest and most important unions. To ban strikes in "essential" industries would tend to make of the union a peripheral institution and to confine it to the unimportant industries in which there are few if any big enterprises.

A permanent no-strike pledge is both possible and necessary in case of grave national emergency such as war. It is both possible and necessary for such services as police, fire brigades, hospitals, etc.—that is, for essential community services which are definitely not economic in character. But to extend the ban on striking beyond national emergency and beyond a very small number of public services really means attacking the principle of unionization itself. Union resentment over President Truman's policy in 1947, which in effect imposed a ban on strikes in essential industries such as coal mining and transportation, was perfectly understandable; and the charge that the President abused his wartime emergency powers to "bust unions" made sense, from the point of view of the unions. Yet, it is no accident that the labor drive to repeal the Taft-Hartley Act foundered on the refusal of Congress to repeal the President's power to stop a strike by court action.

A real solution, which would maintain the union's "right to strike" but would make sure that it is never used in a manner endangering society—the solution which the distinction between "essential" and "unessential" industries aims for but fails to achieve—has still to be found. And of all the solutions to the problems of unionism it will be the most difficult to find.

The Insecurity Neurosis of the Union

A union cannot expect to behave responsibly as long as it fears for its existence and survival. It cannot assume responsibility for wage policy. It cannot accept restraints on the use of the strike weapon. Above all, it cannot assume responsibility for the survival and profitability of the enterprise, cannot acknowledge management's authority as legitimate and necessary, and cannot enforce the contract upon its members. Without the feeling of security the union is bound to be disruptive to society and to the enterprise alike.

There is no other institution in our society that is so beset by an insecurity neurosis. It is rooted in the inborn and incurable inferiority of the union within the enterprise. The enterprise can operate without the union but cannot operate without the management. Even the strongest and most powerful union cannot claim an indispensable function, as does management, but rests its position on contract, legal sanction and political support, all of which are revocable. This inferiority is real and not imagined, as witness the extent to which unions rely on management for their own functioning. Practically all the provisions of the union contract are administered by management. Against management's administration of the contract the union can only complain by means of grievance, slow-down or strike.

Such inferiority must create a feeling of profound insecurity. It shows in the "touchiness" of union and union leader. Anything that is not uncritical praise is apt to be considered an attempt to destroy the union. It shows in the genuine resentment of union leaders when management, during a strike, attacks them publicly, in a newspaper advertisement for instance. The same leaders, however, are genuinely puzzled by management resentment over the terms customarily applied to executives by the union press and in union meetings. The leaders even of powerful and strongly entrenched unions are convinced that management is stronger than the union. A recent poll of American union leaders showed sixty-one per cent of AF of L leaders and seventy-nine per cent of CIO leaders convinced that management is the stronger; only eleven per cent and five per cent respectively held the union to be stronger. In the same poll twenty-nine per cent of the AF of L leaders and forty-one per cent of the CIO leaders expressed the conviction that management was out to break the union, between fifty and sixty per cent of the men in both groups said that management just tolerates the union, and only fourteen and six per cent respectively considered management to have accepted unionism.[2] There was no real difference between the opinions of the CIO leaders and

[2] C. Wright Mills, *The New Men of Power* (New York: Harcourt, Brace & Company, 1948). Pp. 133, 140 and 192.

those of the AF of L leaders who operate mostly in industries where unionism has been accepted for a long time. They should thus feel much more secure, according to the theory of the "mellowing" influence of experience and acceptance upon the union and its leaders. Actually, younger AF of L leaders who have never known the struggle for recognition, and who have spent all their working life in an accepted and strong union, are apparently even more strongly convinced than the young CIO men that management has superior strength and is bent on destroying the union.

This insecurity underlies the union demand that membership in the union be a condition of employment, either by excluding from employment anyone not a member (closed shop), by demanding of a new worker that he join the union within a short period and remain a member (union shop), or, at the very least, by making the continued employment of any union member dependent on his remaining in the union (maintenance of membership).

Insecurity also underlies the need of every union to extend its operations beyond one plant or one enterprise, and to embrace all the workers in a specific skill, or all the workers in one industry.

The first demand raises serious problems of the social order; the second, equally serious ones of economic organization and policy.

Management has been attacking the union demands hotly as "undemocratic" because they force citizens to pay tribute to a private organization before they are allowed to work. The unions have defended their demands by pointing out that to expect the minority to comply with the majority will is "democratic"; that not to allow anyone to profit from the union's activity without contributing to its upkeep is just; and that union security is in the interest of the enterprise itself as it alone enables the union to maintain discipline and observance of the contract.

Both arguments are valid to some extent. But both miss the point. The union needs security. The "open shop" makes it certainly very hard for a union to operate except as a negative and disrupting force. Yet the standard union-security provisions give the union a control over the citizen which no society can allow to a private organization and which a free society cannot even allow to its government without stringent checks on its exercise. Denial of membership in a union with a closed-shop contract is a denial of the citizen's access to a livelihood. In a highly skilled or a highly specialized craft, expulsion from membership in the union may be a sentence of economic death. Control over the number of apprentices in a craft or over entrance to the union gives the union a power over economic and technological progress and a power of monopoly with which no group should be entrusted.

The problem of union security is not too different from that of the powers of professional bodies such as the bar or the medical profession. We have always had groups which had to have police powers over their members either in the interest of society or for their own internal reasons. Officers corps and Civil Service too have to be granted very substantial powers of control over both the conditions of access into, and of expulsion from, their ranks. But the exercise of these powers must be based on rational criteria—a degree, for instance, as the condition of entry into a profession; gross misconduct as the only grounds for removal, etc. They must be exercised in a clearly defined process and by an authority which is both duly qualified and disinterested. There must be some appeal. And the powers must be used not to create an artificial scarcity but in the public interest. If these conditions are not met, the police powers of any private group become socially unbearable, no matter how vital it is for the group to have them or how desirable for society that the group prosper.

It is futile to argue that the union, being a "democratic" organization, would never abuse its power and should therefore be exempt from all restrictions on the police powers of half-private, half-public organizations. This is not only using the term "democratic" in its Moscow meaning. Organized society cannot tolerate the existence of an unlimited and unregulated power of control over citizens. Even if never abused, it is a constant denial of governmental authority and of social cohesion. In practice such a power must, by its very nature, be misused.

Nor are the important instances of misuse confined to corruption or racketeering. Some time ago a taxicab driver in Philadelphia—a city in which craft unions are very strong—decided that he was getting too old for his trade and began to look for less strenuous work. The man was a good union member; in fact, he had been a local union official for years. He was also highly skilled. He had no difficulty getting offers of a job; but in every case the offer required his being accepted by the union. He knew that he could not transfer his seniority to another union and therefore looked for a job only in plants organized by the union to which he already belonged. Yet he still drives a cab. No local of his own union was willing—or able under its by-laws—to take him in except as an apprentice, or so far down the seniority list as to make his employment altogether impossible. And this is by no means an isolated case.

The rules limiting transfers of seniority or of skill from union to union or from local to local are not just "rackets." For every single one a good case can be made out in the name of equity and justice. Together, however, they tend to freeze society and to deny the citizen the enjoyment of "life, liberty and the pursuit of happiness" which every free society must protect. The same applies to other union rules, whether they restrict economic freedom, political and civil rights or discriminate against minorities.

Big Union, and the Concentration of Power

The union's need to expand beyond one plant or one enterprise impels the union towards monopoly. It also powerfully pushes the whole economy in the same direction. In the United States the growth of the large industrial union in the last fifteen years has—next to our fiscal system—undoubtedly been the most effective force for monopoly.

A union must try to make the wage rates uniform in all the plants it covers. It cannot afford to accept for its members lower wage rates than the neighboring industries pay; each union is forever in competition with every other union for members, standing and power. The pressure to extend the union's sphere of activity will tend to level out wage rates for comparable work, first throughout the industry, and then throughout the country.

This may seem eminently fair and just. But it gives the big business an increasing advantage especially over the young and growing enterprise. For the development of a new business requires high overhead costs.

Ability to pay wages is also largely dependent on cash position or on low-cost credit. Very often the real issue in a wage dispute is whether an increase in wage rates should precede or follow an expected increase in the productive efficiency of the worker. The small, and to an even greater extent the young and growing, enterprise is likely to have a much larger proportion of its assets invested in materials, equipment and claims than in cash. It has to watch its cash position much more carefully. It meets with much greater difficulty if it has to borrow, and it has to pay more for whatever credit it can get. A big company may be able to prefinance an increase in productivity for a few years. It may be able to pay higher wages in anticipation of higher productivity, while a small company forced to pay out money it has not yet earned will be driven into bankruptcy.

But under an industry-wide or nation-wide pattern the very biggest company is likely to determine the wage rate. This applies particularly to the system popular in this country today, in which a few big companies, the "wage leaders," establish in their own negotiations the pattern which everybody has to follow. What we have in this country are all the worst features of a wage cartel; uniformity of wages constitutes as effective a cartel as uniformity of selling prices or a division of markets. The only difference is that the open cartel tends to protect the inefficient producer whether large or small, whereas our system simply favors the big, whether efficient or inefficient.

Equally undesirable socially and economically is the effect of union bigness and centralization on the structure of the big enterprise itself. During the last twenty years we have come to realize that it is of the utmost importance for society, for the economy, and for the enterprise itself, that management of the big business be decentralized. The advantages of bigness are obtainable, its disadvantages surmountable, only under a federal system of management organization. Yet the centralization of union relations has brought about greater centralization of managerial control and authority. Local managers have been deprived of authority with respect to one of their most important functions. Independence and responsibility have been taken away from middle management and supervision. For centralized handling of labor relations and a uniform contract make of every decision a "precedent" applicable throughout the whole enterprise, and therefore something only the highest authority in the central office can settle.

Finally, the union drive toward industry-wide or nation-wide unionization leads to "big government" and to centralization of the governmental functions. It undermines local government, which clearly cannot handle industry-wide or nation-wide labor problems. In a vicious circle, this leads to greater concentration of union power, to greater concentration of economic and managerial power, and in turn to greater concentration of governmental power.

Yet the remedy is not to outlaw industry-wide bargaining as a (fortunately defeated) amendment to the Taft-Hartley Act proposed. Such a restriction is bound to remain a dead letter; its only effect would be to make union insecurity an incurable disease. There is a conflict not only between the union need for organization beyond the enterprise and the social interest, but one between two social interests, one demanding an industry-wide union movement, one opposed to its monopolistic and centralizing effect on economy and society.

CHAPTER 13

THE UNION LEADER'S DILEMMA

UNION leadership has become a new center of social and political power. At the same time the inner tensions of unionism place almost unsurmountable obstacles in the path of functioning and responsible union leadership. The complaint that there are not enough responsible union leaders is common in all industrial countries. But considering the odds against them, the amazing thing is that there are so many good, responsible and capable union leaders.

Despite the publicity and prominence of the union leader, neither management nor the public know what he does, what his motives, purposes, his rationale and his code are, what makes a union leader "tick."

The functions, powers and responsibilities of union leadership, if not the very job, hardly exist before a union is accepted and recognized as the representative of the workers in the field. The union leader is therefore a very new thing—newer even than management. Almost all the men at the head of unions today—whether in this country or in Europe—are still men who came up in "prerecognition" days. The conservative old gentlemen who lead the American Railway Brotherhoods look and behave as if they had always been securely in control of their industry. But they spent the greater part of their long lives in a bitter fight for union recognition. The same is true for the leaders of the most powerful British unions; Ernest Bevin, for instance, began his career as organizer of a strike for union recognition. The emergence of the union leader has been incredibly fast—and nowhere faster or more spectacular than in this country. The whole development has been compressed into less than one generation—the period since the First World War in Europe, an even shorter period in the United States. There is as yet no leader at the head of a large union who has come up under the new regime; all the top men of today are "first generation immigrants" who still show clear signs of their origin in the "old country" of prerecognition unionism. Whether an established and recognized union can produce leaders at all is one of the unanswered problems of unionism.

The Union Leader as a Symbol

From the point of view of the worker, the positions of leadership and power in the union movement are, above all, opportunities for social advancement and prestige. Union leadership is a new and particularly attractive avenue of escape out of the working class.

For the union as an institution, the union leader is absolutely essential—as essential as management is to the enterprise. He is likely to exercise greater control over the union than management has even over a nonunionized enterprise.

From the point of view of society, the union leaders represent a new center of tremendous power; they are the "new men of power" as a recent book calls them.[1]

The first of these aspects is rarely mentioned; yet it may well be the most important one. In the hierarchy of union leadership, from shop steward to national president or general secretary, the worker is offered a new system of opportunities. These opportunities, moreover, are not "also" open to the worker in competition with other, more advantageously situated groups, but are largely reserved to him. They are his very own. Even on the lowest levels of this hierarchy the worker finds great rewards, which are no less real for being largely immaterial. The shop steward or committeeman, the officers of a local or the delegates to a union convention usually receive no more pay than the man who tends a machine. But they enjoy real power and prestige. They have the satisfaction of being actors rather than mere spectators, movers rather than tools, leaders rather than the mass. Any step beyond this lowest level offers, in addition, the tangible rewards of an income that is both secure and usually above the worker's income. The middle reaches of the union hierarchy —business agent of a local, secretary of a city or regional council, international representative, etc.—offer economically a middle-class

[1] C. Wright Mills, *op. cit.*

position with much more power, prestige and "nearness to the great" than most other middle-class positions. In the top rank, union leadership leads out of the middle class altogether—though rarely financially —and into a new social and political elite.

It has been said that the key position of the clerical career, as the one route to social advancement open to all, explained in large part the Church's hold on the masses during the Middle Ages; and that the blocking of this route by the nobility, who increasingly monopolized the top positions in the hierarchy from 1250 on, led to anticlericalism and ultimately in the Reformation to actual defection from Church allegiance. It may similarly be said that the key position of union leadership as the one route to advancement reserved to the worker, is one of the major driving forces behind unionization. The opportunities attached to union leadership are probably the major attraction for the active and ambitious minority whose activity and interest organize a union and hold it together. They loom very large in Europe, where the opportunities of union leadership are by and large the *only* opportunities to rise out of the working class—as were the opportunities of a clerical career for the medieval peasant. But even in this country, with its traditional opportunities for the rank and file worker, the opportunities of union leadership are more important than any statistical comparison between, for instance, the small number of union jobs and the large number of foremanships could suggest. The union job is the only avenue of advancement where it is not a handicap but an asset to have started as a worker.

The union itself is completely dependent on its leadership however much the slogans of "democratic unionism" try to play down his role. Union affairs require constant, full-time attention. But as the union serves only partial needs of the rank and file, most members refuse to give the union more than passing and occasional attention except when in the heat of an organizing campaign or of a strike. The efficient conduct of union affairs demands knowledge and experience which the man working at the machine cannot possess.

The discharge of the union functions cannot even be controlled by the membership. All they can do is to throw out one particular set of leaders—but only to put in another, equally uncontrollable one. This, by the way, explains in large part the tendency toward factional feuds "to the bitter end" with which unions are afflicted. There is no way for a dissenting group to operate except by a campaign to turn out the incumbents. Union leadership may be compared to a system of government which has an elected executive without the control of an elected legislature or of a judiciary. The only course open for the members is to follow the leader altogether or to repudiate him altogether.

The union leader is also of vital importance to society. There are few positions in government which carry such power and responsibility as the top leadership of one of the large unions. The power of the national leaders of an important union goes far beyond anything ever possessed by the industrial tycoon, financial giant or monopoly capitalist. And the growth of this new center of power, union leadership, has perhaps been more rapid than that of management.

The American union leader of today probably possesses greater social and certainly much greater political power and influence than his European counterpart ever did. He owes it largely to the traditional independence of the American union from a political party which has made the American union leader an independent estate of the commonwealth. The European union leader has been traditionally committed to a Socialist or Labor party and subordinate to its ideology. True, at times the tail of the union has tended to wag the dog of the party, especially in England. But still, the union has been the tail— and all it could wag when most powerful was one dog of a definite shape, nature and color. The European union is never stronger than a party that depends for its success on either a coalition or the support of independent, nonunion voters. The union leader is always a partner—usually a junior partner—with politicians and intellectuals; he has to support them, whereas the very fact that he and his members have no other place to go makes it possible for the party leaders not to support the union. In this country the union leader is a free agent with the party politicians bidding for his support. Hence, the American union leader enjoys greater publicity, greater prestige and much greater real power. That this is not understood in this country —not even by union leaders in many cases—is the result of the quite extraordinary misunderstanding of European unionism on the part of Americans. The belief of most American union leaders that Europe is much more thoroughly unionized than this country, or the absurd concept of the "more mature" or "more mellow" European union leader that prevails in some business circles, are other examples of the same lack of understanding.

The Union Leader's Job

The union leader's job is a political one: to oppose, control and limit the governmental power of the enterprise. He is, moreover, a spokesman, a representative. His power must rest on express delegation from those for whom he speaks. He must be able to claim that he has both right and power to make decisions for them. This he can only do if he is elected. Even in the Soviet Union, where other elections tend to be a mere confirmation of an appointment already made, the constituents have a real voice in the selection of local union leaders. They can at least choose among a number of approved candidates.

The union leader must therefore always shape his behavior to the end of being re-elected. In order to achieve anything at all, he must stay in power. He need not confine himself to "playing politics"; he need not base his decision only on its effect on his political organization and on his chances for re-election. If he is a smart politician, he will even know that to "play politics" is usually not very good politics. But he will never be able to make a decision without considering its effect on his political future within the union. The more "democratic" the union is, the more real and serious union elections are, the greater will be the pressure of political considerations on the union leader.

The union leader is the governing organ of a union, that is, of an institution. This may seem trite to the point of being meaningless; but it has profound effects on the union leader's behavior. If his first question is: "How is this going to affect my re-election"? his next one must be: "Is it good for the union, will it make the union stronger"?

The union leader must in other words inevitably behave, act and think as a politician. His rationale, his purposes, his point of view must all be political. He must be temperamentally and psychologically adapted to political life. He must be politically minded, must love power, must believe in himself. Union problems, being primarily power problems of mass organization, could not be successfully solved by another type of man. As a political leader he has to weigh expediency against policy, the interests and desires of his constituents against his own convictions and principles, and the good of the members against the necessity to maintain the union as a strong and unified institution.

This is so obvious to the union leader that he cannot imagine why union members, the general public and most managements have the greatest difficulty in understanding it. Managements in particular are sure that the union leader must behave as they do themselves. They assume that the union leader ought to be a person that would be successful on a management team. "The union leader is not the kind of man who would ever have made good in this company," and "He would simply be incapable of running our business," are favorite management criticisms. I know labor relations executives in large corporations who actually pride themselves on never having been able to understand, much less to predict, a union leader's actions; they conclude therefrom not that they themselves have fallen down on their jobs but that "these union fellows are quite impossible, you simply can't do business with them."

It is only fair to add that very few union leaders on their part understand any more about management, its responsibilities, concerns, points of view, its political situation or the personal ambitions and fears of the management people they deal with. Either side considers the other irrational, capricious, unreliable, unpredictable and basically dishonest. This in itself is a major cause of union-management friction and bitterness. A mutual understanding of each other's way of life and mode of action would not by itself solve the problem of union-management relations; but any solution requires such understanding.

Yet the union leader's job can never be entirely a political one. The more successful, the more established the union, the greater the nonpolitical elements in the leader's job. It requires, therefore, two sets of personal qualifications and two sets of objectives and rationales. Once union recognition has been won, the union leader has to become what the union movement itself calls a "responsible" union leader.

Up to the moment of recognition, the union fights an all-out war against the enterprise. The instant a contract has been signed, the union must enforce it against its own members, must discipline violators of the contract in its own ranks, must prevent agitation against the contract, unauthorized work stoppages, etc. The union leader whether he realizes it or not, becomes a management spokesman and a channel for the exercise of management authority over his own men. No union will survive long if it cannot live up to the contract it has signed, that is, if it cannot enforce the contract terms on its own members. To do so, however, requires that the union leader occupy an intermediary position between that of spokesman for the men against management, and spokesman for management against the men.

This tension is greatest when the union is first recognized. But the union leader has to make an about-face every time a new contract is negotiated. His difficulty is greatly aggravated by the conventions which dictate that union-management negotiations are governed by the swashbuckling dueling code of the "Three Musketeers." There is the convention that a union must ask for much more than it can possibly hope to receive—with the corresponding convention that management must offer only a fraction of what it has known all along it will grant. As a result, the union member is led to expect much more than he gets ultimately, and may regard even the most favorable contract as unfair and as a disappointment. And there is the convention of mutual abuse: the small-boy swagger of "bloodsucker" and "racketeer" in this country, the class-war slogans in Europe.

But management and union must live together peacefully after the deal is made. The union leader who up to the moment of signing was forced by etiquette to accuse management of bad faith, exploitation, dishonesty and every other sin, must turn around and make his men abide by his undertaking to these unspeakable liars, exploiters, cheats, bloodsuckers and crooks of management.

Every union leader will be forced to change his basic thinking once he is in power. As long as he was a rank-and-file union member or a contender for the leadership, he could think, speak and act in terms of the desires and needs of the membership. The moment he is in power, his thinking will have as its focus the employer's problems. He can no longer base his actions and policies on what the men themselves would *want* to get, but on what they *can* get—which means on what the *enterprise* can be made to pay or can afford to pay. While the members talk and think in terms of their needs and desires, the union leader will be forced to think and talk in terms of the enterprise's problems. Instead of being member-centered, he will become enterprise-centered.

This is likely to bring the union leader into dangerous opposition to his members—or at least to alienate him from them. It may also put the leader into a painful inner conflict with himself and with his own creed. Even the union leaders who see themselves as "just businessmen," as so many of the early adherents of American "business unionism" did, must believe in unionism as a "sacred cause." Without this belief they would either not stay in union work or become union racketeers.

In addition, the union leader faces the demand that he assume responsibility for the success of the enterprise and for the economic stability of society. The pressure of this demand will become the greater, the more successful, the more firmly established the union becomes. It will finally become a general demand on the part of the public for the "mature" labor leader, who is, above all, a "labor statesman" and who "integrates labor into the national economy" rather than fights for labor's demands.

The individual union leader may resist this social pressure and may affirm, as John L. Lewis has done so often, that he knows no interests other than those of his constituents. He may try to sidestep the issue by asserting a pre-established harmony between the interests of society and the interests of the laboring man. This attitude, which is today widely acclaimed in the person of Walter Reuther, is, however, an evasion rather than an answer. Like Sidney Hillman, he may accept the challenge and try to live up to the demands of society, to be a "mature" labor leader or "labor statesman." That this is not always palatable to the membership is indicated by the remark of the old garment worker, that "Hillman was never really one of us; he worked three months as a pants-presser, and then he was a labor statesman already." But even if a union leader refuses to accept social responsibility—such as, for instance, responsibility for a "rational wage policy" based upon the common weal rather than on the interests of the members—he will find himself judged in the press, from the lecture platform, or in Congress, according to the standards of the "labor statesman"—standards which are not those of the union nor of its members. He will be held responsible for effects of his behavior which have nothing to do with the desires of the union rank and file or with the welfare of the union. Consciously or subconsciously, he will take the public's image of a labor leader into account when planning his actions. Even when he sneers at public opinion and defies public pressure, he cannot escape their impact. Social acceptance, even within the labor movement, goes to the "labor statesman" who pays at least lip service to the demand that the interests of enterprise and economy come before the interests of the members. And so do prestige and recognition, such as the appointment to a Labor-Management Commission in the United States, or to a Royal Commission in England; support by the newspapers, by the universities, etc.; in short, all the satisfactions of personal vanity and all the outward signs of success. A labor leader may resist all this as a temptation of the devil; he may even make a great virtue out of his resistance, as John L. Lewis so skillfully does. But the pressure is still there, and is bound to make itself felt in an even greater intensification of the union leader's basic problem.

The effect on both leader and follower has never been better described than in the first—and for a long time the only—analysis of union leadership, Robert Hoxie's *Trade Unionism in the United States.*

There is a real contest between the leaders and the rank and file. So long as the union is small and the officers work at the bench, there is no friction, but when the union grows and the officers give up work and become paid officials and devote their whole time to official duties, then friction between the leaders and the rank and file almost inevitably arises. The farther up we go in officialdom, the less sympathy and mutual understanding we find. The leaders for the most part reciprocate the feeling of the rank and file. Their attitude is likely to be one of contempt mixed with fear. One trade union leader says that rank and file are ignorant; have to be wheedled, and, when that fails, driven by physical force if necessary. Even leaders who pride themselves on keeping close to the man at the bench speak contemptuously of the crowd. . . .

The causes of the contest between the leaders and the rank and file are partly inherent in the situation. The rank and file are ignorant and impulsive; they do not know anything about business and market conditions and trade. They think all business is making enormous profits, and there is no limit to the amount they can squeeze out for themselves if strong enough. Sometimes they suffer until beyond endurance or are aroused by leaders and then break out, wildly demanding the impossible. Their environment tends to make them radical; they have nothing to lose—no responsibility. All the conditions, on the other hand tend to make the leaders conservative. Responsibility sobers them. As soon as they engage in negotiations they realize the power of the employers, and the limitations in the ability of the employers to meet demands. Moreover, when the leaders get away from the bench, their environment becomes more of the character of the employer's than of the worker's. They no longer deal with the physical, but with the spiritual, in negotiations and in the handling of men. Almost inevitably they develop something of the employer's viewpoint and feeling and thus become unable to see things from the worker's angle and to feel with and for the workers as before. The worker is something to be manipulated. But partly, also, the contest is due to the character of the men who get into power in the unions. Very generally it is not the good worker, but the big, jolly, hail-fellows-well-met, natural born politicians, possessed of considerable administrative ability, men with the latent instinct of the boss and employer, men who love power for its own sake.[2]

Hoxie forecast the actual development of American unionism. He supplied the explanation for the dry rot which was to attack the outwardly successful and strong German labor movement before Hitler, and which destroyed in a decade of apparent union success and union respectability the loyalty and allegiance that had been built up in fifty years of fighting for recognition. His prophecy holds good just as well for the British trade unions of today. For the tension between the union's function as an opposition to the enterprise and its function as part of the very governmental system of the enterprise lies in the nature of unionism. No matter how the union leader reacts to it, or how he attempts to resolve it, the conflict must alienate him from the members. He becomes one of "them" instead of being one of "us."

As soon as a union starts to operate beyond the confines of one plant or of one enterprise, its leadership ceases to operate exclusively in terms of the interest of the workers of this one plant or enterprise. Even in purely local matters the leader is likely to have to give greater weight to the union's position in the industry and in the labor movement, that is, on its position outside the plant, than to the effect on

[2] Page 177 of the 1920 edition (New York: D. Appleton & Co.). See also Benjamin M. Selekman's excellent discussion of the problem of the labor leader in his *Labor Relations and Human Relations* (New York: McGraw-Hill Book Co., 1947), especially the Chapter, "Wanted: Mature Labor Leaders."

the members directly affected. The bigger, the more powerful, the more representative of all the workers in one craft or in one industry a union becomes, the more important becomes its industry-wide policy and the nation-wide effects of its decisions. One good example is the extent to which the leadership of a big union becomes preoccupied with the balance between the various craft groups within the union. Maintenance of internal harmony is inevitably of greater importance to the leadership than the demands of any one of the groups. The more able a union becomes to enforce the workers' demands and desires, the less, paradoxically, will it be concerned with the concrete problems of any one specific group of workers; its concerns will be increasingly with the abstract and the general.

Yet the union leader is dependent upon the membership for re-election. He is always extremely vulnerable to any attack made by a contender for his position. It lies in the nature of his job that he must subordinate the members' interest to his "responsibility" as a union leader. He is always without adequate defense, he is always guilty—and guilty of the worst crime in the union code.

There is never a shortage of candidates for any union leader's job. And there is probably no organization where politics are deadlier or dirtier than in a union. There is also always competition from the outside, from neighboring unions or from rival union movements. From shop steward up to national president, the leader is constantly being squeezed between the pressures of his job and the pressures of his political situation.

One-Man Rule as the Leader's Way Out

The leader can escape this squeeze in two ways: he can outbid opposition by playing up the "anti" character of the union. Or he can establish absolute control over the union, and suppress all critics and potential rivals. He may of course do both at the same time—John L. Lewis has shown how.

If the leader chooses the first course, he will have to keep the union constantly at fighting pitch. He will have to rely on the "ritual" strike. Walter Reuther, for instance, used the strike in 1945 to re-establish the contact with the General Motors workers that he had lost because or his strict enforcement of the no-strike pledge during the War. United Automobile Workers leaders themselves admit today that the strike served little purpose other than to re-establish Reuther's leadership. It certainly was prolonged for three months for that reason, as it could have been settled in December, 1945, on the same terms on which it was finally settled the following March, when the union convention was about to meet.

But the political strike is a union leader's second choice. He would much rather establish his control by centralizing all union power in his hands. When Walter Reuther was on the point of losing out altogether in 1945, he fell back upon the political strike. But as soon as he had been elected president of the union, he at once began to get rid of all actual or potential rivals, to centralize power and decisions, and to put his own men into the positions of authority. Many other union leaders—here or abroad—have done the same. John L. Lewis has driven into exile every single able and independent man in the United Mine Workers and has filled practically every union office with loyal ward heelers. In some AF of L unions criticism of the union leadership has come to be officially considered "anti-union activity" and is punished with expulsion. And few American union leaders have matched Ernest Bevin in the ruthlessness with which he made himself the undisputed and absolute ruler of the Transport Workers.

In other unions the focus of centralization has been a region with three or four regional leaders ruling semi-independent duchies. Dave Beck's control of the Teamsters in the Northwest or the situation in the United Automobile Workers Union before Reuther's recent "breakthrough" are examples. A quite different pattern prevails in some of the building unions, where the national officers are powerless figureheads; where, indeed, there is no "national" union as such but only a loose confederation of local machines with all control in the hands of the practically independent business agents of the large individual locals. Finally, the union may be run not by one leader or by an oligarchy but by a bureaucracy of colorless mediocrities, each of whom alone is quite powerless though he enjoys absolute security of tenure. This was the predominant pattern in the old German unions. It is characteristic of many British unions of today. And it is fast becoming the pattern of some smaller CIO unions.

But the pressures within every union push toward centralized rule, in which local offices lose their independence and autonomy and become patronage jobs of a central machine. Despite all the slogans of "union democracy," the strong union will tend to reserve all real decisions for the leader, and to brand as disloyalty any opposition.

The only union leader who can afford to take any responsibility—let alone to be a "labor statesman"—is the leader who is in such control of the union that there is no danger of opposition from within. Sidney Hillman of the Amalgamated Clothing Workers, for instance, could never have put through his justly famous reorganization of the men's clothing industry if he had not been in complete and undisputed control of his union. To place the industry on a sound foundation, Hillman had to change the job definitions of a sizeable number of clothing workers from highly paid skilled to much less well paid unskilled jobs. True, this saved the industry; without this sacrifice the livelihood of all the union members might have been in jeopardy. Yet this point of view was hardly likely to appeal to that one-fourth or one-third of the membership whose jobs were at stake, nor to the rest, who must at least have wondered whether their leader was putting the welfare of the bosses or that of the workers first. If an opposition movement could have got started, Hillman might well have been thrown out by an overwhelming majority. But Hillman had ruthlessly driven out the Communist faction a few years earlier—and with it non-Communist opponents who refused to accept the Hillman "discipline." He had filled all offices with his own faithfuls. Without such absolute control of the union he would not even have been able to propose a reorganization scheme himself; instead he would have had to fight any such plan, no matter how sound or how necessary.

One-Man Rule and Union Cohesion

Centralized control of the union by a powerful leader and his machine may thus work in the public interest—however much it goes counter to the creed of democratic unionism. But if "responsible leadership" results from union autocracy the price is a very stiff one. While centralized union control may enable the leader to be a "labor statesman," it undermines the vigor and health of unionism and may even threaten its survival.

Centralized union control tends to deprive the worker of the experience that the union is his very own, his community, his fellowship.

This sense of belonging may be even more important to the worker than the tangible benefits of union membership.

Even if the union no longer serves as a community, the worker will go on paying dues. He will continue to obey strike calls and will still look to the union for bread-and-butter gains and for protection against the boss. But the union will be just a utility. If the worker does not consider it "just another racket," though one that works to his benefit, he will look upon it the same way he looks upon his insurance policy: as something very valuable and necessary, which it is worth real sacrifices to keep up, but still as only a scrap of paper. He will cease to believe in the union.

The unions in this country are still much stronger than the—outwardly so strong—unions of Republican Germany with their bitter contempt of the rank and file for the union leader. They are, on the whole, still above the bureaucratic smugness of today's British unionism. But they are also very far below the inner strength of the great CIO drives of ten years ago. They have become respectable, they have become recognized, and their leaders have become established. But what they have gained in mass they may well have lost in energy. It is alarming how fast the leadership of the young CIO unions—particularly of the United Automobile Workers and of the Steel Workers —has become a "top management" and has lost contact with the rank and file. These leaders lack communication with the worker as badly as does the management of the enterprise.

But the greatest damage to the strength of the union—one endangering its very survival—may well be the effect of centralized control on the future supply of leaders. Few institutions are as dependent on their leaders as the labor union. And few institutions would seem as well equipped as the properly decentralized union to select potential leaders, to train them in leadership and to test them in independently responsible jobs at an early stage. In the centralized union, however, these advantages disappear. It will keep the man with leadership potential out of any position of power and responsibility. The very qualities which make a man a potential leader also make him a potential threat to the incumbent. The centralized union will not train its younger men in leadership; on the contrary, it will confine them to routine administrative jobs lest they build up a political machine and a political following of their own. Least of all will the centralized union tolerate an independent local command that would test the younger man.

One look at any one of our powerful unions will show that this is not speculation. Wherever we find a strong, capable leader who has been at the top more than a few years, potential successors are conspicuously absent. There are some able contemporaries who have risen with the leader. But if one of them succeeds to the leadership, it is usually at so advanced an age that the succession problem becomes even more urgent. There may be a few men in the inner circle whom the leader brought in from the outside: the economist, the lawyer, the director of research, the editor of the union paper, etc. These are often capable, even brilliant, people; but the very fact that they are "intellectuals" who have not risen from the ranks disqualifies them for independent leadership—which is one of the reasons why they were brought in in the first place. Finally, there is a large number of union faithfuls—loyal members of the leader's machine, industrious, devoted, usually thoroughly honest, but men without political appeal, without ambition, without ability or willingness to take over the tough job of leading a union.

No industrial country has yet felt the full effect of this development. Today's top union leaders are still everywhere men of the first generation who came up organizing and building the union. But this leadership is dying out rapidly. Of all the major union movements the CIO in this country is the only one with a sizable number of young leaders at the top; and even in the CIO the bulk of today's leadership will die or retire within the next fifteen years. In all other union groups in this country—AF of L, Railway Brotherhoods or independents—as well as in the union movements of England and Western Europe, all but a handful of union leaders are well past sixty. The first great changing of the guards is about to occur. A new top leadership will have to be found among the men now in secondary positions, men who came up in a secure and accepted union, and who, in the great majority, have never had any independent responsibility or any training in the job of union leadership. These men—men who are likely to be well-trained and conscientious, but rather narrow, bureaucrats—will have to tackle the enormous problems of the role and function of the labor union in modern industrial society.

Will Union Leaders Grow More Mature?

Most of the discussions of the problem of the union leader—and in union circles this is one of the most popular topics of conversation —tend to conclude that the solution lies in getting better men into union leadership. The answers are almost always sought in terms of personalities.

At its most naïve the prescription takes the form of a demand for the "honest leader" who will stay close to the members and will not let power separate him from his old comrades and fellow workers. This is the prescription most popular with the rank and file. It has all the appeal of the reform candidate who campaigns squarely on a platform of "good government"—and about as much chance to get the better of the entrenched machine or to make good on its promise if the machine should be beaten.

The answer most popular outside the union movement is hardly less naïve. It is the wishful thought that union leadership will grow more "mature" with age and experience, usually supported by a reference to the "maturity" of the leadership of the older and mellower British unions.

This contrast between the American and British labor leader is based, however, on a misconception of the British labor movement and of the British trade union leader. The British union leader appears more "mature" largely because for a long time he was able to side-step the problems of union responsibility—partly because he had much less actual power over the economy than his American counterpart, but mainly because, being attached to the Labor Party, he was in the opposition. He could always plead that he would do the right thing if only his party had a clear majority. In this country the union leader has not had this easy excuse and has had to face up to the problem of responsibility all along.

The idea that better union leadership will result from mere age is an illusion. Our oldest union leaders with the longest experience have, by and large, shown the least inclination to accept responsibility. Both in years and in seniority, for instance, John L. Lewis is close to being the dean of American unionists. Instead of improving the quality of leadership, aging may actually result in its deterioration. The only thing we can expect to result from the mere lapse of time is a leadership that is bureaucratic, colorless and without sharp corners. But these qualities of the well-behaved civil servant who knows how to stay out of trouble, are hardly all a union leader needs.

The solution does not lie in improving the labor leader. It lies in making it possible for an able and serious man to do a good and responsible job as leader of a union and yet retain the allegiance and following of its members. There is no reason to assume that the union leaders in power today are any less able, mature, competent or willing to accept responsibility than any other group of men in public life. What they lack is opportunity rather than character or knowledge. They are caught in the inherent contradictions of unionism and have to make the best of a very bad job. The solution does not lie in the personality or the character of the leader, nor does it lie in legislation. What is required to give us the "mature" union leader we so urgently need, is a change in the nature and structure of the job.

CHAPTER 14

THE SPLIT ALLEGIANCE WITHIN THE ENTERPRISE

THE future of unionism will be decided within the enterprise. It is there that the basic function of the union lies. It is there that the solutions lie. But it is also within the enterprise that unionism faces its most difficult problem: that of the "split allegiance."

Both management and union must demand the allegiance of the members of the enterprise. Both appeal therefore to the same citizenry, to identical adherents against each other. The worker cannot vote for one or for the other; he owes allegiance to both at the same time. Yet the two are in opposition. This is very much like saying that we have two general staffs fighting each other, each using the same army; or two chess players playing against each other, both using the white figures. Or management and union may be likened to that serpent of the fables who on one body had two heads that, fighting each other with poisoned fang, killed themselves.

There is indeed one precedent for the union-management situation; but it is not a very encouraging one. In the medieval relationship between Church and State both governments of Christendom based themselves on the same citizenship and demanded the allegiance of the individual against each other. Church and State had to oppose each other, yet they had to live together. Each had to claim the allegiance of its members against the other, yet both shared the same membership. Neither could live without the other. But as they could not live together either, they destroyed themselves and their society.

Management and union will do the same unless they can solve the problem so that neither has to abandon its claim to the allegiance of the members. Society cannot stand the "split allegiance," the enterprise cannot stand it, the union cannot stand it. Above all, the individual member cannot possibly stand it; yet he cannot make a decision between the two. What is necessary, therefore, is to convert the "split allegiance" of the members of the plant community into a bearable and functioning "twin allegiance."

The "split allegiance" aggravates all the tensions and conflicts. Each move made by one side to strengthen the allegiance of its members to itself, is regarded by the other side as a direct frontal attack on the allegiance which it claims from the same members and on which its existence rests. This shows in the two most common slogans of management-labor relations: "unfair labor practices" and "union attack on management prerogatives."

An "unfair labor practice" has nothing to do with fairness. It is a management move to undermine the union allegiance of the employee. Granting a wage increase is an unfair labor practice if it is given without prior union demand and announced by management rather than by the union leader. It refutes the union's claim that it protects the employee against management and obtain things for him he could not obtain without a union.

It may even be an unfair labor practice to grant a wage demand too soon, without a show of resistance and a pretense of bargaining; for this too undermines the standing and prestige of union and union leader. For the same reason it is definitely an attack on the political cohesion of the union for management to give in on all grievances. In other words anything likely or designed to strengthen allegiance to management at the expense of allegiance to the union is—from the union's point of view—an "unfair labor practice."

Similarly, all union policies and demands which aim at substituting allegiance to the union for allegiance to management are "attacks upon management prerogatives." Above all, management must resist all union demands that would weaken the authority of its lower ranks—supervision and middle management—to carry out the policies and decisions of top management. Without this authority the enterprise cannot function, cannot discharge its economic responsibilities and cannot maintain its cohesion. But as long as there is a "split allegiance," practically every demand made by the union to safeguard its own authority and cohesion is an attack upon the authority of local management and supervision.

The "split allegiance" puts the worker into an unbearable conflict of loyalties. In the long run it can only undermine his allegiance to both enterprise and union. It demands of him continually that he take sides, that he declare himself for one allegiance or the other. But he must give his allegiance to both. If he abandons allegiance to the enterprise, his job must becomes repugnant and meaningless and something done only because he has no other choice. His own self-respect demands pride in the job, pride in the work, pride in the company he works for —and that means allegiance to the enterprise. By giving up this allegiance he turns himself from a "self-respecting worker" into the "*Lumpenproletariat*" of Marxism. But if he gives up allegiance to the union, he gives up the assertion of his own interests, needs and purposes against the interests, needs and purposes of the enterprise; he accepts domination by a government which is not legitimate; and this too means abandoning his self-respect.

These two allegiances may well be incompatible with each other, as both management and union leadership are wont to claim. But to the worker this logic contradicts all his experience. To him these two allegiances are complementary. He does not see why he must be antiunion or nonunion just because he thinks the company he works for is a "good place to work"—the amazing assumption on which apparently the employee-attitude surveys, so fashionable in this country just now, are based. For him it does not follow from his allegiance to the union that he must be anti-management and anti-enterprise, which is apparently the basis on which union leaders operate. He looks to management *and* to the union. In a recent employee-attitude survey, for instance, the workers listed as things they liked about the company and about their jobs, both policies and practices instituted by management, and "union gains" such as a paid vacation. In their minds, clearly, there was no feeling that they ought not to cherish union gains if they were to be "loyal" to the management and vice versa.

It is to the interest of neither union nor management to press the demand for absolute allegiance, as this can only turn the worker against both. Both sides, therefore, have a real interest in converting the "split allegiance" into a "twin allegiance." That this will be a most difficult thing to do is shown by the medieval experience with the "theory of the two swords," which aimed at creating precisely such a twin allegiance to Church and State. It failed because the two parties could not imbed their conflict in a foundation of co-operation and joint purpose.

They could either go on with their conflict and extend it to all areas—which is precisely what we have been doing in our union-management relations—or they could abandon their conflict altogether—which they could as little do as union and management can. Any solution must maintain a conflict between management and union. But it must also convert it from a destructive into a constructive conflict by underpinning it with a foundation of co-operation and joint purpose in all non-conflict areas.

It is the union that stands to lose the most from continued "split allegiance," at least in the long run. Our experience so far may seem to contradict this. But if pressed to the point where he has to make a final decision, the worker will have to decide for the enterprise. His situation is that of the medieval citizen caught between Church and State. To anyone analyzing the situation in the thirteenth or fourteenth century, it would have appeared as if the battle were going strongly against the State; the one thing the medieval man would cling to at all cost would have seemed to be the Church. Yet, in the showdown he chose the State—if only because he depended on the day-to-day performance of routine administrative functions which only the State could provide.

In such a showdown between enterprise and union the weight of society and government will ultimately come down on the side of the enterprise. For society can manage without union, however undesirable the political consequences of a suppression of unionism. It cannot possibly manage without the enterprise and its management. To press its claim for absolute allegiance would appear to be the height of folly for the union. The very survival of the union movement would seem to depend on its finding a resolution of the conflict in a functioning "twin allegiance."

The basic problem of the union's relation to the enterprise cannot be solved as a problem of the balance of power, which is the way we have been trying to solve it all along. A balance system with only two powers is practically unmanageable; it has no elasticity at all and must break down as soon as there is the slightest shift. Actually there are not two "powers" but only one power—the governmental authority of the enterprise necessarily divided against itself. A balance-of-power solution can only make permanent warfare inevitable.

Neither can the problem be solved by making laws. A great deal can and should be done legislatively. The jurisdictional strike and the secondary boycott both require legislative treatment and will yield to it. Union control of its members must be made subject to judicial review, which can only be done through law. But the major problems lie outside the sphere of the legislature. Indeed they lie outside the sphere of the national government.

We cannot expect from the union that they themselves solve these problems. Above all, we cannot demand of the union leader that he learn to behave "responsibly" and "statesman-like," nor expect that such responsibility will come by itself with the "maturity" of the union movement. Before we can expect of any union leader that he behave "responsibly" and "statesman-like," we must make it possible for him to accept responsibility without endangering the allegiance of his members, the cohesion of his union, and his own hold on his office.

The only thing that will make it possible for union and union leader to accept responsibility for enterprise, economy and society, is a solution of the basic problems of unionism.

This, in the first place, means structural changes—changes which will lessen, if not eliminate, the union member's opposition to profitability and productivity, lessen the union's basic insecurity, settle the dilemma of the strike, etc.

Secondly, it means that the initiative for these solutions has to come largely from management. For management—no matter how strong the union—is the dynamic and determining factor in the enterprise, and its final governmental authority. But this means that management must accept the union as legitimate and indeed as essential, and learn to understand how a union functions and why. Both conditions are absent today.

Above all, the solution of the problems of unionism depends on the resolution of "split allegiance" into "twin allegiance." In the last analysis every union problem hinges on this. Make it possible for the union to function *within* the enterprise and yet to discharge its opposition role, and all the other problems of unionism become solvable. The basic insecurity of the union would then disappear or at least become a subordinate rather than, as at present, the compelling motivation of union action.

FOURTH PART: The Problems of An Industrial Order: The Plant Community

CHAPTER 15

THE INDIVIDUAL'S DEMAND FOR STATUS AND FUNCTION

THE economic relationship is neither the whole nor even the most important part of the individual's relationship to the enterprise. The "cash nexus" of the economist is not really a "nexus," that is a bond, at all. It does not make the individual a *member* of the enterprise. It does not satisfy the individual's demand for social status and function.

Social status and function are terms of relationship, of "belonging," of identification, of harmony. "Status" defines man's existence as related in mutual necessity to the organized group. "Function" ties his work, his aspirations and ambitions to the power and purposes of the organized group in a bond that satisfies both individual and society. The oldest term for status is "personality"; the oldest term for function is "member." Together, status and function resolve the apparently irresolvable conflict between the absolute claim of the group—before which any one man is nothing in himself and only a member of the species—and the absolute claim of the individual, to whom the group is only a means and a tool for the achievement of his own private purpose. Status and function overcome this conflict by giving citizenship to the individual.

Man must have status and function in his society in order to be a person. Without it he is either the "caged spirit" of Oriental philosophy, senselessly and meaninglessly caught in a senseless and meaningless life, or just "Homo sapiens" and one of the more brutish apes. But the group's own cohesion and survival also depend on the individual's status and function; without it the group is a mere herd, never a society. And only a society that gives status and function to its members can expect their allegiance. Status and function of the individual member are requirements of individual and social life. They are verified by all historical experience. They are at the same time value-terms: demands on society flowing from the Christian concept of the nature and destiny of man. Their realization is doubly imperative to Western society. Because it is a society it will lose its life, because it is Western it will lose its soul, should it fail to realize them.

During the last two hundred years, "status" has not been a popular word; it has come to stand for *status quo ante*, the status of an old, obsolete, hated regime, for privilege in a static, rather than for opportunity in a mobile, society. It would be cowardice, however, to abandon a good word only because misuse has made it unpopular; there is certainly no other one to take its place. At the outset I should emphasize, therefore, that "status" does not exclude social mobility. Indeed, in our society social mobility is a prerequisite to proper status. The phrase of "equal opportunities for everybody" expresses in slogan form a major requirement of adequate status-realization today, as does the American promise that "every boy has a chance to become President." For status is both what the individual is objectively and what society recognizes in him.

In its simplest form status may be given by a friendly word from one's neighbor; in its most elaborate form, by the pomp and majesty in which society clothes the holder of a great office in which it represents itself. Whatever the form, the essence is that the individual's social position represents, as in a microcosm, the structure of his society; and that the social order mirrors, as in a macrocosm, the basic convictions regarding the nature of man which this particular society holds. The caste system of the Hindu is a true status system, as was the feudal system of the Middle Ages—but so was the completely mobile, unstatic, and apparently chaotic "free market" of the nineteenth-century economist, where social position depended entirely upon economic effort and economic success.

Similarly, "social function" is a two-way relationship. The oldest analogy is the relationship between the human body and its members —used, according to the Roman fable, to settle history's first sit-down strike, that of the plebeians against their senatorial masters. In the body each member must function if the whole body is to function; and the functioning of the body is in turn necessary to each member. This analogy is, however, misleading. The members of the human body have no ends of their own; they exist only as parts of the whole body.

But the members of the body politic are entities in themselves, biologically and spiritually. It is only in their social existence that they are not sufficient unto themselves. To have adequate social function in a society, the member must, in serving the ends of society, serve his individual ends, purposes and aspirations. And in serving his own individual ends, purposes and aspirations, the member must also serve society's ends.

The relationship is not one of identity. In fact, identity between the ends of society and the ends of the individual would destroy both society and the individual—as Aristotle asserted against Plato more than two thousand years ago. What is needed is a relationship of harmony under which two autonomous sets of purposes and needs are fulfilled in one and the same movement.

Status and function are closely related to each other but they are not inseparable. The ideal "free market" of the classical economist was a society which knew only status. The ideal tribe of the modern cultural anthropologists is a society which knows only function but no status. I would consider either society unable to live. Indeed, the absence of "function" in the market society is considered by one competent observer to have been the major reason for its collapse.[1] And the supposedly status-free tribe of the anthropologists seems to me to reflect the romantic illusion of the "noble savage" rather than actual observation.

A society that gives no status must appear as oppressive to the member; it does not give "justice"—the foundation of commonwealths. A society that fails to give function must appear without pattern, meaning or purpose, hence as irrational, demoniac, unpredictable.

A society without status must always see in the member—just because he has been born a human being—a potential rebel to be held down by threats, magic or bribes. He is always a menace, always conspiring. If there is no social function, the member's life and work, his aims, hopes and aspirations must appear to society as frivolous and meaningless, if not downright vicious and criminal. He can, as in the theory of market society, promote public virtue and welfare only through his private vices.

A society without status must become a tyranny over a cowed but despised mob. The denial of status underlies all totalitarianism, whether of the Right or of the Left. A society without function must go insane,

[1] Karl Polanyi, *The Great Transformation*.

collectively and individually. One such handicap a society may conceivably overcome by means of police terror or by magic ritual, by bread or by circuses. But if both status and function are lacking, the allegiance to, and the cohesion of, society will be broken.

The concrete society of the West has to demand of the industrial enterprise that it fulfill that promise of status we call Justice, which is expressed by the slogan of "equal opportunities"; and that it organize function according to the belief in the Dignity of Man as it is expressed in the responsible participation of citizenship.

This is not "theory"; it is not just an abstract conclusion from abstract premises. The worker himself makes the demand; whether it is fulfilled or not decides whether the worker considers the plant community a success or a failure.

If the industrial enterprise were one of many subsidiary institutions of industrial society, we would not have to be too much concerned with the basic promises and beliefs which the enterprise realizes through status and function. In all but the most primitive society there are important institutions which fail to realize the beliefs, promises and values of the society. There are even some institutions which are organized on beliefs, promises and values radically different from, if not opposed to, those of "their" society. Such are the Christian churches in the modern secular state, a professional officers' corps or the liberal arts college in the businessman's society of the American tradition, etc. The existence of such dissenting institutions is the specific difference between "primitive" and "civilized" societies. It is the latent energies of these nonconformist institutions which enable a society to change, to adapt itself to new conditions and to new ideas, to recover and to build. Their abolition, the dreary uniformity of *"Gleichschaltung"* in Nazi or Communist totalitarianism is not only a relapse into barbarism; it seriously weakens society. The frightening inability of post-Hitler Germany to develop any kind of functioning social life shows this dramatically.

The enterprise is however both subordinate to, and dominant in, society. It is representative and decisive but an institution of our society. This means that the beliefs, values and promises of society are binding upon the enterprise. It means also that the extent to which the enterprise succeeds or fails in living up to those beliefs, values and promises will decide the success or failure of our society.

Indeed the beliefs, values and promises which are being realized in the representative institution are *the* real beliefs and promises of a society; they are its character and its order. If fulfillment of these beliefs and promises in the representative institution is inadequate to sustain faith in their reality, the whole society will be found wanting. If the order actually realized in the representative institution is in conflict with the professed social beliefs and promises, the whole society will appear irrational. In either case the cohesion, even the survival, of society, is threatened; society is in crisis. Insufficient performance and nonsupport on the part of the representative social institution are the only causes of social collapse and social revolution other than natural catastrophe or foreign conquest. In an inadequate society the people are increasingly susceptible to the lure of new beliefs and of a new allegiance. In an irrational society they will be forced to search for the security of new beliefs and of a new allegiance.

What Is "Fulfillment"?

The demand is, however, for efficient rather than for absolute fulfillment, for adequacy rather than for perfection. At best, even the most successful society operates at a very low rate of fulfillment. If it were measurable quantitatively—as we measure the thermal efficiency of an engine—we might find in the stablest and most successful social order which to its members appears completely rational, a rate of fulfillment of less than five or ten per cent. We deal after all with the social order of men not with that of angels. But there is a point below which the efficiency of social fulfillment may not fall without making society itself appear despotic, arbitrary, irrational and meaningless. Where this point is we do not know. We do not even know whether it is the same for all societies, whether there is a general law of social effectiveness or whether different societies—or the same society at different times—have different social melting points. But pragmatically we are usually able to tell whether a specific society in a given age fulfills its basic order sufficiently, whether it is above or below the critical point, in what direction it is moving, and also where action has to be taken to prevent disintegration or to restore cohesion. The question is not whether our industrial society is perfect; we assume that it is, at best, grossly deficient. The important question is whether it fulfills the promise of equal opportunities and the belief in citizenship right now and in the countries of the West sufficiently to be accepted by the individual as a functioning social order.

CHAPTER 16

THE DEMAND FOR THE MANAGERIAL
ATTITUDE

THE plant community obviously does not serve primarily either society or the individual; it is part of the enterprise. The "plant community" is one aspect of the human resources of production and their organization. No social order of the plant community can function and survive unless its requirements agree with the enterprise's demands on its human resources. Indeed the social order of the plant community has to contribute to the most efficient utilization of the enterprise's human resources—and vice versa.

The intellectual's traditional view—expressed in Aldous Huxley's *Brave New World*, for instance, or in the slogan of the deadening monotony of the assembly line—assumes that the demands of individual and society and the demands of the enterprise are in head-on collision. This view is rarely based on first-hand acquaintance with conditions in an industrial plant. It is often not much more than sentimentalism; because the enterprise's interest is in economic performance, it must be "sordid" and "antisocial."

Fortunately we have ample evidence on the subject, and the evidence is completely unambiguous: *The demands of the enterprise on the plant community and the demands of society and of individual are in harmony. The enterprise must demand that the individual assume a "managerial attitude" toward his job, his work and his product; but that amounts to the same thing as society's demand for the individual's responsible participation as a citizen. The enterprise must demand the fullest utilization of the abilities and ambitions of its employees; its demand for people to fill supervisory and executive positions is practically insatiable, which means that the enterprise's interest and the demand for equal opportunities run parallel.*

This does not mean that there is no problem of a functioning plant community, nor does it mean that the mass-production plant is the Earthly Paradise. Undoubtedly the plant community today is in very bad shape and fails to satisfy either individual or enterprise. But whatever the cause for the lack of social fulfillment in the industrial enterprise, it is not a conflict between the interests of the enterprise and those of society and individual.

The Managerial Attitude

No part of the productive resources of industry operates at a lower efficiency than the human resources. The few enterprises that have been able to tap this unused reservoir of human ability and attitude have achieved spectacular increases in productivity and output. In the better use of the human resources lies the major opportunity for increasing productivity in the great majority of enterprises—so that the management of men should be the first and foremost concern of operating managements, rather than the management of things and techniques on which attention has been focused so far.

We also know what makes for efficiency and productivity of the human resources of production. It is not primarily skill or pay; it is first and foremost an attitude—the one we call the "managerial attitude." By this we mean an attitude which makes the individual see his job, his work and his product the way the manager sees them, that is, in relation to the work of the group and the product of the whole.

The demands for a "managerial attitude" on the part of even the lowliest worker is an innovation. There was neither room nor need for it in the pre-industrial order. It has come into being because mass-production technology depends on social integration. Because of the "specialization" which makes mass production possible—"specialization" which, as we discussed, is very different from the traditional division of labor—the mass-production technology demands an integration of the individual operation into a unified whole. It is this whole, the team, the pattern, the organization, which produces in the modern industrial system. This "whole" does not exist in the individual operations themselves. It is a highly abstract thing. But at the same time it is necessary for the functioning and cohesion of this pattern, that the individual operator see it as a whole and understand his own function within it.

The need for the "managerial attitude" on the part of the worker and the effects of this attitude on his productivity are the greater the more his work is organized on the mass-production pattern. There is very little demand for a view of the whole among the men in traditional crafts, such as tool makers, machinists, electricians, etc., even when they work in a big mass-production plant and are in every respect—save their own work—subject to the same social forces as the mass-production workers. But to the unskilled or semiskilled worker the need for a view of the whole is urgent and pressing.

In the most comprehensive study of mass-production workers we have ever conducted, the *General Motors Contest* of 1947, this showed dramatically. The mass-production workers in their essays used their own work to develop an integrated picture of the whole. The craftsmen felt no such need; they concentrated on their own job; if they mentioned plant or product, they treated is as something that existed on a different level, almost on a different planet, from their own work. Contrary to popular impression, the highly skilled men had less knowledge and understanding of the whole than the unskilled men, many of whom showed amazing imagination and integrating ability. Where the assembly-line operator produced a tremendous vision of a universe of production all revolving around the screw he puts on a fender, the skilled model maker talked with love and knowledge about the characteristics of the wood he uses.

The productivity of the skilled craftsman is little affected by his ability or inability to integrate, by his having or lacking the "managerial attitude." He too, of course, wants to know and to understand —but as a matter of curiosity, interest or information. But to the mass-production worker, manual or clerical, the desire to know and understand is a primary motive of action. The greatest contribution of the skilled man is his skill itself; in it lie his pride and satisfaction as well. The people who do not have the artisan's traditional skill, including a great many men who are normally classified as skilled or semiskilled, have their pride, their satisfaction, their contribution, in plain fact their "skill," in the ability to integrate, to see their work and the whole in its mutual relationship and to find fulfillment of their demand for function in the "managerial attitude."

This contradicts completely the slogan of the "deadening effect" of mass production. But it also denies the basic assumption of the chief proponent of mass production, the scientific-management movement, with its theory that ease and speed of operation are the only factors controlling efficiency and productivity. Insofar as this meant the reduction or elimination of *manual* skill, the assumption has indeed been proven. But the scientific-management school also intended to eliminate the worker's attitude as a factor in production—or rather it rarely occurred to the industrial engineer steeped in scientific-management thinking that attitude is a factor in production and productivity. Yet our studies show that the reservoir of productivity that lies in attitude is no smaller than the one that has been tapped through the mass-production principle. The "managerial attitude" among the production workers leads to an almost explosive increase in productivity and efficiency—maybe even a doubling of output. This is certainly much more than could be expected in any properly engineered plant from the further application of the scientific-management methods of time and motion study, breakdown of the operations into unskilled, component parts, synchronization of materials-flow and human operation, etc. In fact, as we shall see, a major chance to increase efficiency, and to eliminate real obstacles to worker satisfaction, lies in modifying scientific management methods wherever they hamper the development of the "managerial attitude."

The group to whom the "managerial attitude" is most important is the group that is even more characteristic of the modern enterprise than the mass-production worker: the new industrial middle class of supervisors, technicians and middle managers. If the efficiency of the enterprise depends on the attitude of the production workers, the very strength and functioning of the enterprise may well depend on the attainment of a "managerial attitude" by the middle groups. For these groups are the organization itself, the nerve and circulatory systems of the enterprise.

Unlike their ancestors, the skilled artisan, supervision, middle management and technicians need no skill in the handling of tools or of materials. Their "skill" is the ability to integrate. They have to organize the men under them into a productive team. They have to apply technical and scientific knowledge to the product and processes. They have to fit the work of their department into the work of the whole and to project the whole onto their own work. Top management can set the pattern, but middle management and supervision must live it.

It is only from supervision and middle management that the individual worker can obtain a view of the whole. To the man on the machine his supervisor is "management" and stands for the enterprise. We will have to give the individual worker direct experience in understanding and seeing the whole. But supervision and middle management will always be the main channel of communication and understanding between the enterprise and the individual worker.

To the top men, on the other hand, supervision and middle management are "the organization." Though the executive sees the whole, he sees it as a complex of figures and data, and as a highly formalized abstraction. Only through middle management and supervision can he get the "feel" of his own organization. And the enterprise is bound to lack adequate leadership in the future unless the future executives—the middle management, technicians and supervisors of today—acquire the "managerial attitude."

During the last few years American management has begun to realize the importance to the enterprise of this middle group and its attitude. But so far very few managements understand that of all the groups, the industrial middle class finds it hardest to see the whole and to understand its own function. The production worker deals at least with something tangible and immediate: a process, a motion, a product. He handles a strip of metal, pushes a lever, operates a machine. The middle group handles blueprints, pushes paper forms and manipulates concepts and figures—all highly abstract. The worker works in a group of equals; the supervisor and middle manager, often the technician also, work by themselves. The worker can point to a part in the finished product and say: *I* put that one on. The man in the middle group can only say "We," without really being able to say who is embraced by this plural nor where he stands in this collective. The very group that ought most to have a "managerial attitude" faces the greatest difficulties in attaining one.

But why do we call this relationship to the whole the "managerial attitude"? Would not "understanding" be sufficient? The reason for my choice of the term "managerial" is precisely that the social order of mass production requires more than intellectual awareness. Every member of the plant society has to be convinced that his own operation, however small, is vital to the success of the whole. He must be willing to assume responsibility for the whole. The old nursery rhyme that begins, "For the want of a nail the shoe was lost," and goes on to "For the want of a nail the kingdom was lost" describes very well the structure of modern mass-production technology. Under modern integration there are no unnecessary or replaceable operations; therefore every single operation is essential. It also prescribes the attitude which the individual member of the society must take toward his own work. And this attitude which centers the whole in one's own work is the attitude of the "ruler" rather than that of the "subject"—it is a "managerial attitude."

The Enterprise's Need for Leaders

The dependence of the mass-production technology on intellectually and technically trained men is a reversal of all historical precedent. In pre-industrial society the number of trained men—and especially of intellectually and technically trained men—which the society could afford was severely limited, as was also the education society could afford to let them have. The great danger was always that there would be too many such men rather than that there would be too few. These men would normally cease to do manual labor. In all pre-industrial societies only manual labor is directly productive; hence a man not doing such labor is a burden on the entire economy. The economy of a pre-industrial society is much too close to subsistence to allow more than a very small fraction of the population not to be immediately productive.

This is the explanation of the "class" school system of the European Continent which gives such offense to the American observer. It is perfectly true that the European upper school is traditionally a school for the children of the upper and upper-middle classes. But the absence of the lower and working classes is the result neither of deliberate exclusion nor of high fees. In fact, the fees of the high schools in France or Germany were not only lower, even in terms of local incomes and purchasing power, than the expenses for social activities and sports in the "free" American high school; these schools, being state-owned, have been granting exemption from fees to the children of poor families as a matter of routine and without attaching any social stigma to the request. But while the lower-class family could thus have afforded to support the child in school, it could not afford to do without the support from a child old enough to work. It was so close to the margin of subsistence that it could not normally, or without real sacrifice, afford to allow an adolescent member of the family to be unproductive even for a few years.

This also explains why the very "highest" civilizations, the ones that produced an unusually large class of educated men, all went in for a deliberate extension of slavery through conquest, slave raids or degradation of their own native lower class. To support a large class not working with their hands, the number of manual workers had to be increased, control had to be exercised that they would really be productively employed, and an increasing share of their product had to be directed to the economically unproductive educated class. This explains also the persistence of the "cultured farmer" or the "cultured mechanic" as the ideal of the moral reformer from Hesiod to Emerson. The "farmer who read Greek while leading the plow" was indeed a perfect symbol; on no other basis could a pre-industrial society hope to reach a high level of culture and education without destroying its own moral and social basis by degrading the majority into beasts of burden. But Emerson's New England farmer was hardly a very efficient producer; and in Emerson's own lifetime he forsook both the Greek authors and the respectable poverty of New England transcendentalism for the Midwest's rich soil, its farm machinery and its pamphlets on profitable farming.

In the industrial society of the mass-production technology the situation is radically reversed.

It is the nonmanual worker, the intellectually and technically trained man, who is the most productive member of the community. A local of the United Automobile Workers, one of the most militant of American labor unions, recently protested against an increase in production standards in a plant: "It is fully proven that higher productivity cannot come from working men harder but only from improved techniques, better tools, better design and new processes so that responsibility for higher productivity rests entirely with management and must not be unloaded on the worker." Nothing could be more directly opposed to the pre-industrial concept of productivity, including the union's own labor theory of value.

In an industrial society it is therefore not the trained men whose number must be limited; on the contrary, the question is how many untrained men the society can afford. The productivity of an industrial society is directly proportionate to the supply of intellectually and technically trained men. Untrained men—including manually skilled men—can be replaced by machines within very wide and elastic limits. But the size of the trained force is an absolutely controlling factor—next in importance perhaps to the availability of water and energy supplies. This showed in Russia's industrialization program, on which lack of adequately trained technicians, supervisors and middle managers has been the major brake. It was also shown in our war-production program, where the major bottleneck was not shortage of materials or shortage of labor, not even shortage of transportation, but shortage of middle management technicians and supervision.

The industrial enterprise depends, therefore, on the greatest possible discovery and utilization of the abilities of all employees. It cannot depend on the "educated classes," that is, on a necessarily small group in possession of a socially accepted title to positions of responsibility and leadership. Promotion in industrial society is not just a reward to the individual. Systematic discovery of abilities, systematic selection for promotion, systematic recruitment into the middle class is a necessity of the social order itself. "Equal opportunities" are not only necessary to satisfy the individual member's demand for social status. They are equally necessary for the enterprise's efficiency, function and cohesion.

The problem of the enterprise as a social institution is radically different from its problems as an economic or as a political institution. *In the social area there is no conflict.* On the contrary, the objective needs and purposes of enterprise, member and society are in harmony. The "managerial attitude" which industrial society must demand of its members is in harmony with the demand that the individual achieve that "dignity of the person" in which a Western society believes. The demand for the maximum utilization of human abilities runs parallel with the individual's demand for status, and with our society's promise of equal opportunities.

At first sight this may seem to be in complete contradiction to the conventional view of an industrial society, the view which William Blake a hundred and fifty years ago expressed in the symbol of the "satanic mill." But to read our conclusion as an assertion that status and function, dignity of the individual and the justice of equal opportunities are indeed *realized* in our industrial society, would be an absurd misunderstanding. To be sure there is a great deal more fulfillment of status and function in the plant society than is generally realized; every study of the worker and his job brings that out clearly. But every study also brings out that there is not enough fulfillment. The plant society today at best barely satisfies the minimum required to give our society cohesion. It does not appear an entirely rational society to any of its members and appears entirely irrational to many. The conventional picture of industrial anarchy is overdrawn, sometimes to the point of the grotesque. But even when it is a caricature, it caricatures something that really exists.

The correct conclusions from our findings are very different indeed.

Research and analysis—and every one of our conclusions is completely supported by factual research into concrete situations—indicate *that the individual can be given status and function in the industrial enterprise.* They disprove the popular belief that the industrial system is by its very nature destructive of human community and individual dignity. Indeed, they prove this belief to be a sentimental nostalgia for the "good old times" which never existed. More striking perhaps, and equally contrary to popular ideas, is the finding that "monotony" is not a real problem at all. The member of the big mass-production plant does not, indeed, find it easy to obtain satisfaction and fulfillment in his work. But the reason is not "monotony"; it is not the "starvation of man's creative instincts," as the pet phrase of the glorifiers of the "idyllic" agrarian society of yesteryear would have it.

The correct conclusion is not that the industrial enterprise *of necessity* gives status and function but that it is inherently capable of doing so. What all our studies uncover is the *potential*—most convincingly, perhaps, in the *General Motors Contest*, which, by inducing the worker to take a "managerial attitude," if only for a moment, showed what our industrial society could be. The 175,000 entries in the Contest leave no doubt that it could be a society in which the demand for function and status is fulfilled.

The more fulfillment of social status and function the enterprise gives, the more will the enterprise itself benefit directly in higher productivity and profitability, that is in better economic performance. The slogan of modern personnel management, "The happy and contented worker is an efficient worker," is a dangerous half-truth; but it is correct in proclaiming an essential harmony between the demands of member and society on the enterprise and the social demands of the enterprise on its membership.

Any step toward the social integration of the plant community will be supported by the natural forces within the enterprise. It will cut with the grain, will be carried and furthered by the *"élan vital"* of the social body itself, and will in turn strengthen the social body. It is likely to have disproportionately large results in increased fulfillment of status and function. The famous Hawthorne studies undertaken at the Chicago plant of the Western Electric Company twenty years ago showed that even mere gestures, unsupported by any action, will have that effect, though of course not permanently. The operators on an assembly-line job, for instance, reacted with greater productivity to any change in their working conditions even to a marked change for the worse. The important things were not the actual conditions but the gestures of concern for, and interest in, the worker. And despite all our mistakes, despite philosophies and policies which could not have been more effective had they been designed to deny status and function, we find a great deal of status and function in every single situation we study.

Europe probably presents a much less bright picture. But it is unlikely that studies of the European worker would produce anything that would decisively change these conclusions about the character of the industrial society. The disintegrating forces have only been allowed to work a much longer time, the constructive forces have been hampered much more thoroughly, than in this country. But the basic conclusions from American experience and evidence should, by and large, be valid for Europe as well.

The obstacles to status and function in the plant community must, however, be very great. Otherwise we could neither explain the general belief in the reality of the "satanic mill" one hundred years after the conditions were remedied which Blake had attacked. We could not even explain the actual situation which, though much better than is popularly believed, is still far from satisfactory, and, at best, just barely passable. Only very great obstacles could account for the difference between the plant community as it is, and the plant community as its own natural forces would want it to be.

We can further conclude that these *difficulties must lie within the enterprise*. They have nothing to do with the "system." The Marxist criticism of the "system" may be valid. But it is irrelevant to the social situation of the industrial enterprise, which will not be basically different whether the "system" be Capitalism, Socialism, Communism or Fascism. Private or public ownership of the means of production, market determination of prices, central planning are very weighty matters. But they have no more bearing on the social functioning of the industrial enterprise than the conjunction of two planets has on the cause and cure of pneumonia. To blame the social ills of industrial society on the "system" instead of the internal policies of the enterprise, is a form of social astrology and pure superstition.

Finally, we can conclude that the only way to overcome these difficulties and obstacles is through *concrete changes in policies and practices*. They cannot be overcome through propaganda or good intentions. They cannot be overcome—as one highly vocal school seems to believe—by psychoanalyzing the worker to "adjust" him to the plant-situation. The difficulties are neither illusions to be dispelled by information and indoctrination, nor "personality problems" of the worker and the result of factors outside the plant, such as childhood traumas or mother-in-law trouble. The difficulties are objective, concrete and real. They are difficulties rather than conflicts. They lie within the enterprise rather than in some abstraction called the "system." Hence they can be attacked and overcome. But they are concrete, impersonal and real, not imaginary or psychological. Hence they require for their overcoming, concrete, radical and major changes in the policies, the organization, the practices, and even in the philosophy of the enterprise.

CHAPTER 17

MEN AT WORK

MASS-PRODUCTION technology creates new social conditions. It gives an altogether new meaning to the *placement* of the worker in his job and to the relationship between a man and his work. There is a new relationship between the work of the *individual* and the work of the organized *whole*, and between the *individual* worker himself and the other workers on the *team*. Every one of these new conditions and relations creates obstacles to social satisfaction and fulfillment—and also to efficiency and productivity.

However, the problem is not "monotony," as is so often asserted. The popular concept of monotony as stifling a man's creative impulse is a romantic fable. "Monotony" as a disintegrating factor is startlingly absent in the Hawthorne material, even though the operations studied were among the most monotonous and most repetitive in industrial history. Equally emphatic is the evidence of the *General Motors Contest*. Some of the most monotonous operations in the automobile plant proved actually to yield the greatest job satisfaction and to provide the most stimulus to the imagination.

The monotony slogan is not only a false explanation of the phenomena we have to deal with; it is a misleading one. It leads to the attempt to feed the worker's imagination and creative energies outside of the job in the form of "cultural" and "leisure" activities, and to a neglect of the problems of the job. But the answer lies in the job and in the operation, which have to be made meaningful and satisfying. Outside compensations for the dreariness of the job cannot help at all.

Fitting the Man to the Job

In mass-production technology placement becomes a social problem. However specialized his product itself may be, the worker in a traditional craft or industry performs a variety of processes in the course of his work. He constantly changes tools, rhythm, speed and posture. He is almost bound to find at least one phase of the work congenial to him. Take the cultures where crafts and trades are hereditary. There are always plenty of misfits, people who loathe the trade they were born to, and who try to break out of it. But in a hereditary craft system the great majority is at least able to adjust itself to it, if not to enjoy it positively. In a pre-industrial system the problem of placement is not a social but an individual, an atypical rather than a general problem.

Under modern industrial conditions, however, each job embraces only a very small number of operations. This means that the industrial system can give a useful life and meaningful, productive work to the handicapped: the old and infirm, the disabled, even the mentally backward or retarded. But it also means that the worker who is not placed right is *misplaced*. Since there is only one phase to the job, the worker has to find satisfaction in this one phase; there is no compensation in other phases of the job, such as there usually are in a pre-industrial technology. Placement in modern mass-production industry is either right or wrong, either successful or unsuccessful.

Right placement is not only in itself a major source of job satisfaction; it is a prerequisite to any satisfaction or function fulfillment. *The misplaced person is likely to be a displaced person in the industrial community.*

Right placement is also one of the most fruitful ways of increasing productivity and efficiency. At present the productivity of the mass-production plant is geared, by and large, to the output of the wrongly placed worker. The "standard" of performance for any one operator is the amount of work that can be turned out by an "average person," that is, by someone without obvious physical or mental handicaps but also without any pronounced ability or liking for the job.

How low this "average" efficiency is, is shown by the experience of one man who, alone among the ten or fifteen assembly-plant managers of a large corporation, gave some thought and attention to placement. Where the other assembly plants consistently operated at ninety per cent or less of the "standard" set by the engineers in central office, his plant worked at one hundred and twenty-five or one hundred and thirty per cent of standard. Yet, the other plants resorted again and again to the "speed-up," whereas he kept the pressure fairly low. Where the other plants were plagued by labor friction and "quickie" strikes he had almost no labor trouble. And his is by no means an isolated experience.

It is not only the badly placed man himself who feels alienated by the job and who performs inefficiently. The well-placed man in an environment of bad placements may be even more of a problem. He will be under strong pressure not to produce up to his capacity; ordinary human decency and the informal code of the plant forbid his setting a pace that his badly placed fellow workers cannot maintain. He will want to do well at a job he likes, to show his ability and to win recognition for it. But he also feels loyalty to his fellow workers and desires to be "one of the gang." He is thus apt to be badly frustrated and in conflict with himself.

Industry has at last begun to realize that placement is a real problem in the modern enterprise as shown by the mushroom growth of all kinds of "infallible" tests for all kinds of jobs, aptitude tests, personality tests, etc. Not one month goes by without the discovery of another such Chinese torture claimed by its inventor to be the definitive answer to the placement problem. But it is very doubtful whether any of these gadgets, however scientific, will contribute much to the solution of the problem. Indeed, the skepticism of the old operating man against the "scientific solution"—though in most cases based only on hostility to newfangled ideas—is probably well founded.

These tests are mostly designed to place a man at the time he is hired. Like all entrance examinations, they measure promise against a highly simplified abstraction of future situation and environment. Even if "scientific" tests would give us reliable placement data, they could be successful only after a man has been in the plant for some time—and then mainly as a check against the experience of the man himself and of his supervisors.

Any test can measure only a few facets of a man's personality. But placement is a matter of the whole man—his abilities, his interests, his emotions, his values—and of the men he is working with. Finally, all tests must assume either that the job is an unskilled one or that it requires one or two specific and identifiable skills. However, the very fact that placement is a problem refutes this assumption. If the job were really unskilled, there would be no placement problem. And the skill needed—which is really the ability to obtain constant satisfaction out of one particular job—is not a skill in the old sense but a configuration of inclinations, abilities and temperament—things which by their very nature are almost impossible to define or to measure.

The so-called scientific approach may well be the lazy man's way out and an attempt to avoid coming to grips with the problem. The solution probably requires neither scientific tools nor much outlay of money. But it requires an understanding that placement can be done only after a man has worked in the plant for some time, and a willingness to let the men themselves work the problem out together with their supervisor.

Fitting the Job to the Man

Even if we learn to fit the man to the job through successful placement, there would still remain the problem of fitting the job to the man.

All modern industrial operations are based on the division of the work into elementary and repetitive single motions. This principle was first developed some fifty or sixty years ago by Taylor and Gantt as the principle of "scientific management." It was the basis on which modern mass-production industry was built; and to it we owe the efficiency and productivity of modern industry. By now, this principle has been extended not only to practically all industrial operations proper but, far beyond manufacturing, to office work, distribution, etc.

The principle itself is productive and efficient. But it is very dubious, indeed, whether we yet know how to apply it except to machinery. There is first the question whether "specialization" as it is understood and practiced today is a socially and individually *satisfying* way of using human energy and production—a major question of the social order of industrial society. There is also the question whether "specialization" is an *efficient* way of using human energy and production—a major question of the technology of an industrial society. To break up complex operations into their constituent simple components is provably the best way to obtain maximum output and productivity. But is it in accord with human psychology and physiology to assign each elementary operation to a separate worker, as does our assembly line in manufacturing and office work? Is it efficient and conducive to maximum output?

Scientific management answers this question in the affirmative. But the answer is not really a "scientific" one. It rests on the premise that man is a machine tool. Undoubtedly, the most efficient way for a machine tool to be designed is for one specific purpose and for one specific operation. And a man undoubtedly will perform a series of five repetitive simple motions faster than a complex of five different motions. But man is not a machine tool and most certainly not a single-purpose machine tool. And from his efficiency to perform a series of five repetitive motions no conclusion can be drawn on his efficiency to perform five thousand. In other words, it is very dubious whether the unimaginative and unthinking application of machine tool principles to man does not: (a) fail to utilize man's real efficiency; and (b) lead to real and tangible inefficiency in the form of fatigue, stresses and strains.

Our evidence on this point is perhaps not conclusive. Nobody has yet studied the human being in production except in a few unrelated aspects. The worker himself rarely tries to bring his attitudes and reactions out into the open. But though only fragmentary, the evidence is highly suggestive. It indicates that the application of the assembly-line principle to the human being, that is, the tacit assumption that man is a badly designed, single-purpose machine tool, is psychologically and physiologically unsound. We have concrete evidence that it is a wasteful, unproductive and inefficient use of man as a tool of production, that it is poor engineering, and that it leads to tension, frustration and dissatisfaction which set up barriers between a man and his work.

Our evidence is partly physiological: muscular and nervous strains develop in people who are being used as single-purpose machine tools. They result in that unique phenomenon "industrial fatigue," which, as we know, tends to be the greater the less physically or mentally exacting the work is. On the production line, the worker works at the speed of the slowest and at the rhythm of the jerkiest man on the line. We know from our fatigue studies that an artificially low speed of operations produces more fatigue than short spurts of excessive speed, and that nothing sets up as much muscular and nervous resistance as jerky rhythm. We know that human beings most efficiently overcome fatigue and strain by varying speed and rhythm as they work.

Partly our evidence is psychological; even viewed purely as a machine, man is not a single-purpose tool. His productive capacity does not lie in maximum efficiency for any one operation but in his ability to combine and integrate an almost infinite number of operations. To use him as if he were a badly designed, single-purpose machine tool is to use him inefficiently and poorly. Even a machine is damaged if used in the wrong way.

Our best evidence is the experience of World War II.[1] In some cases it was not possible to set up the traditional assembly-line-in-space; instead the work had to be organized in what might be called an assembly-line-in-concept. The work was actually broken up into elementary operations; but each man did a series of these operations instead of just one. To the engineer's surprise, this resulted in an increase in efficiency and production instead of in a drop. In addition, there was a noticeable change in the atmosphere. Instead of the tension, hurry and drive of the normal mass-production environment, whether industrial plant or clerical office, the atmosphere was unhurried and unrelaxed, the rhythm even and strong, the people friendly and easygoing.

We have yet to learn how to do the second half of the job of which Taylor and Gantt did the first half fifty years ago. They split up the operation into its constituent motions; we shall have to put the motions together again to produce an operation that is based both on the unskilled elementary motion and on the specifically human ability and need to co-ordinate.

The Worker and the Work Team

The problem of fitting the man to job is not exclusively an engineering problem. It is just as much a problem of group work. Just as we must not set one man apart from his abilities, we must not set one man apart from, or against, the men he works and lives with.

The individual in mass-production technology needs to be a part of the community of his fellow workers. This was established and proven by the pioneers of "scientific management" a full half-century

[1] Examples can be found in my *Concept of the Corporation* and in my paper, "The Human Factor in Mass Production," Production Pamphlet No. 175, American Management Association, 1947.

ago when they found that differentials between the wages of individual workers and between the wage levels of groups of workers are usually more important to the worker than the absolute wage rate. For social prestige and standing in the community of his fellows matter more to the worker than the economic reward for his work.

Elton Mayo and his associates, working in the twenties and thirties, showed that in every industrial enterprise there is an "informal" social organization of the workers as well as of supervisory and managerial personnel. They found that it is this informal organization rather than management which actually determines rates of output, standards, job classification and job content. Without employing formal sanctions other than the disapproval of the group, this organization effectively directs the member's behavior. All later research has borne this out. In the *General Motors Contest*, for instance, "good fellowship" or "good relations with fellow workers" showed as leading causes of job satisfaction.

Our studies also show, however, that the member's need for integration with the group, for this relationship to the community of his fellows, is not at present sufficiently satisfied. Indeed they show that mass-production technology tends to isolate man from man.

The traditional automobile assembly line provides a visible example of this social isolation. If the men on one position fall behind, the men at the next position cannot come to their help and thus restore the rhythm. They are confined to their own operation; they do not even have the tools or the equipment to take over some of the load their fellow workers cannot carry. If the men at one position go ahead because they are abler or more skillful workers, the rest of the men do not benefit. Indeed, the others are lucky enough if they escape without being penalized by a higher production quota and a speed-up for what in any other team relationship would be of benefit to all, namely the ability of some of the members to do more work and to assume leadership.

The automobile assembly line is not at all an extreme example of this social organization in isolation. Altogether, the extreme is to be found in clerical work rather than in industrial operations. The business machine operations in a bank, insurance company or mail-order house carry much further the split between the complete integration of the process and the complete isolation of the operator.

This social effect of the assembly-line principle is the target for most of the attacks on modern industry. It gives substance to the charge that mass production is inhuman and antisocial. It was, for instance, this aspect of mass-production technology on which Charlie Chaplin focused his "Modern Times." The film was a caricature, but a caricature of something that undoubtedly exists.

The "assembly-line-in-space" undoubtedly isolates. But though this social atomization is characteristic of most present-day uses, it is almost certainly not inherent in the principle. It is another result of the fallacious analogy between man and the single-purpose machine tool which permeates our industrial thinking and practice. Wherever during World War II we replaced the traditional assembly line by an "assembly-line-in-concept," social isolation was immediately replaced by the closest social integration. At the same time productivity and output increased.

To give one example: In one of the big aircraft engine plants there was not enough time to study and lay out each motion and each operation. As a result the men who put on the cylinder heads had to work out the details pretty much on their own. There were about a dozen crews of six men each, working in neighboring aisles on the same job. Under normal conditions each of these crews would have done the work exactly the same way, at exactly the same speed and with the same motions. But because the details of the work had been left to the men, each crew actually did the job a little differently. One thing, however, they all had in common: they worked as a group rather than as six individuals. On one location the six men rotated, each man doing only one operation at the time but doing the entire operation during a full cycle. In the next aisle two men would do the same operations over and over again while the other four rotated, with the two fixed positions rotating from shift to shift. In yet another location the six men would work as two groups of three with each man occupying the same job all the time, but with the two teams changing places after each completed cycle.

In the department where the cylinder heads were put on, actual productive efficiency was considerably higher than in the rest of the plant—so much so that the crews sometimes had to stand idle to give the rest of the plant a chance to catch up. In this one department of an otherwise hectic plant the atmosphere was unhurried. A casual observer might have felt that the men were taking it easy—in the same way in which a good tennis player seems to be languid and unhurried when the game is really fast. Tempers were even, little jokes passed between the men and were appreciated all the more for being obviously in the family. There was conversation between the aisles—something entirely absent in the rest of the plant—a spirit of friendly competition, but also a willingness to come to the other crew's rescue when things went wrong.

Another example, showing the inefficiency as well as the social disruptiveness of the individual's isolation, is provided by the postwar experience of a Midwestern plant producing electrical equipment. In the assembly of small switches, eight women work together, as a team, with altogether about twenty such teams. Seated at a round table, the eight used to pass the work from one to another apparently without organization. In an efficiency move, the work was reorganized on assembly-line principles. Each woman was assigned one operation. Parts and subassemblies which formerly lay in disorderly heaps in the middle of the table, were brought by overhead conveyors to each worker's place at the speed at which she was supposed to work. Lighting was improved, the height and shape of the seats was changed to give maximum comfort, etc. To make the transition easy for the workers, the standard of output was left unchanged for a trial period. Yet, the workers immediately began to complain that the standard was much too high; in fact, they could not maintain the "new" speed and fell behind. Poor and defective work went up sharply. Absenteeism and illness increased, together with small accidents and with complaints about headaches and eyestrain. Friction and fighting among the workers—almost unknown before—became general. The most revealing symptom was the general complaint that the seats were too close together. There had been no change in the distance between work places; but where formerly there was a closely knit team, there were now eight isolated individuals each demanding "living space."

The plant manager was intelligent enough to realize what had happened. He had the imagination to ask the workers themselves to work out the solution. As a result, they kept all the innovations that had to do with comfort and ease of operation: lighting, new seats, overhead supply of parts, etc. But they threw out everything that confined one worker to one operation. They restored the team. Efficiency not only went up to the old mark but passed it by a fair margin; it has stayed up ever since, that is for two years or so. The thing that baffled the industrial engineers most was that when they first tried to find the cause of the trouble, they discovered that the standard—which was actually the speed at which the workers had been working all along— was indeed very high measured by industrial engineering norms.

The basic trouble is not only a view of man as an inanimate machine tool but a failure to understand the nature of mass production itself. There is, for instance, the general use of individual production quotas and of individual incentive wages. Both tend on the whole to isolate men and to set them against each other.

There is nothing wrong with the idea of a production standard. Indeed mass production could not operate without it. There is also nothing wrong with the idea of a relationship between output and monetary reward. But *individual* quota and *individual* incentive are socially disruptive in many cases, as they run counter to the basic structure of mass production. They result from the same confusion between analysis and application that leads from the correct analysis of the operation as a series of elementary motions to the confinement of the worker to one such motion. To *analyze* the work in terms of individual quota and individual incentive is indeed necessary. But it does not follow that it should actually be performed on this basis any more than it follows that we should spell out *c*, *a*, *t*, whenever we want to say "cat" (and the alphabet is indeed the oldest and most imaginative application of "scientific management").

The antisocial effect of individual quota and individual incentive is, in most cases, purely unintentional, if not the very opposite of what is intended. Very few managements even realize that these policies have a social impact. They adopted them partly because they are traditional, partly because they are easy and seem obvious. That does not, however, lessen their effect on the group. The informal organization of the plant may mobilize to sabotage them which preserves the plant community but destroys efficiency. Or the incentives may be so great as to be irresistible, in which case productive efficiency is achieved at the price of social atomization and of hostility among the workers to each other as well as to the enterprise. Yet an incentive system should be, and can be, a source of group cohesion, of allegiance to the enterprise and of efficiency.

In the three areas, placement, relationship between operation and human being, and relationship between the men on the same job, we deal primarily with operating problems. The solutions lie primarily in operating practices. The problems themselves, however, are social: the wrong techniques create dissatisfaction, friction and social tension; they reduce the efficiency of the enterprise's human resources.

Still it might be justified to call these problems technical. The task is not to do something new, but to do properly and constructively things that have to be done anyhow: to employ, place and train people; to lay out the operation and the job; and to establish performance and pay standards.

The Need for Integration

We have mentioned before the individual's need for integration into the community. We may call this need by many names, the need for "identification," the need for "self-respect," the need for "rationality." It is always the same need, and it is perhaps the greatest need of the individual in the industrial society of today. If it goes unfulfilled, both the work of the whole and the work of the individual become meaningless. Nothing is more fully established by all our studies than this need and its importance.

One indication is the strength of the resistance to changes in the work and operation of the individual. We have discussed the resistance to technological change. But there is throughout the plant a deep resistance to change altogether. It reflects the precarious hold the worker has on the understanding of his job and of his work, which makes any change a threat to his inner security.

The individual by himself, unaided, can rarely satisfy his need for understanding and integration. He needs new organs to see the whole and himself in it. In mass production the whole, as well as each man's relationship to it, can be seen easily only from the top.

Again World War II supplied us with dramatic proofs of the importance of integration. It made both management and workers conscious of the need for meaning and purposes in the work, and of the difficulties in satisfying it. It also showed us how the difficulties could be tackled.

War production in many cases—at least in this country—meant little change in the worker's actual operation. But it meant a complete change in the meaning and purpose of the work; the same humdrum routine job was suddenly vitally important to the national effort. The worker suddenly saw that there could be pride in the work, that the job could have meaning. It also made the worker realize how very little he knew about his operation and about plant and product. The resulting demand for information overwhelmed management. It showed that the worker is not just out for the pay check but is profoundly interested in the work, the place he works in, the process and the product—the lesson the Hawthorne studies had brought out so strongly a decade earlier. It also showed that satisfaction of the demand for function, for information and understanding, leads directly to more efficiency and to higher production.

Equally startling was what happened after the War. Instead of making door hinges for cockpits, the worker was again making door hinges for passenger cars. They were the same hinges, and the worker performed the same operations. But the meaning had gone out of the work. The result was a letdown, a deep feeling of frustration and dissatisfaction—perhaps even more noticeable in Great Britain than in this country. What is usually explained as "fatigue"—the sudden drop in productive efficiency after the war—was probably very largely this disappointment, this feeling of being deprived of the satisfaction and meaning which the worker and the work had had during the war. The wave of postwar strikes in this country may have had a similar origin.

To understand why it is so difficult for the mass-production enterprise to relate the worker's work with the work of the whole, we may refer again to the analogy between the social organization of the modern plant and the acting troupe or the symphony orchestra. The analogy was valid enough to illustrate what we meant by "integration." But it does not go any further. However unimportant a walk-on part, it is "acting"; it is of the same kind as the work of the star. The budding young actor is probably grossly mistaken when he tries to imagine the star's work as a projection of his own. But at least he believes that he understands what the star is doing. There is no such imaginative relationship between the shaping of a piece of sheet steel and the completed turbine, the punching of cards in a business machine and the banking business. By projecting steel-shaping or hole-punching, the imagination can reach only more and bigger steel shaping and hole punching.

It is not the size of the operation or even its variety that creates the difficulty, but precisely the kind of integration which makes a product in the modern industrial process. In itself this process is one of the greatest and most creative achievements of the human mind, a concept of great daring and a feat of synthesis and ordering. But the whole concept, the whole product, the whole order, can be put together only by starting out from the final product, which only the men at the top can do with ease. It is as if we had an orchestra in which only the conductor hears all the instruments, while each musician sits in his own soundproof cell out of sight and hearing of any other instrument. By using the most rigid rules of time-keeping, we might produce a symphony in this fashion. But no musician would know what he was doing nor would any of them be able to say what they contributed to the end result—perhaps not even with a complete score in front of them.

What the worker needs is to see the plant as if he were a manager. Only thus can he see his part; from his part he cannot reach the whole. This "seeing" is not a matter of information, training courses, conducted plant tours, or similar devices. What is needed is the actual experience of the whole in and through the individual's work. Wherever in our research studies we find an individual worker who has successfully established a meaningful relationship between his own operation and the work of the whole, we find a man who has the "managerial viewpoint" and who projects the whole productive process onto his own individual operation.

There is, for instance, a General Motors worker who runs a scrap-baler—in itself a completely unskilled, dirty and monotonous clean-up job—and who succeeded in identifying himself and his own operation with the whole process. He did it by reconstructing production—which he may never have seen—through the kind of scrap which it threw out. What matters is not whether his reconstruction was accurate or not, but that a man engaged in the most monotonous task is able to see himself as a part of the whole. What matters even more is that the only way in which he could do this was by starting out from the whole, by looking at his own job "managerially." This scrap-baler has imagination of a rare kind; while by no means unique, he is certainly the exception rather than the rule. And even he would probably never have succeeded but for the *Contest* with its spur to the "managerial attitude."

There is another aspect to the same problem: the worker needs to be able to endow the product with usefulness.

A pre-industrial society as a rule is close to subsistence; and it turns out a small number of products. The social importance of practically every activity is immediately apparent—as witness Plato's division of all activities into toilers, soldiers and philosophers, or the almost identical classification of all human labor in Germanic law into the three estates: the *Wehrstand*, the *Naehrstand* and the *Lehrstand* (the defense estate, the feeding estate and the teaching estate).

Our industrial society, however, is very complex and far removed from subsistence. Few of its activities are essential in the sense that society could not go on were they to cease. Few are directly related to social effectiveness. The social meaning of few products or activities is obvious or striking.

Also, in the craftsman's work in pre-industrial society social usefulness was secondary compared to the pride of skill itself. Even today, the one group in the mass-production plant which is not at all worried about the social function of their product are the highly skilled workers. The same is often true when the work itself is dramatic, for instance, in a steel mill. The social meaning of the product was, of course, also no problem at all during the War. But how does one endow can openers or lamp shades with social meaning and purpose? Yet the worker demands—especially after the experience of the War— that his work be meaningful.

This demand showed strikingly in the differences in emphasis, in the *General Motors Contest*, between the workers in plants turning out products of obvious meaning for instance truck engines, and workers in plants turning out "undramatic" products such as the wiring for the same trucks. In the one group pride in the product was not only high, but an obvious source of major job satisfaction. In the other group—maybe a plant with better working conditions, stabler employment and better personnel management—pride in the product was either absent or defensive: "Though nobody ever sees our product, I know that it is important." Yet anything connected with the automobile enjoys high visibility and high esteem in the American culture. How much greater must be the need for a social meaning of the product in less glamorous industries?

There is one way to solve this problem, as shown by both Soviet Russia and Nazi Germany: by creating the perpetual excitement of the "National Effort." But except in actual war, this can lead only to hysteria. Worse still, the effort can be sustained only by playing with the danger of war. The stimulus is habit-forming, and greater and greater doses are required to keep up the intoxication. Altogether there is no better way to make war inevitable than to rely on the appeal of the National Effort to give social cohesion and meaning. If, however, we fail to solve the problem of the meaning and function of the product for the individual in industrial society, we may well find ourselves forced to use the false emotional satisfaction of the "production battle."

The key to the understanding of the problem as well as to its solution is that the problem does not exist for management, though it exists for supervision and the lower ranks of middle management almost as much as for the rank and file. From management's point of view the product is obviously meaningful. The reason is, of course, that management does not see can openers or lamp shades but a business with problems of manufacturing and engineering, buying and selling, financing and accounting, etc. What is needed here is again the "managerial attitude."

The worker is pathetically eager to know as much about the business as possible. But all our evidence also shows that the worker is as unable from his vantage point to see the business "managerially" as he is unable to see the relationship of his process to the work of the whole.

CHAPTER 18

IS THERE REALLY A LACK OF
OPPORTUNITY?

OPPORTUNITIES for advancement in the industrial enterprise are greater than they have ever been in any society. Statistically, opportunities are increasing apace; the industrial enterprise depends on a steady increase in the executive and middle-class positions. Every major company in this country has had to start systematic recruitment and training programs for supervisory and executive personnel, as the supply is not equal to an ever-increasing demand.

And yet it is becoming increasingly difficult to rise in industrial society; the promise of equal opportunities is being fulfilled less and less. Outside of the United States this is perhaps not so important. The rise from the rank and file into the management was the exception in Europe rather than the rule. In this country, however, the promise of equal opportunities for every one in industry has been regarded as a basic promise, as one of the foundations of "democracy."

The key to the riddle lies in the character of the "skill" required of the new middle and upper groups, the industrial middle class and the executive group. These are not "skills" in the traditional sense, based on experience and long practice. Theoretical knowledge and administrative ability are required. A rank-and-file job, however skilled, will not give the worker the knowledge needed for a supervisory job; nor will it give him an opportunity to demonstrate his ability for supervisory work. A supervisory or middle-management job, by the same token, will not give the knowledge needed for an executive position nor an opportunity to show executive ability. As a result, the chances of a working man to be promoted to supervisor, or of a supervisor to be promoted into the managerial group are actually becoming smaller, even though the number and proportion of supervisory and managerial positions are increasing. The increased demand tends to be filled by direct appointment of men from the outside rather than by promotion up the ladder. At the same time, the irrelevance of the worker's performance as a criterion for performance as a supervisor, and of the supervisor's performance as a criterion for managerial performance, means that promotions are not rational and understandable to the group out of which the promoted man comes.

The Key Position of the Foreman

The first-line supervisor, the foreman, occupies the key position in the problem of opportunities. On the one hand, he is what the term originally meant: the senior man in the rank-and-file team, the noncommissioned officer of industry. But in American industry the foreman has traditionally also been a member of the management group, a second lieutenant, rather than a long serving noncommissioned officer. On this traditional position of the foreman as the bridge between the two major groups within the enterprise rests the worker's opportunity for advancement into the executive and managerial group. It is this traditional position which is meant by the management claim that the "foreman is the first line of management" and that unionization of the foreman is therefore a direct attack upon the cohesion and function of the management group.

The long-serving sergeant of industry, the foreman, is not a "skilled" worker in the sense of being a craftsman. However, like the skilled craftsman, he needs long experience—experience not in the use of specific tools or of specific techniques, but in the routine of his department and in the job of each man in it. Like the skill of the craftsman, this skill, while requiring native ability, is fundamentally a product of time.

As a member of the management team, however junior, the foreman needs a completely different set of qualifications: knowledge of organization, knowledge of technical processes, understanding of policies. The ability required for this job is intellectual ability rather than skill. The training required for it is education in principles rather than long exposure. It is therefore becoming more and more difficult to combine the qualities needed for the leadership of a small group of workers with those needed for participation as a junior member in the management group. The two require different, if not conflicting, qualifications. It may even be argued that the long exposure necessary to be a good foreman in one sense of the word, makes a man unfit to be a good foreman in the other sense of the term.

Caught between conflicting demands, the foreman's job has become increasingly difficult. He has to know more and more; he has to be able to do practically everything—and carry a heavy load of paper work in addition. A recent manual for foremen put out by a big company listed seven hundred and fifty subjects—from the company's balance sheet to the use of the company's product and to its labor policy—on which the foreman is supposed to be expert enough to advise his workers. Yet, it left out everything directly related to the foreman's own job and the job of his department; that he knows all he needs to know about the techniques, the tools, the processes as well as about the management of men was apparently taken for granted.

Even the paragon of this manual will hardly be trained adequately for a managerial position. The foreman's job may have become so unlike that of the worker as increasingly to exclude promotion to it from the ranks and to require recruitment of specifically trained men from the outside. At the same time, it may have lost so much of its earlier executive function as to preclude promotion from it into the executive groups.

Fifty years ago the foreman was not only the "first line of management"; he was pretty close to being the last line of management too. He ran his own department. Not so much earlier, in the years after the Civil War, it was not at all uncommon in American industry to find foremen who were actually the managers, running their departments at their own economic risk. "Top management" confined itself to selling and financing without taking any direct part in manufacturing. Foremanship was an executive position.

Today the foreman's task, while extremely heavy and difficult, is almost entirely without executive elements. The foreman has no authority; what he has not lost to the new management groups above him, he has lost to the union. He makes no decisions, he does not, as a rule, any longer hire the people who are to work under him. He takes no part in the formation of policies; indeed, it is a rare foreman who is even told what the policies are. And this is not just shortsighted or ill-considered policy. The foreman's department is much too small to make him a member of management in anything but name. At the same time, his responsibilities are much too heavy to allow any expansion of his scope.

The Break in the Promotion Ladder

One important result is the almost general complaint that promotions are not being made on merit but by favoritism, whim or prejudice. Of course, there is always justification for such a charge; only the decision of the Recording Angel is based on complete knowledge of a man. But the belief is as strong in plants where management has tried to develop a rational, objective and impersonal promotion policy as it is in plants that depend on the "hunch" of the superior. The qualities that make a worker outstanding are not too relevant to his qualification as a foreman; the qualities that make a foreman an outstanding foreman are not too relevant to his promotion into middle management. Thus even the most rational decision is likely to appear incomprehensible, irrational and arbitrary to the group out of which the man is promoted. Hence the strong pressure for seniority as the sole criterion for advancement; at least it is a simple, clear and indisputable criterion, however little it may have to do with merit or with the qualifications for the job.

In practice, the ladder of promotion tends to be broken. One trend is to preserve the character of foremanship as executive training; in which case workers usually no longer have a chance to be promoted. Foremen are then recruited directly from colleges, engineering schools and business schools, or out of special training courses for "management trainees." Or foremanship is regarded as the end of the worker's promotional ladder. Candidates for executive positions either come out of a few staff departments, or are recruited directly from the outside; in fact, some of the graduate business schools, especially Harvard, are organized to turn out "crown princes" who go directly into junior executive positions, usually on the staff of a senior executive, thus by-passing the shop altogether.

The first approach is followed most consistently perhaps by the American Telephone Company, which recruits men directly from the colleges into supervisory positions. The chemical industry also has few openings for rank-and-file workers in the supervisory ranks. In organic or synthetic chemistry a man has to have a good science or

engineering degree to be able to perform any but rank-and-file
functions.

The General Electric Company on the other hand promotes from
the ranks to foremanship but reserves higher positions to executive
trainees recruited directly from the graduate schools. The railroads
have probably carried furthest the exclusion of the foreman from promotion into the executive ranks. Railroad foremen, almost without exception, come out of the rank-and-file group; but they are also likely
to be so old as to have practically no chances for further promotion.
The foreman's "team leader" qualifications are preserved. The older
foremen probably do a better job working with the men under
them than the bright boys from engineering school who are not
likely to understand the men or be respected by them. But at the same
time the typical railroad foreman is a noncommissioned officer and
nothing but that. He has only skill, no understanding or training; and
he is most unlikely to become a candidate for promotion to a genuine
executive or managerial job.

That the development is not something peculiarly American—let
alone something peculiarly "capitalist"—is indicated by the experience
of the only other country where the worker once had the opportunity
to become an executive: Soviet Russia.

Twenty years ago, when the Russian industrialization drive started,
opportunities for the worker were practically unlimited. The positions of the managerial group of prerevolutionary days had become
vacant; there were in addition, all the positions in the new industries to
be filled. The Russians promoted every worker who showed any ability
at all as fast as he could learn the new job. From 1926 until 1936
Russia knew indeed unequalled opportunities; a boy fresh from the
farm could be almost certain of attaining quickly a major position
if he showed ability and industry. But while Russia got good gang
bosses out of the ranks, she did not get good technicians and executives out of the gang bosses. Very soon she found out that it was
on these that the performance of industry depends. Hence in 1936,
practically overnight, the whole policy was changed. Able workers
now can make a good deal of money; indeed, under the Russian incentive system their wage is three or four times the average. But
they cannot become executives or even supervisors. Supervisory positions above that of "gang boss" are reserved for the graduates of the

technical schools and universities who are to be the future executives, and who in turn are usually the children of technicians, executives and government officials. The extremism of the change in policy is indeed typical of a regime based on ideological absolutes such as Communism. The change itself, though, was not ideologically motivated but was a reaction to the realities of the industrial situation.

In this country the tremendous pressure for a college education is a sign that our younger generation does not believe any longer that opportunities for advancement from the bottom really exist. They believe that the only chance to rise to the top is by starting well above the ground.

Even though middle-class and executive positions are rapidly in-· creasing, the popular impression that opportunities are shrinking is thus founded in experience. Moreover, opportunities in our society as a whole are shrinking owing to the emergence of the enterprise as the central social institution. The enterprise recognizes only one prestige system: the economic prestige system; and only one contribution: contribution to economic performance. It has no room for the prestige, satisfaction and authority that come from personal standing in the community, from group leadership, from social and civic responsibility. It knows only *promotion*.

It is his plant community however to which a man looks for the fulfillment of his aspirations for success and for social recognition. As a result, the opportunities and advancements outside of the plant community have lost much of their satisfaction.

Only a small minority can be promoted. Out of ten workers only one can be promoted to foreman. Out of twenty foremen only one can become plant superintendent, while the odds against any worker's becoming general manager are about three thousand to one. The chances for promotion in the industrial enterprise, though greater than in any previous system, are still very small.

Also the enterprise can only fulfill the demand for opportunities of those people to whom economic advancement offers the most meaningful success. And this is a small part of the human race. Eventually advancement itself loses much of its satisfaction. Because there is always one more step ahead, promotion will tend to become a mere "raise." The manager of a large division within a big company who, when asked about his job to which he had just been appointed, immediately began to talk about the importance and prestige of his superior's job, was exceptional only for his frankness.

The enterprise needs all the talent and ability it can get. It certainly cannot depend for managerial personnel on an upper class and leave unused the abilities and talents of ninety per cent of its members. That in American industry—and in American industry alone—the managerial positions were not reserved for the educated or well-born but were accessible to the worker, was a major reason for the emergence of this country as the leading industrial power. It was not our natural resources, not our technical skill or our great good luck—important though all three were. It was our fuller use of the human resources of leadership, ambition and ability, one-sided though it may have been, which gave the American economy its dynamic quality. If the opportunities for advancement in the plant community are cut off, enterprise and economy are made poorer, just as much as through the destruction of any other productive resources.

The popular substitute for advancement from the ranks—a college education for all able young people—is really not acceptable. The abilities which make for scholastic success are not the abilities the enterprise needs. By asking the schoolmaster to pick management, the enterprise will deny itself the very men it needs most: the entrepreneur, the innovator, the risk-taker. The process is also self-defeating. All but the very poorest will go to college and will then expect a managerial position as of right, being too proud for subordinate jobs but unable to find any other. To make the degree the passport to promotion is certain to debauch education; it will become "quickie" training in the latest fad and in readily salable skills. But a free society requires an educational system dedicated to training of character and to the education of leaders.

Altogether, society cannot be satisfied with economic satisfactions. It must demand the prestige satisfactions of a genuine community. If the enterprise fails to offer these, its members will not only rightly feel that opportunities are shrinking or absent. They will also seek these satisfactions outside the enterprise and against it. One of the major attractions of the union has been that in union activity and union leadership, the individual is offered a chance to satisfy his needs for the social satisfaction and prestige that are denied to him in the enterprise. But if prestige satisfaction can be found only in the union, it is found in opposition to the enterprise.

And that the very cohesion of our society would be endangered were we to lose faith in the social justice of equal opportunities, hardly needs documentation or argument.

CHAPTER 19

THE COMMUNICATIONS GAP

ENTIRELY different in texture and character from the problems discussed so far is the problem of *group relations* in the plant community. It is commonly called a problem of "communications"—the ability of the various functional groups within the enterprise to understand each other and each other's functions and concerns.

We can say flatly that there is no communication today. The functional groups within the enterprise do not understand each other; each is unable to imagine what the other one is doing and why. The problem is usually presented as one of "communications between management and the worker." The term is misleading. We do not deal with two groups, "management" and "the worker," but with at least three: top management, middle management and supervision, and the rank-and-file workers. Socially and politically, the three groups are clearly differentiated. And "communication" between the middle-management group and the top-management group is as difficult and usually as completely absent as is communication between either group and the workers.

The term "communication" tends to have a purely technical meaning in industrial usage. It refers to the means of conveying rather than to what is being conveyed, to the telephone rather than to the conversation. As a result, the "communications problem" is usually considered a technical one of bringing information within the reach of the worker or of management. But there is no dearth of technical facilities; most of the programs for "communication"—plant newspapers, training conferences, letters to the employees, employee-attitude surveys, etc.—duplicate already existing facilities and present information already available to all groups. What is lacking is the willingness of each group to listen and its ability to do so, in other words, understanding and imagination rather than information.

This lack of mutual understanding rests on the differentiation of function between the three groups. Each group sees the same thing, the enterprise, from a different viewpoint and within a different angle of vision. What the one sees as obvious and plain fact, the other simply cannot see at all.

Top management sees the whole in terms of its economic performance, efficiency and productivity, and as one unit in a complex and competitive economy.

Middle management and supervision see the enterprise as a complicated machine, as a collection of "departments" and technical functions, and as sufficient unto itself rather than as a unit in the economy. More often they do not even see that much; each man's vision is confined to the technical function in which he is engaged. He is usually much more conscious of the political and social aspects of the enterprise than top management; he is much less conscious of the economic aspects. Every member of top management knows whether the enterprise is doing well financially or not. Few members of middle management are likely even to be able to find out how the company is doing, let alone to relate financial data to their own work. On the other hand, it is quite typical for top management not to know that a strike is brewing, while middle management is fully aware of the trouble and understands the real issue.

Either management group sees only a facet of the whole: top management sees the enterprise as an economic performer, middle management as an administrative entity, or at best as a social and political unit.

The worker is incapable of seeing either of these facets. From his position no management function makes much sense, neither top management with its focus on economic responsibility, nor middle management with its focus on technical functions and on the enterprise as an organization. What determines his vision is his job and the jobs of the people working next to him, his relationship to the job and to his fellow workers. Even if he knows what is going on in other parts of the plant, he cannot put these parts together to come up with an understanding of the whole plant, let alone add to it the invisible functions: selling and buying, engineering and research, finance, or the planning for the future which is top management's major responsibility. Yet while the worker sees only a facet, it appears to him nevertheless that he sees the "whole."

The Other Side of the Mountain

The root of the problem is that the enterprise has more than one aspect; and each group is concerned primarily with one aspect. Yet what each group sees supplies a complete explanation of the phenomena within its ken and thus looks completely convincing. It is often only by standing outside the enterprise that one can see how incomplete and limited each viewpoint actually is; from within the enterprise each viewpoint appears complete.

The man who has risen from the ranks to a managerial position usually cannot even remember how the enterprise looked to him a few years before when he himself was a worker. He is like the bear in the nursery song who went over the mountain, "and all he saw was the other side of the mountain." As very few people realize that they cannot remember, they think that they still know and base policies and practices on this illusion.

A man promoted from one group into the other has to acquire the new vision and blot out the old one to be able to do his job. This explains the hesitation of so many workers to accept a foremanship. On the one hand, they are naturally anxious to get the bigger job, with the income and prestige it brings. But even if they do not fight shy of the new and frightening responsibility, they generally—particularly in large plants—fear the new climate and the new social situation. The promotion will upset the friendships they and their families have outside the plant, and the social relationship they have established with their fellow workers inside the plant. It will force them to change their behavior, their code and their basic views. But unless a man makes this change to the point where he, so to speak, puts on a new skin and certainly acquires new eyes and ears, he will not last long as a foreman.

A similar break is required of the man who moves from middle management into a top-management position. Perhaps this break is even more difficult because the dividing line is not so clearly marked. The worker become foreman will no longer be accepted as one of their own by his former fellow workers. This may make the change very painful; we know from a good many foremen that they at first felt lonely, isolated and naked. But by the same token the transformation will be faster and more thorough. The man, however, who is promoted from middle management into top management will not go through any comparable "initiation rite." Socially, there is much less of a break between the two management groups, at least outwardly, than there is between worker and middle management; functionally, however, the break is probably even sharper. As a consequence, there are many more men in top management who fail to perform their job adequately because they have never completely acquired the top-management point of view than there are foremen who fail for the corresponding reason.

The lack of communication between the three groups makes it very hard for each group to understand what the others are seeing. It makes it equally difficult for each group to understand what the others are doing.

This greatly sharpens all the differences and conflicts we have discussed so far. It makes it difficult for management to understand, for instance, that the worker is talking about wage as income, and for the worker to understand that management is necessarily talking about wage as unit cost. It makes it difficult for management to see that the worker cannot relate his work to the product as a whole, and for the worker to understand that management sees only the whole and hardly ever the constituent parts. It equally aggravates the problems of the middle-management group, especially its difficulty to fit its own job into the work of the whole. It explains to a large extent why top managements fail even to realize that their concerns, policies and decisions are not understood by middle management and vice versa. To the worker who does not understand what the management groups are doing and why, management decisions will become arbitrary and irrational. To top management who does not understand the worker, the worker's behavior become irrational and incomprehensible. Middle management, caught in between, understands neither the worker's actions nor top management motives, rationale and actions.

This lack of understanding and imagination extends over the whole area of decisions and actions, attitudes and behavior. It pertains to managerial policies and functions, whether economic, engineering, plant lay-out, production methods or personnel policies. Perhaps there is even more understanding for the function of management among the workers—and consequently more respect for management—than there is understanding and respect for the worker and his function on the part of top management.

During the last few years industry as a whole, and management in particular, have become aware of the communications problem. Without this awareness—by no means general even today—the problem can certainly not be tackled. But awareness is not in itself a solution, nor are the measures which management have taken so far to establish communications particularly effective. By and large they consist of flooding the plant community with information material. But the worker is neither willing nor able to accept and to understand the information management pelts him with. What is needed is not information but new organs of perception, new eyes and ears for all three groups.

The solution, therefore, lies in the sphere of institutions rather than in that of information. Top management will have to develop an organ for "listening," so that it knows what the worker and middle management want to be informed about, and why they do not understand what to top management is so simple and clear. Similar "ears" will have to be grafted onto middle management and the worker. The present management efforts are, by and large, like the attempt to establish "communication" between a Chinese and a Spaniard by putting them both on the telephone; unless one of them knows the language of the other, the most perfect telephone system will not enable them to talk to each other. Today industry hardly has the telephone; certainly there is no common language.

CHAPTER 20

SLOT-MACHINE MAN AND DEPRESSION SHOCK

IT WOULD be completely wrong to conclude from this discussion of the problems in the plant community that the enterprise fails completely to give status and function.

Actually, the promise of status and function is fulfilled to a very considerable extent. Even the most casual contact with the industrial plant brings out the pride, the identification, the satisfaction of such groups as foundrymen, railroad workers, operators of heavy mechanized equipment, etc. Quantitatively there can be little doubt that at least in American industry the positive greatly outweighs the negative in the actual work relationship.

This cannot be emphasized too strongly. It is proof that the enterprise can be made a functioning institution. It also means that the natural forces within the enterprise will establish social health to the extent to which we overcome the obstacles.

But the picture changes completely when we shift from the quantitative to an appraisal of the *trend*. The trend is toward less, rather than toward more, social fulfillment.

Whenever the individual in the industrial situation can be induced to take a "managerial attitude," whenever he can look at his work and his job as a whole, the positive elements will dominate; the *General Motors Contest* showed this very clearly. But in the absence of any special effort, the individual is likely to be moved mainly by the negative factors. To see the positive requires a special effort; above all, it requires imagination. The negative factors are therefore usually taken for the normal and for reality. They will determine attitude and behavior. Unless the "managerial attitude" becomes normal and is supported by everyday experience, the negative and disintegrating tendencies, the unsolved problems, the lack of satisfaction, are likely to become increasingly the determining and dynamic factors.

The negative factors enjoy high visibility and carry decisive impact partly because practically all our human-relations thinking assumes that the problem is exclusively one of the "worker." It assumes that there are no social problems of the clerical, supervisory and executive groups. Most of our research studies have for instance focused on the rank-and-file worker. But the position of the white-collar groups is probably even less satisfactory; and it is these groups which are decisive for the social order and for the social atmosphere of the industrial enterprise. Their attitudes and behavior determine the attitudes and behavior throughout the plant.

Secondly, the one area in which we can bluntly assert that everything is negative is the area of communications. This prevents the positive factors from becoming effective. Only disappointment, dissatisfaction, disillusionment, opposition and complaints are voiced and thereby made concrete and conscious. The positive is taken for granted. To formulate it requires effective communications between the groups.

Finally—and this is really the decisive point—nearly all the negative tendencies are *obstacles to the imagination*. The positive satisfactions are largely to be found in concrete and tangible things and achievements. The disintegrating and negative forces, however, involve the intangibles. They involve precisely the experiences the individual needs to have to be conscious of status and function fulfillment, and to be able to project himself onto the whole and the whole onto his work.

The pattern and rationality of the mass-production principle are so abstract that their understanding makes very large demands on the imagination of the individual. The task therefore is primarily one of organizing the imagination. We must actively induce, coax, even force the member of industrial society, whether rank-and-file worker, middle management or top executive to see the society he lives in. To do that he will have to be given new organs of perception; for there is nothing more difficult than to overcome barriers to the imagination. It can be done only by giving the individual a genuine experience, either the actual external experience or the internal experience of symbol and ritual.

In this task our greatest difficulty lies in the forces that govern the attitude of management and employees in the plant. Management is obsessed by a concept of human nature that prevents it from seeing or understanding the plant community—the concept of the "slot-machine man." The worker is in the grip of a panicky fear that makes him intensely suspicious: the "depression shock." If the concrete obstacles to social fulfillment in the plant impede the imagination, the concept of the "slot-machine man" and the "depression shock" paralyze it.

The "Slot-Machine Man"

The "slot-machine man"[1] is not a creature of industrial society. He is the feeble-minded child of eighteenth-century rationalism, in whom the features of his father have become a ghastly caricature.

According to this concept, man is little more than a machine. What, therefore could be more natural for an engineer than to apply to him the principles of progressive engineering, and to reconstruct him as a single-purpose, high-speed machine tool? Man, according to the concept, is also an automaton responding to monetary stimulus like a chewing-gum vending machine. What could be more natural, therefore, than to attempt to use individual wage incentives as the basis for the social organization, for the integration of man into the enterprise?

Without the pseudoscientific and actually thoroughly fallacious concept of the slot-machine man, the mass-production revolution would probably never have succeeded. It needed so gross an oversimplification, so mechanistic a concept of man and society, to subvert and ultimately to replace the old pre-industrial society. The more radical a revolution, the simpler, the more distorted have to be its slogans. And the mass-production revolution has been one of the most radical revolutions in man's history. To the concept of the "slot-machine man" we owe, therefore, the achievements of the mass-production revolution in no small degree.

But the price was indeed a very heavy one. When management

[1] Elton Mayo's term is "rabble hypothesis."

looks at the worker, it does not really see the worker but sees the caricature of the "slot-machine man" instead: a greedy, lazy, shiftless automaton interested only in the pay check. And when the worker looks at management, he too sees what the "slot-machine man" concept has conditioned him to see: a fat parasite in cutaway and striped trousers, clipping coupons. These stock caricatures mold the concrete policies of both groups.

Here again there is no difference between Capitalism, Socialism or Communism. Indeed the country where the concept of the "slot-machine man" has become official dogma is Soviet Russia—and with good reason as it was Marx who, inheriting the concept from Ricardo, gave it universal currency. But belief in the concept is almost as general in the West, though a good many adhere to it but subconsciously. In the West and in the East, in Communism or in a free-enterprise society, however, it will have to be overcome if the individual is to have status and function.

The "Depression Shock"

As potent a disintegrating force as the "slot-machine man" is the "depression shock" from which the workers all over the Western world suffer as a result of their experience in the nineteen-thirties.

The Depression with its chronic unemployment made the people aware of a central fact of an industrial society: that social effectiveness, citizenship, indeed even self-respect depend on access to a job. Without a job man in industrial society cannot possibly be socially effective. He is deprived of citizenship, of social standing, of the respect of his fellow men, if not of his family and, finally of self-respect. No amount of economic relief can possibly offset the social destruction of chronic unemployment in an industrial society.

It does not matter so very much how many unemployed there are actually; what matters is whether they consider themselves "unemployed" or not. We may have numerically fairly large unemployment and yet have psychologically no unemployment whatsoever; the unemployed will be reasonably sure that theirs is but a temporary predicament, a lull between jobs. This, for instance, happened in the transition from war to peace in 1945-46 when for a few months unemployment in some parts of the country reached very high proportions. On the other hand, there may be little unemployment, and yet we may have a "depression psychology," if the unemployed feel that they are not likely to find a job soon, if ever. We can stand, socially, even considerable unemployment if the individual and the workers as a whole can predict how long it will last. Precisely because the impact of unemployment is social and psychological, it is uncertainty and unpredictability which make it unbearable.

The Depression also destroyed the belief that the access to the job is controlled by rational forces. It destroyed—or at least undermined —the belief in the rationality of our economic system altogether. The forces which determine the worker's life and livelihood have come to be regarded as demons: beyond his control, beyond anyone's rational control, unpredictable and forever lurking to pounce and to destroy. The worker feels the same fear of the economic forces that his primitive ancestor felt of the unseen forces of nature. It is this fear I call the "depression shock."

The "depression shock" is by no means confined to those workers who actually were unemployed for any length of time during the Depression—by and large a minority. The worker who was fully employed all the time from 1929 to 1939, who never missed a day's work, and who was actually never in danger of being laid off, suffered as much socially and psychologically as the unemployed, perhaps even more. The fear of being laid off next payday did as much damage as real unemployment. And there can have been very few workers during these ten years who did not live constantly in this fear. It is not limited to men who were of working age during the depression, but has hit even harder those who, as children, grew up in a family living under the threat and fear of unemployment. Our entire working population for a generation to come will thus live under the impact of this experience.

Insecurity—not economic but psychological insecurity—permeates the entire industrial situation. It creates fear; and since it is fear of the unknown and the unpredictable, it leads to a search for scapegoats and culprits. The "depression shock" makes the worker intensely suspicious of any innovation. It makes him timid. It also leads him to feel that action is futile; he'll lose his job anyhow so why try to make it meaningful?

To overcome the "depression shock" is thus a major task. Only if we restore the worker's belief in the rationality and predictability of the forces that control his job, can we expect any policies in the industrial enterprise to be effective.

Our evidence indicates that by and large the American enterprise still satisfies the minimum requirements of status and function. However, our evidence also indicates that the factors which are decisive and dynamic are not the sources of satisfaction and fulfillment but the obstacles, that, in other words, the trend in American industry is toward the social melting point. It is not too late to reverse this trend. In no other area can we hope to achieve so much so fast. All the basic forces—the objective requirements of society, the objective requirements of the enterprise, and the objective needs and requirements of the individual—work in the direction of making the industrial enterprise a functioning institution. But we certainly do not have too much time to do the job—perhaps another fifteen, hardly more than another twenty-five, years.

CHAPTER 2 1

THE THREEFOLD JOB OF MANAGEMENT

MANAGEMENT as it emerged during the last generation is the new ruling group of our society. Because the enterprise is necessarily big, even the management of the moderate-sized business controls a greater concentration of resources than even the "merchant prince" of pre-industrial society. The decisions of management affect the lives and the livelihood of a large number of citizens and ultimately of all citizens. Its policies and principles determine very largely the character of our society.

The proper organization of management is the enterprise's business —its first business. But the function of management, the obstacles to the proper discharge of this function, and the organization needed to enable the enterprise to produce a functioning management, are more than technical problems of interest only to the business executive. Management's ability to function largely determines how well the enterprise carries out its economic responsibility as a trustee of a part of society's productive resources. It also decides how well the enterprise discharges its governmental and social functions. The structure and organization of management are a real and direct concern of the citizen.

As an organ of the enterprise, management can be responsible only to the enterprise and for the enterprise—to no one else and for nothing else. The question to whom the enterprise is responsible, is indeed important. The divorce of ownership and control, which separates the enterprise's power and authority from the legal title of individual private property, has also made it very acute. But the question to whom management is responsible is a simple one to answer. Management is an organ of the enterprise; and the essence of any organ is expressed in its function for the body it serves. Management as the governing organ of the enterprise must be responsible for the survival and prosperity of the enterprise.

Concretely, this entails three major responsibilities which together constitute the top-management function:

> (1) Responsibility for the survival of the enterprise in the economy, that is, for its profitability, its market and its product.
>
> (2) Responsibility for the organization of the enterprise's human resources and for their efficient use.
>
> (3) Responsibility for an adequate and orderly succession to top management itself.

All three responsibilities involve the making of decisions rather than their carrying out. The management function is a policy-making function. Management does not do things. It decides what should be done. Even the job of getting things done—to paraphrase a popular definition of the management function—is not properly the job of top management.

The first and the third responsibilities deal almost exclusively, the second very largely, with problems the enterprise will face five or ten years hence. The management job is thus largely a job of projecting the future onto the present. It deals with what is going to happen rather than with what is happening, let alone with what has happened. It is not only a policy-making, but also a planning job.

What is Our Business?

It is management's first responsibility to decide what economic factors and trends are likely to affect the company's future welfare. Management must make sure that five or ten years hence the resources of the enterprise will be at least as productive economically as they are today. It must make the decisions *today* on the problems that will confront the enterprise *tomorrow*. This function can perhaps best be expressed by saying that *it is management's responsibility to decide what business the enterprise is really in.*

This may seem pointless. Surely, it needs no rigmarole and analysis to find out what a company's business is. Is it not even, in most cases, stated in the name of the company? Actually, the decision what business an enterprise is really in—that is, the decision what its product is, what its market is and what its outlook is—is anything but obvious. It requires careful and difficult analysis of a very high order. It also implies a very difficult decision what business the company should aim to be in. Only a few managements have so far been able to answer these questions.

It may seem obvious, for instance, that it is the business of a railroad to provide transportation. But one particular railroad—to give an actual example—found that its real business was the development of the region it serves rather than the physical movement of freight and people. As a result, management decided that the development of the resources and facilities of the region was the proper business of the company and that anything that contributed to the economic growth of the region, including even the development of competing forms of transportation, such as air services, waterways and highway transportation, would contribute directly to the economic performance and profitability of the railroad.

Another example of the difficulty of the decision is provided by two large automobile companies. Faced by an automobile market that had become purely a replacement market—the situation in this country from 1929 on—each management asked itself the question what its business really was. One decided that it was to market and to service durable consumer goods; it decided that the productive equipment which represents the bulk of the company's capital investment was only a necessary adjunct to the intangible asset of its dealer organization. The other company decided that its major business was the production of motive power; it saw its main asset in its engineering and production staffs. Accordingly, one company decided to expand by taking up distribution of goods other than automobiles, produced by other companies. The other company expanded by adding trucks, tractors, locomotives, Diesel engines, airplane engines, etc., to its production line.

The decision also involved a change in the management in each company. In the one company sales executives are considered the logical candidates for top jobs; the company has drawn heavily on men with mail-order and retail sales experience. The other company has built up a top management of engineers, metallurgists and research physicists.

To give yet another example, a fairly large company which had developed a market in patent medicines found in analyzing its business that it was not really in the patent medicine business, but that its salable commodity was its ability to develop small and unsuccessful businesses producing branded goods for mass distribution. Its product was neither patent medicines nor pharmaceuticals, but primarily promotion. Its market was the capital market rather than the consumer's market. This involved a change in the direction of the company's expansion; its major business has become the acquisition of small and none too successful companies in a wide variety of fields: drugs, perfumes, household cleaners, even reprint books. These businesses are put on their feet and then resold again.

Only on the basis of such an analysis of the proper business of the enterprise can it be decided what the function and the objectives of management are. Unless management first finds out what the enterprise's business is, it does not even know what it actually manages.

The analysis of the nature of its business can alone isolate the economic factors likely to affect the future of the enterprise. It alone enables management to prepare for the future and to make the right decisions. It will show which developments—though apparently important—can really be disregarded, and which trends—perhaps hardly yet visible—have to be watched carefully. It makes it possible to decide how to react to a new development. Is it a danger or a boon? Can it be used to make the enterprise stronger and how? Does it force the enterprise to change its nature and its business?

The decision what business the enterprise is engaged in also includes decisions what to do about developments in economic and social policy that are likely to affect the future economic performance and prosperity of the enterprise. It is not only the duty of management to foresee such developments. It is its duty to promote trends likely to further the prosperity of the enterprise, and to take preventive action on those likely to weaken the enterprise. Most managements today shirk this responsibility altogether. It is not enough, however, to protest against public policy and to label as "subversive" all advocates of regulation and restriction. In every single case public regulation and restriction of business have grown out of a failure of management to develop by itself workable policies and practices; the fundamental fault is management's failure to realize that the public reaction to its business decisions is as much part of the enterprise's business as are new markets or new products.

It is certainly a vital part of the management job today in this country to work on the development of a mass capital market that will channel the savings of the middle classes into productive investment. Our mass-production and mass-consumption system simply cannot operate with a "carriage-trade" capital market such as ours still is.

It is the responsibility of every big-business management to work on the development of policies to support small—and especially young and growing—business, and to develop a workable code of behavior for the relations between the big enterprise and its small partners: suppliers, dealers, etc. Otherwise big business will inevitably be subjected to increasingly strict and increasingly more punitive controls.

It is part of management's job to develop policies on plant-location and on the distribution of work and orders between the several plants of one company—which can only be done in close co-operation with local authorities and with the union. It is management's job to develop policies for the conservation of resources—especially water—and for keeping air and water clean. And, of course, every single one of the problems discussed in this book, whether that of security for the worker, that of union relations, that of plant-community government, that of management organization or that of management-succession is also one in which failure to act on the part of management will inevitably lead to public regulation which can only be restrictive and punitive.

A management that refuses to accept the duty to look ahead to the public pressures of tomorrow, and that fails to anticipate these pressures by *positive* action, is simply refusing to manage and guilty of betraying its responsibility for the economic performance of the enterprise.

Finally, the decision what business the enterprise is in includes the development of gauges to measure the performance of the enterprise, and of proper performance controls.

The design of the proper controls is so important to the welfare of the enterprise that it might well be considered a major management responsibility in itself. The industrial enterprise is so large and so complex, and so many things happen at the same time in so many different places, that it is as impossible for a management to "play by ear" as it is for the pilot of a four-engine jet bomber to "fly by the seat of his pants." Yet the pilot endangers only a small crew if he flies without proper controls. An enterprise operating without them endangers directly thousands of people and indirectly the entire economy.

So far we have practically no measurements and controls in the enterprise. Managements are forced to "play by ear," if not by "hunch." All we have, by and large, are gauges of the financial situation. We have only the most primitive tools to measure efficiency and productivity, to measure standing and success in the market or the utilization of human resources, etc. We do not even have a usable gauge of profitability; for accounting—apart from its confusion between current costs and future costs, and from its conventional assumption that the value of money is stable—is by definition focused on the past rather than on the future. The development of reliable gauges and controls is, therefore, one of the biggest jobs confronting management.

To a large extent it is a technical job. A gauge must be reliable, or at least its margin of error must be known. It must react fast, in contrast to most of our measurements today, which do not register a change until months or years later. It must also require very little energy. "The direction of large masses and large forces by small effort and small energy," is the definition of a "control." A system under which it takes three men to check what one man is doing is not control; it is systematic strangulation. Yet in far too many of our enterprises mountains of forms and triple checks are mistaken for controls.

But above all, gauges and controls must measure and direct what is relevant and important. They must disregard what is unimportant. The better gauges and controls function, the fewer there are. A system that were to try to control everything would be so swollen as to be unsupportable. It would also not control anything. If the number of dials on his panel goes into the hundreds or thousands, a pilot is worse off than if he flies "by the seat of his pants." He cannot watch all the dials. He does not know which to watch and which to neglect. But he has been trained to rely on the dials and not to use his own judgment. Similarly, a management overwhelmed by "facts" will not be able to pay attention to any of them. At the same time, it will not dare to use common sense and judgment. It will "play hunches" and pick out one "fact" as the sole basis for its decision. The designing of the proper controls, therefore, requires above all a decision what business the enterprise is in. Without this decision all the controls in the world would no more give control than a clock face tell the time without a movement.

The Enterprise's Human Resources

The second function of management is the organization and efficient utilization of the enterprise's human resources. In the industrial enterprise it is not individuals who produce but a human organization.

The job of making and of keeping the human organization productive implies responsibility for the most efficient design of the individual's work, the grouping of man in a work team, and the ordering of the small teams into a productive whole. It includes the organization of supervision and middle management, who, in the last analysis, are the core of the body we call the enterprise. Finally, it includes responsibility for the efficient and productive organization of top management itself. Indeed this comes first; for no organization can be more efficient than its top management. Faulty organization at the top inevitably means friction, dissatisfaction, inefficiency and unproductivity down to the lowliest wheelbarrow pusher. And it is in the organization of top management that there is usually the most room for improvement.

In most institutions the organization is two-dimensional: in Army, Church or State, for instance, individual and group have to be integrated into an order. But in the enterprise the organization is three-dimensional: individual, group, and physical equipment have to be welded into one whole.

The organization of the human resources is by necessity a top-management function. Policies, practices and attitudes can be effective at the bottom only if they are being lived at the top. The many top managements who are completely unaware of their responsibility for the organization of the human resources—including those who have not yet realized that there is such a thing as human resources—nonetheless determine the character of their organization as completely as if they had a conscious and clear policy. Just as any farmer practices soil conservation or soil depletion whether he knows it or not, every management builds human resources or erodes them.

Responsibility for the human resources cuts across all departments and all functions and embraces the whole enterprise. It can only be discharged by the same organ that decides what the company's business is. Just as the economic decision is partly determined by the kind of human organization that the enterprise has in its employ, so the kind of human organization that the enterprise requires will be largely determined by the nature of the enterprise's business. To mold the enterprise's personality to its objective economic needs, and to adapt its economic decisions to its character and to that of its organization is therefore necessarily a top-management job.

The Problem of Succession

The third major function of management is to provide a functioning management. This means that management has to provide for its own succession. Like all administrative bodies, management is basically self-perpetuating. It is tomorrow's management that will determine whether the enterprise will prosper ten years hence and indeed whether it will survive. Even the ablest management cannot foresee the future. Even the best decisions made today regarding the future are necessarily guesses. But today's management can at least make sure that there will be available to make tomorrow's decisions men who are fully qualified, fully trained and fully tested in actual performance.

Every institution depends for its survival on a clear principle of orderly succession. At any time an institution must have a government fully recognized as the legitimate holder of power and capable of exercising this power. If there is no orderly succession, any change in the personnel of the government is likely to produce convulsions and disturbances which may threaten the very life of the institution. And the accession of a new government without adequate powers, even if it succeeds to the title legitimately and in an orderly fashion, is likely to have similar results.

It is the fatal weakness of dictatorship that there is no legitimate successor to the dictator. Every dictatorship in history has broken down, after the death of the dictator, in civil war, fights between pretenders and demoralization of the body politic. For a dictator's power rests on nothing but his own personal strength and the allegiance to him, neither of which can be transferred. Also, no dictator can possibly allow one man to become recognized as a successor. If he tolerates any strength at all, there must be at least half a dozen potential successors to prevent any one from overthrowing the dictatorship.

This problem of the succession is perhaps the oldest problem of government. Every known form of political organization is in the last analysis rooted in an atttempt to solve the problem of the succession. In the earliest solution, in the primitive tribe, succession follows the magical powers of the chief transferred by an act of the gods or by a conveyance of the magic properties which gave the chief his authority and his wisdom; the story of Jacob and Esau is only one of many illustrations of this principle. There have been many similar attempts since, but very few of them have been much more successful.

The great historical stability of the principle of hereditary monarchy is due precisely to its success in solving this problem. But even hereditary monarchy is beset with the risk either that there may be no heir or that the heir may be a child, sometimes not yet born, feeble-minded or crippled. If this happens, the new government while legitimate does not have the power to discharge its functions.

Indeed the only really succesful solution so far is that of the American Constitution, under which there is available always a successor to the presidency who is legitimate, who can be expected in practically all cases to be physically and mentally capable to hold the job, and who has immediately the full powers of the presidency in his hands. But even this solution is not perfect. It requires of the second-highest man in the government, the Vice President, that he stand by and wait. In practice this has made the office insignificant and the holder a nonentity.

No institution can depend for its survival on a supply of geniuses. Any institution must be organized so that men of not much better than ordinary ability can run it—at least in normal times. But at the same time no institution can ever entrust the quality of its leadership to luck. It must attempt to select the best available men for the succession, train them and test them.

The problem of the qualification of the successor, of his selection, his training and his testing is as old as that of legitimate succession—

and fully as difficult. Though it has occupied some of the world's best minds, it has rarely been solved. If it is the great strength of the American political system that it always provides a legitimate government with full powers, it is its greatest weakness that it has no rational system for the selection, training and testing of the candidates for the top job. Even the British Cabinet system—the best training school and proving ground of leadership ever seen anywhere—is not perfect. The triple test of vote-getting ability in the country, parliamentary leadership in the House of Commons and administrative ability in a major cabinet office, while formidable, does not really test the ability for the supreme command of the Prime Ministership, especially in times of crisis.

The enterprise faces particular difficulties in the selection, training and testing of top-management candidates. In every other institution the selection, training and testing of leaders is either built in and does not require special provisions and a special body responsible for it, or it is the responsibility of a separate organ outside and beyond the governing body itself, a Council of Elders, a Board of Examiners or the High Priests. In the enterprise, however, the development of leaders is not automatic; on the contrary, the structure of the enterprise tends to inhibit the development of properly trained and properly tested leaders. But there is no objective yardstick of qualifications and performance, and no special organ for the selection of successors. Most enterprises are still in the primitive tribal stage where succession goes either by age or by magic.

These three responsibilities do not, of course, comprise everything with which top management has to concern itself. Even the best organized management will have to deal with a multitude of other matters, large and small. But these three responsibilities comprise the *management function*. They are the responsibilities which must be discharged in any enterprise and which are decisive for its functioning, survival and prosperity. They are the responsibilities which only top management can discharge and which cannot be delegated.

WHY MANAGEMENTS DON'T DO THEIR JOB

ONLY a few managements today adequately discharge their responsibilities, although there is no shortage of tools, gadgets and techniques for the job. There is little understanding on the part of top management of what its function is, if there is indeed any understanding that top management has a responsibility and a function. There is little ability to discharge the function. And few enterprises are organized so as to permit management to devote itself to its proper job, let alone so as to give effectiveness to management decisions.

We are not concerned here with the competence or incompetence of individual managements. Nor are we concerned with the fact that management is so new—there is not even a word for it except in English—that there has been little time to develop a tradition and standards of management. We are only concerned here with the objective obstacles in the structure of the enterprise to a functioning management. It is objectively difficult for a management to understand and to discharge its function. The structure of the enterprise also makes it difficult for top management to be effective. Finally, the structure of the enterprise makes it difficult to provide adequately for the succession.

The first obstacle lies in the nature of management itself. The job of top management is radically different from the work and responsibility of the operating executives. Yet top management personnel must be recruited from operating executives. The atmosphere in which the future top manager spends his formative years, the work which he is trained to consider important, the things which he learns to pay attention to, are all different from the atmosphere, the work and the angle of vision of the top-management job. The future top manager is likely to be ignorant of the nature of top-management responsibility and incapable of understanding what the job involves.

The emphasis in the early development of an executive in the enterprise is on qualities and abilities which unfit a man for a top-management position. During these early years there is a heavy premium on increasing specialization. Mass-production technology demands of a man that he become more proficient in an increasingly smaller area as he advances. In addition, the enterprise, large or small, places a premium on mental departmentalization. It is bad manners to display curiosity about another function or another department. This is partly the result of a normal and healthy political situation in which departments and functions compete with each other for budgets and prestige. But it is also an unintentional by-product of the principle that each executive have a clearly defined function for which he alone be responsible. The result, however, is that a man who shows too much interest in the enterprise as a whole, and who tries to obtain a general view, is not likely to be promoted.

Moreover, every operating job is by nature strictly circumscribed, if not subordinate. What is valued in an operating executive is his ability to carry out the duties assigned to him. He is neither expected nor permitted to be independent—if indeed he is consulted at all in the making of the policies which he has to carry out.

In the operating job, the accent is on doing things; the outward trappings are those of "busy-ness" and industry: the heaped desk, the ringing telephone, the long hours, the bulging brief case taken home in the evening. The operating executive is trained for fast action. He is trained to give immediate results and to demand immediate results from his subordinates. He is expected to know the answers to all the questions about his own function and job. And—worst of all—he is trained to concentrate entirely on concrete and precise "data" and to admit no other "facts."

But the top-management job requires a general understanding. It requires a view of the whole. It demands tested ability for an independent command and the willingness to assume the responsibility for a decision. It asks for detachment, patience and the ability to take the long view. The top man needs to think rather than to do; his is a questioning attitude rather than a ready acceptance of orders. Whereas the operating executive will measure his job in terms of the number of tons of steel turned out yesterday, the top manager must think of the factors affecting steel consumption over the next ten years. And nothing in top management's job has the comfortable certainty of the operating executive's "data"; at best top management deals in approximate magnitudes, but more often in intangibles such as trends and assumptions.

After he has been promoted into top management, the former operating man will cling to his comfortable departmentalization, instead of assuming responsibility for the whole. He is apt to define his job in purely departmental terms, to be satisfied as long as "his" department runs smoothly and to be neither interested in, nor even aware of, the problems of the enterprise. This applies often even to a company's president. As a former operating man, he may be afraid to make decisions or to tackle basic problems. And he will be slow to deal with the future, if not actually afraid of its vagueness and intangibility.

Other institutions too have serious problems of obtaining the proper kind of top command, of selecting, training, preparing and testing potential successors. But they do not normally face a split between the work of the junior executive and that of the man at the top. A bishop's field of action and decision is very much wider than that of a parish priest. But to a large extent the responsibilities and functions of the bishop are not too dissimilar to those of the parish priest. A commanding general also has a much broader area of decision, but his functions are not too different in kind from those of a regimental commander. Above all, there is little in the qualifications and the training of the parish priest or the regimental commander which unfits them for the top job; the atmosphere and the climate in which either lives is the same, by and large, as that in which the bishop and the commanding general live. In Church or Army, training and development follow in a logical progression from the junior to the senior job. In the enterprise a radical break is required. A man who has been brought up to be a specialist has to be converted all of a sudden into a "generalist." A man who has been brought up to be a subordinate member of a functional organization has suddenly to assume independent command for an entity; and until he reaches the point at which he has to assume top-management responsibility for the whole there is usually no opportunity to test him in an actual independent command or in any but purely functional and specialized activities.

Even a capable and well-selected top management is up against real obstacles to the proper discharge of its duties. The top executives will find themselves under great pressure to spend their time and energy on activities which only they can perform, but which are at best incidental to the top-management job. In a large enterprise, for instance, they carry a heavy ceremonial load. They have to open this and that, make speeches both within their business and on the outside, serve on committees and boards of civic and business institutions, etc. They are expected to maintain personal relations between the enterprise and its major suppliers, its major customers, the bankers, the important government agencies, etc. In other words they are both the enterprise's king and its prime minister.

Another important obstacle, of an entirely different nature, is the "executive mind," the divorce of the top men in a large enterprise from both the realities of the enterprise and the realities of the society in which they live. This "executive mind" is very much like the "military mind" of the professional army officer and has a similar origin. The man in command of any large organization, a bureaucracy, an army, a church, a large university, or a business enterprise, works on a high level of abstraction. Matters for his decision must be presented to him as matters of "policy," that is, in terms of abstract principles. Otherwise the executive would have to study the whole problem himself, for which he has neither the time nor usually the information. Every problem that comes to the top must be grossly oversimplified. It must be made capable of a fast "yes" or "no." But actual problems are never so simple and never so clear-cut.

Also, the management group of any large organization lives in very great social isolation. They are likely to find themselves thrown increasingly with people of the same social set, the same business, if not confined to the company of their own top-management group. This leads to a narrowing of the imagination and of the understanding of which perhaps the best example is the inability of American management during the last twenty years to understand the temper of the American people. Management's decisions are thus apt to be made in a vacuum.

It must be emphasized that the "executive mind" is as necessary as is the "military mind." It is perfectly true, as Clemenceau said after World War I, that "War is too important to be entrusted to generals." But nobody has yet found a way to entrust it to somebody else— and the latest example of the amateur military leader, Hitler's "intuition," is unlikely to encourage imitation. The managers are the only ones to whom the management of the enterprise can be entrusted. It is the function that makes the "military mind" and the "executive mind." Civilians turned generals will be forced to develop the "military mind," as our experience with the civilians in uniform during World War II amply proved. Similarly, outsiders put into a management position will have to develop the "executive mind."

The Ineffectiveness of Management

The cleavage between the job of top management and that of the operating people adds another difficulty to top management's ability to perform its duties. The executive groups below the top do not understand what top management's job is. They are apt to see only the immediate problems, and those as problems of specific departments and specific functions. They will not only lack the understanding for the top-management function; they will find it very difficult to make out what top management is after, on what it bases its decisions and why it acts the way it does. In a great many cases operating executives even feel—and feel deeply—that top management pays no attention to the real problems of the enterprise, but chases a will o' the wisp of its own imagining. Top-management decisions are therefore likely to meet with a lack of understanding and sympathy, if not with resistance.

The enterprise depends on the operating people for the execution of management decisions. A company may be organized along semi-military lines, with all decisions handed down from the top as orders which operating management is expected to obey unquestioningly. But actually the operating executives are always in a position to sabotage these orders. If they neither understand nor sympathize with them, they will at best be lukewarm in carrying them out.

The problem is likely to be much less serious if the operating executives take part in the formulation of policy and of decisions. In fact, the military model of organization is an extremely poor model for the industrial enterprise. Yet with the maximum of consultation, the operating people are still likely to lack a real understanding of the top-management job. They simply cannot see things from top management's point of view; their own point of view as conditioned by their own job remains a different one. They may reach a point where they accept top-management decisions even though they really do not understand them. But it is very difficult for them to put themselves into top management's place.

As an illustration, there is the case of a big metallurgical company which for many years had in its top management two outstanding men to whom the success of the company was largely due. These two men did a pioneering job in the analysis of the economic factors determining the enterprise's business and in projecting them on the future. They also did an outstanding job of building a strong management team. Everybody in the company had the highest respect and great personal affection for them. Yet when they retired, their program and policies were forgotten within a year. The operating people had never really understood them. They had been willing to follow along because of their respect for the two men at the top. But the policies had never become their own. They had never understood what the two men were after and why.

These obstacles to the formation and to the effectiveness of a functioning management explain the great prevalence of one-man rule and of overcentralization as forms of management organization despite their universal condemnation.

One-man rule, indeed, often solves the problem of the management function—provided the one man is extremely able. But it does so at the expense of the future. What is the outlook for an enterprise in which, as in one of our largest merchandising companies, one man, now seventy-five, has held dictatorial power for twenty years and has fired any subordinate who dared have an idea of his own?

Excessive centralization is always the result of management weakness rather than of management strength. Overcentralization provides the top men with a perfect excuse for not coming to grips with the enterprise's real problems. It gives them the illusion of being feverishly busy and so overloaded with work as to be unable to do anything else, which means in effect unable to do the top-management job proper. It also gives top management the illusion that its orders and decisions are carried out. Instead, overcentralization always goes hand in hand with an efficient system of sabotage of top-management orders.

Both one-man rule and overcentralization are lazy men's ways to sidestep a problem—one-man rule the way of the strong lazy man, overcentralization the way of the weak lazy man. Yet, because they create the illusion that the enterprise has a functioning management, they will continue to be attractive until we learn to overcome the obstacles to the effective discharge of the management function.

CHAPTER 23

WHERE WILL TOMORROW'S MANAGERS
COME FROM?

SINCE operating experience and performance are likely to unfit a man for top management, it would seem logical to try to obtain top-management candidates from elsewhere. This reasoning underlies the two most popular policies of American management today with regard to the problem of the succession.

One is the increasing dependence on "staff" people as the reservoir for top-management positions. Men who have had very little or no operating experience, who have actually never worked in the enterprise proper, but who have spent most of their working life in the central office as assistants on policy decisions, are increasingly preferred in the promotion to top-management rank. These men obviously have a view of the whole—which is the reason why they are being picked. But they have usually been less tested in an independent command than the operating people. In fact, most of them have never been in charge of any organization larger than a private secretary. Also these men, while they see the whole, often lack any knowledge of the actual operations of the enterprise; they do not have the "feel," of the place; they do not know the people and are not known by them. They also tend to be rather contemptuous of the operating people. It is after all the staff's job to be critical of operating performance. The staff men have thus spent many years trying to "sell" the operating people on new ideas and to overcome the resistance of the organization. They are in turn regarded by the organization as outsiders and as "starry-eyed dreamers" who are completely impractical. The operating organization bitterly resents their promotion and tends to ascribe it to "pull" and favoritism. Their decisions, when in the top command, therefore meet with resistance and sabotage.

Hardly more satisfactory is the attempt to provide special training and a special ladder of promotion for a few hand-picked "crown princes." Increasingly, young men are being promoted to top-management positions. These young men are not, as they were fifty years ago, the sons or the relatives of the owner or of the top-management people; anything that smacks of nepotism is now frowned upon. The young men who have taken the place of the boss's son of yesterday are usually brilliant college graduates who were picked for a rapid career the moment they entered the company's employ. Outwardly it appears as if these men have to climb the same ladder everybody else has to climb. They begin as clerks or as apprentice engineers, and go through the customary steps. Actually, this appearance of a normal career is an illusion, if not a mere concession to the proprieties. The brilliant young candidate as a rule does not even spend enough time in any one job to get a thorough training. He spends just enough time to become familiar with the jargon of a department.

Unlike the staff man, the "crown prince" is usually thoroughly tested in independent commands. At an early age he is given important assignments and important responsibilities; from the first his job is that of a future top manager in training rather than that of a genuine subordinate. But his assignments will all be "special" assignments. He remains an outsider, who is not likely to accept the organization or to be accepted by it.

This attempt to solve the succession problem is less rational than the succession by inheritance of fifty years ago which modern management so virtuously spurns. At least the special training and promotion of the owner's son was honest and out in the open. Everybody knew that the young man would inherit sooner or later. The "crown prince by birth" had a title to the succession. It was to the interest of the whole organization to have a man so obviously destined for the top position well trained, well acquainted with the organization and well prepared. The "crown prince by selection," however, is resented by everybody. While the owner's son had an obvious claim and title, the claim of the graduate of the Harvard Business School to possess superior intelligence and ability is not likely to be taken in good grace by people who have grown old in the service of the enterprise. That they call it "cradle-snatching" shows what they think of it.

There is no escaping the need for a policy that will make operating men capable of succeeding to the top-management positions. During the next few years the development of such a policy may well be the most urgent task of American management. Our big businesses are still managed by the "brilliant young men" of 1929—the men who took over in the early years of the Depression. But these "brilliant young men" are all by now well in their late fifties and early sixties. Their average age is sixty—the highest it has ever been in this country. Within five years—ten years at the very latest—successors will have to be found for every one of them.

The first obstacle is the lack of any yardstick to measure performance, and especially to measure potential top-management performance.

Every one of the traditional yardsticks developed to measure executive and administrative potential is inapplicable to the enterprise. The oldest of all objective measures, and the one with the longest continuous history, is the competitive examination around which the Chinese built their entire governmental structure, and which is being increasingly used in the government service of every Western nation. But examinations can only test knowledge, whereas the enterprise needs a test of ability and character if not of performance.

Equally inappropriate is the criterion of success developed in Church or Army: a combination of length of service and adaptation to a codified tradition. In both these institutions the emphasis is not on ability to change, let alone on ability to initiate change, but on ability to conform to an unchanging standard of conduct and personality developed over a long period of time. But in the enterprise the management job consists very largely of the management of change, if not of taking the lead in changes. Neither seniority nor the yardstick of a traditional pattern can be applied.

Where there is no way to predict performance, we have to use experience and judgment. But the enterprise does not normally provide the experience that alone would count: experience in an independent command. The qualities which make a first-rate lieutenant are likely to unfit a man for an independent top position. The enterprise usually cannot test a man in an independent command until he has reached a position where incompetence or mistakes may endanger the very survival of the enterprise. Methods of predicting a man's potential—by psychological tests, for instance—are a very poor substitute for an actual test under "battle conditions." At best they can eliminate the grossest misfits.

If selection as well as evaluation of management personnel has to be based on judgment, there must be an authority to make these judgments. It must be an authority thoroughly familiar with the problems of the enterprise and with its personnel. At the same time it must be completely untouched by the personal ambitions and political struggles within the management group.

Such an authority does not exist in the enterprise. By law and custom the Board of Directors constitutes this authority. But there are very few Boards which actually assume it or which would be capable of discharging it. The great majority of Boards do not even concern themselves with it.

Altogether the Board of Directors is an anomaly. It does not function, and usually cannot function as the representative of the stockholders, which according to law it is supposed to be. It is much too far away from the company's affairs to have any real knowledge of the company's problems. The normal Board member spends at most a day or two each month with the company. More and more companies have replaced their outside part-time Directors with inside full-time Directors who are members of management and therefore themselves interested parties in the decisions of the Board. The selection of management personnel, their training and development, their promotion, the replacement of top executives and their appraisal are thus either left to chance or to the uncontrolled decision of top management itself.

That the "withering away" of the Board is not a weakness inherent in the corporate form of organization, but one that lies in the structure of the enterprise, is indicated by the Russian experience. In the Soviet Union the top-management position is held by the various ministries in charge of specific industries; the manager of a plant, even of a big plant, has only operating and day-to-day duties. The job of selecting successors is considered a foremost responsibility of the head of the ministry, who is usually not a technician or a former operating man but a Party politician. Yet, despite the minister's political power and his independence of the organization, he is apparently quite incapable of controlling the personnel decisions of his ministry, or even of ensuring that leaders are being developed and trained. The neglect of the job of supplying adequately trained and tested successors has been a constant and loud complaint since the beginning of Russia's industrialization. The reasons given are very similar to those given for the failure of the Board of Directors: the minister is too far away to know what goes on; he is too busy to pay much attention, etc. Just like our Boards, the Soviet Minister of Light Metal Industries or of Mining apparently tends to postpone decisions on top-management personnel till it is too late to do anything but appoint the man with the greatest seniority to the vacancy. That the decision can be postponed for a long time explains in large part why decisions on succession are so often shirked altogether.

CHAPTER 24

IS BIGNESS A BAR TO GOOD MANAGEMENT?

CAN bigness be blamed for these difficulties of the management function? Is the big enterprise too big to be manageable?

There is certainly a limit to the size of the enterprise beyond which it tends to become unmanageable. In the giant enterprise top management can hardly find out what goes on. Its decisions take far too long to filter down. The whole organization becomes so complicated, so unwieldy and so bureaucratic as to be in danger of breaking down at the first emergency. Where the point lies at which bigness becomes too big is probably impossible to say theoretically. Also, new techniques and tools constantly increase the manageable size. But certainly the industrial corporation which, for its management, requires six levels of vice presidents with six to twelve men on each level—the whole held together by five executive vice presidents and a president —has passed the optimum point, if indeed it has not become unmanageable altogether. Similarly, there is the well-known American corporation whose vice presidents have to wear name badges at their semiannual staff meeting because they are too numerous to know each other's names Under such conditions top management clearly cannot function effectively.

The worst examples of excessive size are not likely to be found in a free-enterprise economy but in a nationalized economy. In fact, the worst examples of unmanageable size to be found anywhere are probably the recently nationalized industries of Great Britain, especially the coal industry, the transportation industry and the electric power industry. Just as bad are the industrial monsters into which the Russian economy is organized.

But the enemies of bigness attack neither the few giant corporations nor the nationalized industries. They object to the ordinary large enterprise. To say, however, that the large industrial enterprise is unmanageable because it is big, is not merely wrong—the opposite is true. One of the reasons why the enterprise has to be of considerable size is that only the big enterprise can have a functioning management.

The management function is not the result of bigness. It is the result largely of the technology and economics of industrial production, regardless of size. Because industrial production requires fixed capital, that is, an investment that will only yield results after a good many years, somebody must make the decision what the business of the enterprise is. Because the organization must be productive, the enterprise's human resources must be systematically organized. That, finally, the nature of industrial production creates the need for a management and sets its function—just as the nature of the State creates the need for a government—underlies management's responsibility for its own succession. In an industrial society the management function has to be discharged.

People have often wondered why there are so very few *small* Gothic churches. There are small churches galore in the earlier Romanesque and in the later Renaissance and Baroque styles, but not in the Gothic. The main reason was the need for a management of the highly complex organization and technology necessary to build in the Gothic style. Only a large project would justify this organization and support the necessary overhead.

Similarly, only the fairly large enterprise can discharge the management function of industrial society. Management is by necessity expensive; the ablest, most experienced and most expensive people have to be kept out of immediately productive work. Also, the size of the top-management group does not increase very much with an increase in the size of the enterprise—up to the point at least where the enterprise does indeed become too big to be manageable and where the vice presidents no longer know each other. An enterprise with an annual turnover of five million dollars and a force of a thousand men needs about the same number of top people as an enterprise ten times as large. And neither the quality required nor the salaries are likely to be much lower in the smaller business. The cost of such a top management might cripple the smaller business but it can easily be borne by the larger one.

The same applies to the tools which enable top management to perform its job, for instance, research or personnel work. Our technological progress tends to become more and more the result of organized research activities. But only the large enterprise can afford to maintain an adequate research staff and to engage in long-range research work. Only the large enterprise can afford to do systematic work on the organization of its human resources.

Even more relevant to functioning management is the fact that the small enterprise cannot easily work systematically on the supply of successors. Only the fairly large enterprise can be organized federally and thereby solve the problems of a functioning management.

This is not an answer to the indictment of bigness. Still left are such important counts as the charge that bigness is monopolistic. All our answer states is that bigness is not the cause of the management problem. If we did not have the big enterprise, we would have the problems of management function just the same; and they would be much harder to solve. For the only alternative—a government discharging the management functions—would not only be bigger than the most gigantic independent enterprise. It would suffer from all the problems of the big enterprise—only much more so.

CHAPTER 2 5

LABOR AS A CAPITAL RESOURCE

THE first requirement of a functioning industrial order is to get rid of the proletarian. Industrial society cannot afford him. But industrial society also has the means to do without him. The modern industrial order is extremely sensitive to the poisoning effect of a proletariat. But it—alone of all the civilizations above the primitive stage—can also rid itself of the poison, and can convert the socially destructive proletariat into the very basis of social strength and cohesion. In fact, the proletarian is obsolete and an anachronism.

The proletarian does not sell himself like slave or bondsman. He sells his labor. And his labor—the only thing he has—is bought and sold as a commodity; socially and economically the proletarian *is* a commodity. We have known all along that the proletarian is incapable of acting as a citizen for all that he enjoys the political status of a free man. The present-day argument of the union movement that "political democracy" is a sham without "economic democracy" is only a reformulation of Aristotle's famous statement about the artisan, made more than two thousand years ago.

But an industrial society—even if not organized in a popular government—demands the active and real citizenship of the worker. It demands acceptance of the principle of profitability from the worker. It loses its social cohesion if the worker is a proletarian. At the same time it demands that labor costs be considered unit costs of production and that both wage burden and employment be flexible. It must find a way to get rid of the proletarian, that is, of labor as a commodity, and yet maintain labor as a flexible and controllable cost.

In this country this is primarily a job of prevention rather than one of cure. One of the central facts of American life is that there has, so far, never been a proletariat in the European sense—with the exception of the "poor white" and Negroes of the Deep South, who live, however, in a nonindustrial society. The absence of the proletarian is perhaps the most striking difference between America and Europe. It has many reasons: the American tradition of rising from the bottom —that is, basically, the absence of hereditary, privileged classes; the frontier; the American respect for manual labor, so unlike the intellectual arrogance of Europe's humanist tradition. Above all, America escaped the soul-searing suffering of early industrialization in Europe —the horrors of Lancashire around 1830, of Saxony or Silesia around 1850, of the industrial suburbs of Paris under Napoleon III, of the Belgian Borinage of 1870, of the Vienna tenements of 1890, etc. In its eastward march through Europe, industrialization broke not only the bodies but the spirits of entire generations; and the scars show to this day in fear, in resentment and in that sullen defiance that goes by the name of "class pride" or "class consciousness." By contrast, early industrialization in this country produced the model factories of 1830 Lowell, Springfield and Newburyport—righteous and stifling, unbearably regimented, suffering from all the weakness of paternalism; yet conceived essentially as social utopias to "uplift" the worker both economically and intellectually. America too knew the "satanic mill" of course; and the model factories were always an exception. But however bad conditions were, especially after the Civil War, we never experienced on any considerable scale the horrors of child labor, of the fourteen-hour day, etc. All the stains on the record of industrial development in the United States—land grabs and railroad swindles, racketeering, monopoly exploitation and bribery—are harmless children's pranks compared to the proletarianization of the European worker. They affected the pocketbook of the people; proletarization affected their soul.

This is all the more reason, however, to prevent the formation of a proletariat in America. And we can only be sure of our immunity if we eliminate the treatment of labor as a commodity.

In Europe the conversion of the proletarian into a citizen is, obviously, both infinitely more difficult and infinitely more important. Indeed, it is the central problem of European society and civilization. For the new industrial territories: India, China, South America—countries plagued by a rural proletariat—there is nothing more vital than to be able to industrialize without creating an industrial proletariat in the process.

A high standard of wages or of living will not avert proletarianization or remedy it, vitally desirable though it undoubtedly is. The only thing that is absolutely effective against the poison is the adoption of the principle that *labor is a capital resource in an industrial economy*. The worker's wage must be considered to be fully as much a provision against the future costs of staying in business as it is a current cost.

Actually, labor is not a commodity in an industrial economy. It is one of the foremost characteristics of such an economy that it can resolve the *economic* conflicts. It can do so partly because of its wealth. But above all it can do so because industrial production focuses on the future and does not, therefore, demand that labor be considered exclusively a current cost. The economic reality of an industrial system itself makes the proletarian obsolete by requiring the treatment of labor as a capital resource.

CHAPTER 26

PREDICTABLE INCOME AND EMPLOYMENT

THE cornerstone of economic policy in a developed industrial society is a policy that gives the worker the knowledge what income and employment he can expect.

A predictable income and employment plan, while not a panacea would banish the uncertainty, the dread of the unknown and the deep feeling of insecurity under which the worker today lives. It could not be a guarantee of absolute security. But it would make it possible to work systematically on decreasing the uncertainty of employment confronting the worker. Above all a predictable income and employment guarantee makes it possible for the worker to have a budget and for the enterprise to have flexible labor costs.

What a Predictable Income Plan is Not

We had better say first what a predictable income and employment plan is *not*. It is not, and must not be, a guarantee of full employment, that is, an attempt to guarantee absolute security. This attempt has become very popular lately under the name of the "Guaranteed Annual Wage." A predictable income and employment plan should indeed guarantee an annual income. But it guarantees a minimum rather than the maximum, as the "Guaranteed Annual Wage" of our popular discussion would attempt. Moreover, it guarantees a flexible minimum geared to predictable economic conditions. A guarantee of full employment is like an attempt to make man immortal; a guarantee of predictable income and employment is like a life insurance policy.

In fact, the pressure for the "Guaranteed Annual Wage" makes it imperative that we go to work right away on predictable income and employment. The worker, especially in the United States, has for the first time become aware that his economic insecurity is not God-given and necessary. He has caught a glimpse of the promise of security which he will never forget. Unless we do something fast to satisfy the legitimate demand—in a manner which the economy and the enterprise can stand—we will be forced into giving guarantees of full employment under the name of the "Guaranteed Annual Wage."

Such a guarantee could, however, do only harm to the worker and the economy. The economy could not live up to it. It would have to default on it at the first minor business setback. There is practically no enterprise which could afford to pay wages for work not done for any length of time without going into bankruptcy. A guarantee of absolute security would not be worth the paper on which it is written. It would give the worker an illusion of security which is bound to be cruelly disappointed just at the moment when he most needs real security. In the first test, the whole idea of predictable security for the worker would be thoroughly discredited, with the workers losing all faith in the economic system and in the honesty and competence of management. The fact that every single employment guarantee developed during the optimism of the twenties —and there were quite a few—collapsed within the first years of the Depression should be conclusive proof of the folly of any attempt to eliminate economic fluctuations by paper guarantees against them. In every company which was forced to suspend its employment guarantees during the Depression, the workers are deeply suspicious of, if not opposed to, any new plan for employment security.

In contrast to any guarantee of full employment, a predictable income and employment plan should be able to outride even a serious depression successfully. In fact it plans for a serious depression all along. Yet to be reliable and valid, it does not impose a major risk on the enterprise.

A guaranteed prediction of income and employment does not mean a "right to the job." As far as the "right to the job" is meant to imply protection against arbitrary dismissals, an orderly procedure for layoffs, a grievance procedure to settle problems of discipline, etc., there is of course everything to be said for it. But the slogan has come to mean a demand for employment and income regardless of economic circumstances. The "right to a job" is as much of an illusion as the "Guaranteed Annual Wage" and is bound to dissolve in thin air in any economic setback, let alone in a depression. At the same time it could freeze the economy. It would keep in business the high cost, low-efficiency producer at the expense not only of the efficient low-cost producer but of the whole economy, including the worker. It means subsidizing obsolescent industries and restricting, if not stopping, technological progress.

If this seems exaggerated, the recent demands of John L. Lewis for the "right to the job" of the coal miners supply proof that it is not. Lewis proposed that the coal mines adopt an industry-wide employment program based on the "right to the job" under which nobody could be laid off in any mine until all mines had cut down production by about one-third, that is to thirty hours during forty weeks in the year. His purpose was to prevent unemployment among the workers of the marginal high-cost mines, and to prevent displacement of miners through technological improvement. If this should really be the only way to "stabilization," it would justify the contention of the most extreme advocates of *"laissez faire"* that violent instability is vastly better for everybody, including the worker, than any economic stabilization.

John L. Lewis' plan would go far beyond the most extreme cartel. A cartel too keeps going the high-cost and low-efficiency producer at the expense of the efficient enterprises, of the economy, and of the consumer. But though it weakens incentive, at least it does not block technological improvement. John L. Lewis, however, would actually make technological improvement impossible; under his plan companies installing improved machinery would have to cut their total output so as not to threaten the employment in the less efficient mines.

Yet, like the demand for the "Guaranteed Annual Wage," Lewis' demand for the "contractual right to the job" is a serious symptom of the pressure for income security and of the need for a plan to relieve it.

How To Predict Income and Employment

The starting point of any predictable income and employment plan is the fact that even at the bottom of the depression of the thirties, the American worker put in almost two-thirds of the man-hours he had worked at the peak of the boom. Even during the most precipitate decline in business activity and employment during any twelve-month period, the decline from the near prosperity of 1937 to the deep depression levels of 1938, man-hours worked in the great majority of American industries did not fall by more than twenty to twenty-five per cent. No business, to be sure, can foresee the future. But every large enterprise can project its past experience on the future and can thus predict what is likely to happen if the worst economic disasters were to recur. Certainty is impossible; but probability is attainable. And while this probability will apply to a pattern rather than to an individual, three centuries of insurance have shown us that probability in the great mass is sufficient to make the individual case insurable.

The projection of the past on the future will not always be easy technically. Conditions have changed greatly during the last twenty years. New products have come into existence and new processes have been developed. The lay-out of the work has been changed. The wage structure is different. Old plants have been razed and new plants have been built. Finally, union contracts have come into existence which regulate the manner of lay-offs and the distribution of the work between different categories of workers, etc. In its first attempts to estimate the effects of future business declines on employment, managements will certainly make mistakes. It will take patient work over several years to develop dependable methods of projecting the economic past into the future.

But even at the start the margin of error should not be so large as to invalidate the attempt. It is possible for any management to say with fair accuracy what effect a cut in business of ten, twenty, thirty or forty per cent would have on employment. It is possible to say how many hours of work and what work would still have to be performed even if, say, 1932 conditions returned. It is even easier for management to calculate the maximum decline in business and employment that is likely to occur during any twelve-month period. It is therefore possible for management to say how many hours of work there will be over the business cycle, and—perhaps even more important— what proportion of the labor force can expect to be fully employed within any twelve-month period ahead.

To establish this pattern will in itself have a tremendous impact on the worker. At present our entire working population is convinced that it lives in complete insecurity. Even the man who worked full-time right through the Depression is as basically insecure and as much obsessed by the "depression psychosis" as the man who was unemployed for five years. If the projection of the past on the future did nothing but replace the threat of the unknown with a known expectancy, it would mean a great deal. For the facts are strikingly at variance with the popular impression. To give but one example: Practically every member of one management told me recently that their company had kept only a token force in the mills in 1932 and that it had laid off between 1937 and 1938 "at least one-half of the workers." The actual figures show that this company worked fifty-eight per cent of its 1929 man-hours at the very bottom of the Depression; the drop in man-hours between 1937 (a very good year for the company) and 1938 (when the company ran up a heavy loss) was less than twenty-five per cent. If managements overrate the impact of a depression—and most of them do—how much more must it be overrated by the workers.

Once we have the pattern, we can also come to grips with the causes of insecurity. We can convert the prediction of total man-hours to be worked into a prediction of job and income for the individual worker or at least for groups of workers. *This conversion of a general pattern into a specfic insurable expectation is the most important step.* It is also the technically most difficult task. It requires a lot of time to work out and may have to be modified considerably in the light of later experience. I have found that in a large company it takes almost two years to arrive at a prediction of individual jobs and incomes, as usually both figures and statistical techniques have to be developed on the job.

If the plan were to stop at this stage, it would still be of value. It would be the first step toward enabling the worker to budget. It would provide him with a powerful incentive to build up reserves in good times. Knowing the risk he is facing, a worker, especially in the more highly paid and more highly skilled categories, could, so to speak, set up his own income guarantee. Certainly people cannot be expected to have an incentive to provide against the risks of the future if those risks are completely unknown and incalculable. The only rational behavior is to live in the present and to get the most out of it. If, instead, the risk becomes limited as well as calculable, the building up of reserves becomes meaningful and attractive—even though no worker could build up enough reserves to tide him over a prolonged period of unemployment.

The prediction of income and employment should be underwritten by the enterprise. This imposes upon the enterprise an obligation for fixed weekly payments of a minimum amount to the workers who, according to the prediction, can expect a minimum of employment during the next twelve months. This risk, while very small, is unavoidable. The guarantee should contain an escape clause which provides for an automatic revision of the guaranteed weekly payments should the downward plunge in any twelve-month period prove unexpectedly precipitate. The enterprise should also set aside once and for all a guarantee fund to cover the difference between the predicted drop in employment during a twelve-month period and the point at which the escape clause begins to operate. A comparatively small sum—something like five per cent of one year's wage bill at full employment, or between $100 and $200 per worker—will take care of this; and it is an expense that has to be incurred only once. After a few years, moreover, the cost of providing against this one and only necessary risk should become very much lower. Indeed, this is the kind of risk which would require only a very small premium if covered on an insurance basis; for the risk of the few enterprises that at any one time are likely to suffer an unexpectedly precipitate decline is likely to be counterbalanced by the great majority of enterprises which stay within their prediction.

This question of the risk involved has been discussed in detail because it is essential that a predictable income and employment plan be virtually riskless. The guarantee should actually be much more conservative than the prediction—for the same reason for which a life insurance company, to be really reliable, should base itself on a higher mortality rate than its actuarial tables indicate. It is more important that a prediction be reliable and survive the test of bad times than that it be favorable. It is much more important to the worker to know where he stands, and to be able to count on an expectancy of income and employment, than to be given promises which may not be honored when the critical period comes. If any plan assumes risks, it should do so only after it has been in existence for some time, that is, after the basic idea is thoroughly understood by both management and workers. The risks should be closely calculated and amply provided for; they must also be strictly limited as to both amount and duration.

We have already mentioned that the prediction leads logically to a promise to pay a weekly installment to workers with a certain minimum employment expectancy during the next twelve months, *whether they work or not*. Obviously, in order to qualify for such a payment, a man must have a fairly good employment expectancy. Every worker's employment expectancy can be predicted; but only those workers with a fairly good expectancy can be guaranteed a definite income. The actual guarantee will vary considerably from industry to industry, and from business to business. A company that can guarantee in advance fifty weeks of work—full employment—in any twelve-month period to more than four-fifths of its workers would be exceptionally stable. A company that could give such a guarantee to fewer than three-fifths of the men on the payroll would be exceptionally unstable or exceptionally badly managed. Even such a company should normally be able to guarantee thirty weeks of work or so to another ten to fifteen per cent of the men.

The administration of a plan which pays the worker an income each week, while he does not work, is anything but simple. The amount paid will usually be a percentage of the man's normal income. It will be considered an advance against his wages repayable when he comes back to work, etc. This requires complicated bookkeeping and a lot of explanation. That it can be done is proved by the example of the few companies which today have employment and income predictions in force, such as the Hormel Meat Packing Company in Austin, Minnesota. But even if a company should find the difficulties greater than those which Hormel overcame successfully, the weekly payment is essential. It gives the worker a minimum income with which to pay for the essentials of life, and prevents the collapse of himself and his family into destitution.

Improving the Income and Employment Prediction

Once a guaranteed income and employment prediction has been set up, it can be greatly improved. Employment can be made more stable and income expectancy can be a good deal greater. Yet the enterprise would not have to shoulder additional burdens. Indeed, the enterprise stands to profit substantially.

That fluctuations in operations are wasteful, uneconomical and expensive has become an axiom of good management. A plant which operates under extreme seasonal fluctuations obviously has to be large enough for its peak volume of business, while its average volume of business over the year may be very much lower. The equipment needed only for the peak business has to return a much higher profit in order to earn its keep—which in effect of course means higher costs of production for the entire plant. One company in an industry not particularly subject to seasonal fluctuations estimates, for instance, that one-third of its equipment is needed only two months in every year. It has therefore to yield four or five times as much income per unit of production as equipment in constant use.

Work at the peak is also rushed, expensive and inefficient, especially repairs, maintenance, plant expansion and other work on capital equipment. A gang of track workers on the railroad, for instance, has to interrupt its work and stand back for several minutes every time a train passes over the tracks. During the busy season, track-layers may have to stand idle two minutes for every minute they actually work. The less traffic, therefore, the cheaper are track repairs.

In 1941 one of the large automobile companies had to pay four to six times as much as in 1938 to have the inside of a plant painted. Neither the cost of materials nor the wages had gone up much; but in 1938 the plant was working on one shift while in 1941 it ran on two and three shifts. In 1938 the painters worked in an empty plant and the paint was dry by the time next day's shift reported for work. In 1941 the painters had to work around men and machines going at full speed. To stabilize work, both by evening fluctuations in volume and by planning work on equipment and buildings for the slack periods, entails therefore very substantial benefits for the business.

At the same time it is the one way in which an *employment* prediction can be greatly improved. In fact, one of the most widely publicized employment guarantee plans in existence today, that of the Procter and Gamble Soap Company in Cincinnati, started out as an attempt to economize by cutting seasonal fluctuations rather than as a plan to give income and employment security to the workers.

To stabilize operations, the pattern of operations has to be studied carefully and plant maintenance and expansion projects have to be planned—something only a negligible handful even of the big companies have done so far. Reserves earmarked for such projects have to be set up. This, needless to say, does not impose an additional burden on the enterprise. The sum which would normally be spent on maintenance during a good year would still be charged as maintenance expenditure against operating income. The only difference would be that it would not be spent right away but would be kept in reserve to be spent when business falls off.

The only way to improve the *income* prediction is through a tie-up with unemployment insurance. In fact, unemployment insurance payments should be regarded—and set up—primarily as supplementary income to the payments under a predictable income and employment plan. This would be particularly important in the severe depression years. A combination of predictable income and unemployment insurance should make it possible in most industries to guarantee at least half the labor force a full year's income even in pretty bad years, with another twenty-five per cent guaranteed two-thirds of the full income or so. Without unemployment insurance payments the senior half could normally expect only seventy per cent, the marginal quarter only fifty to fifty-five percent of the full income in a bad year.

When unemployment insurance was set up, nobody thought of predictable income plans. As a result, our laws today actually block the development of income and employment predictions. A worker who works full time—forty hours—for thirty weeks in a year receives in most States unemployment insurance for all or most of the rest of the year. With unemployment compensation at two-fifths to two-thirds of his normal wage, his total annual income will amount to eighty per cent or more of his normal full income. Under the present laws, however, the worker is likely to lose his unemployment payments if there is any form of employment and income guarantee. The man who works thirty hours for forty weeks obviously works as many hours as the man who works forty hours for thirty weeks. But in most States the worker is legally eligible for unemployment benefits only during the twelve weeks during which he is totally unemployed. And if he receives any payment from his employer during this period—as he would under a predictable income and employment plan—he is not eligible for unemployment benefits at all.

This is contrary to the public interest, which requires the maximum of support and encouragement for predictable employment and income plans. It is also entirely incompatible with the fact that unemployment benefits are insurance payments rather than the "dole," and that they come out of the contributions made by employers and employees rather than out of charity or tax money. If unemployment insurance were written by private insurance companies rather than by the government, the regulatory agencies or the courts would have outlawed the restrictions long ago as an indefensibly sharp practice. As it is, a change in the laws was recommended several years ago by a government committee studying the problem of income guarantees; however, nothing has been done so far.

A predictable income and employment plan requires close co-operation with the union from the very start, or at least as soon as management has worked out the predictability pattern. The union must understand what management is after, and what the provisions of the guarantee plan mean. A guaranteed minimum weekly payment as an advance to workers temporarily out of work presupposes joint management—union administration to overcome the worker's suspicion that the plan is used to rob him of something that is properly his.

To make the plan workable, union rules will have to be changed. The insistence on strict seniority as the basis for lay-offs may, for instance, work serious injustices, especially in companies and industries where long service is the rule. It may mean that the men who need an income prediction the most, the men between twenty-five and forty years of age who have to support both small children and dependent parents, may be without any security at all, while the old men near retirement age who have no family obligations may have a practically absolute guarantee of full employment.

Most plans will also demand that men can be shifted fairly freely between different departments and different occupations. Otherwise employment and income predictions—if at all possible—would vary greatly within the plant. In one department men with no seniority at all may still enjoy practically full employment while in the department next door men with twenty years' service are in danger of long-term unemployment. Such freedom to transfer freely goes against the rules, if not against the basic philosophy, of a great many unions, especially the craft unions. To avoid labor trouble, it has to be planned and agreed upon beforehand. And it requires that men be trained in advance for work in several departments or in several occupations; a continuous policy of rotation between departments and occupations must be followed which few union contracts in force today permit.

There are also some legal problems to overcome. One of them has already been mentioned: our present unemployment insurance laws. Another one would be the approach to depreciation allowance on the part of our tax authorities; unless it is changed, any attempt to stabilize operations by postponing maintenance work will be difficult.

How Much Can Be Guaranteed to How Many

A guaranteed income and employment prediction cannot prevent depression or cure it. Its only purpose is to make depression unemployment bearable by making it predictable, and to eliminate—or at least to cushion—the destructive effect of unemployment on the workers' social and economic life and on his family. This should have some effect on the severity of a depression, of course. It might even be argued that it will prevent the collapse of an economy into panic, such as we witnessed in 1932 and 1933. But an income and employment prediction is not a means to exorcise depression.

Also, such a plan does not protect the worker against several other major economic risks. It is not a guarantee against technological unemployment. In fact, every plan must state explicitly that nothing in it is to be read as curtailing management's rights to change processes, methods, tools and products. In addition, every plan should provide for an automatic review at frequent intervals—three or five years—to adjust the prediction to technological changes.

An income and employment prediction is also no guarantee whatever against the decline of a business or of an industry, against bankruptcy, going out of business, suspending production and other risks of economic death or severe economic illness. These risks shared by everybody who is dependent for his livelihood upon a particular business or a particular industry, cannot be covered. Individually they are very serious risks. But for the economy as a whole they are incidental rather than central.

Perhaps even more important than these reservations and limitations is the fact that not every enterprise can make a meaningful prediction; and without ability to predict there can be no guarantee. *By and large, ability to predict is confined to the larger enterprises employing a fairly considerable body of men.* The small enterprise, even if its economic position is good, cannot as a rule assume that its past experience provides a reliable indication of its future expectancy.

Even among the enterprises large enough to make a meaningful prediction, there will be a number whose prediction is not good enough to satisfy the minimum requirement for security of a minimum number of workers. These minimum requirements are probably quite low. If sixty per cent of the workers can expect sixty per cent of their income in the depression trough—which means if the total man-hours worked are not expected to fall below thirty-six per cent of full capacity pro‚ duction as long as the enterprise stays in business—the guarantee will be meaningful. Similarly, if two-thirds of the workers can expect to earn three-fourths of their last year's income during any succeeding twelve-month period, if in other words the decline expected in any twelve-month period is not likely to be greater than fifty per cent, a basis for a meaningful and effective guarantee exists.

Yet some industries and enterprises could not underwrite such a minimum. There are, first, the industries producing heavy capital equipment, such as railroad equipment, electric generating equipment or machine tools, which may see their entire business disappear at the first sign of a turn in the economic tide. During one depression year, for instance, the whole United States railway equipment industry turned out only three locomotives, which means that practically all locomotive companies were closed down completely.

There are many enterprises which can make meaningful income and employment predictions only if operations are stabilized and if unemployment compensation is fitted into the guarantee. Otherwise the portion of the working force that could be covered would be too small for the plan to do much good. Here belongs the steel industry the automobile industry, the farm equipment industry and the other industries producing durable consumer goods. For entirely different reasons, guarantees would be difficult in industries subject to sudden changes in fashion, such as the dress industry. Here the number of jobs in the industry as a whole is comparatively stable; but the number of jobs in any given enterprise is subject to extreme and unpredictable fluctuations. One false guess on the turn of fashion may wipe out a business altogether. A meaningful guarantee would have to take in a whole region, such as the garment industry in New York City or the garment industry in California.

It is precisely these industries in the intermediate group in which a guarantee, however, is the most badly needed. A worker in a locomotive plant knows that he is living under the risk of complete unemployment. A worker in a consumer's goods industry with stable sales can usually, even in a very bad depression, be made to understand that he has fair security. The worker who feels much more insecure than his actual employment expectancy warrants is mainly to be found in the industries where fluctuations are normally great without being extreme.

In some industries and enterprises the employment prediction may differ radically from occupation to occupation without much hope that an enterprise-wide pattern can be set through the transfer of men from one occupation to another. In the railroads, for instance, the pattern of employment in maintenance of roadbed and track is reasonably stable over the years; the major fluctuations are seasonal. The considerable force employed in the repair and maintenance of rolling stock has about the same expectancy of employment as the production worker in the automobile industry. It runs a considerable risk of insecurity with total unemployment confined, however, to extreme depression periods. To give this group a meaningful guarantee would require stabilization of operations and a definite tie-up between the guarantee and unemployment compensation. Finally, train and engine crews fluctuate directly and immediately with the volume of traffic, which is outside the control of the railroad. Here a guarantee would be very difficult to establish.

With all these reservations, however, a very substantial proportion of our working force can still be given a meaningful guarantee sufficient to tide it over the worst spots and certainly sufficient to enable it to plan twelve months ahead. Perhaps only a third of the total working force could ever be given such a guarantee (short of a wholesale adoption of profit-sharing and a switch-over to an anticyclical business policy). But only one-third of our working force today is unionized, for instance; yet the unions dominate the scene and determine the political and social atmosphere of all industry. A guarantee to one-third of the workers that they will receive at least one-half of their full income even in the worst year (and that, to repeat, is a conservative figure) would have a startling effect on the economy. It would go a long way toward bridging the gulf between wage as income and wage as cost.

It would also have a direct effect on the employment security of the majority who are without any guarantee. The workers under the guarantee will be able to keep up their basic expenditures during bad times and thus provide purchasing power for the whole economy.

Above all, a guaranteed income and employment prediction would give the one thing no worker has or has ever had: ability to plan for the future. And it is inability to plan for the future and the need to live for the day that more than anything else make the proletarian.

CHAPTER 27

THE WORKER'S STAKE IN PROFIT

THAT the worker must have a direct stake in profit and profitability in his own interest as well as in that of the enterprise has been understood for a long time. Profit-sharing plans have, therefore, been tried many times during the last hundred years. Just now they are again being preached as the panacea for all our industrial ills. Yet, practically no large company shows any interest in profit-sharing nor do any of the unions in the major industries. And the actual experience with profit-sharing plans has, by and large, been very disappointing.

The main reason is that practically all profit-sharing plans aim at making the worker a "partner" by giving him a financial interest outside of, and separate from, the job. But the worker is already a "partner"—if by partnership we mean having a stake in the business. His stake is in his job; and it is infinitely greater and more important to him than any financial reward outside of the job could be. It is precisely because he sees *his* stake, the job, subordinated to, controlled and ultimately threatened by, the primacy of profitability that he rejects and opposes profit.

The profit-sharing dividend of most of the plans which is entirely outside of the job, will at best appear to the worker as "parsley on the soup," a pleasant but unessential relish. He may even resent it as emphasizing an order of values and priorities that he considers hostile to him. There is an old story of one of the Rothschilds who fell into a turbulent river and was rescued by a beggar. The grateful banker offered a partnership to his rescuer. "That's the gratitude of the rich for you," said the beggar in disgust. "Now you want *me* to be responsible for *your* debts." The worker often feels exactly the same way about the traditional profit-sharing plans.

In addition, the traditional profit-sharing plan fails to establish a relationship between worker and profit except in the small business. In a larger enterprise—let alone in the very big enterprise—the relationship between the worker's effort and the enterprise's profit is much too remote and vague to become visible under the usual scheme.

Furthermore, the individual worker's share in the profit, even in a prosperous company during a very good year, is bound to be very small. In the great majority of industrial companies total profit is at best one-tenth of the wage bill. Even if the entire profit were distributed to the workers, each worker would receive an amount so small as to be practically meaningless. It would create resentment and hostility rather than give the worker a stake in profit. The discrepancy between the company's ten-million-dollar profit and the eighty dollars the worker receives as his share is far too great. It is likely to make the worker feel that he is being cheated somehow. Certainly, the worker's profit-sharing dividend will be less than the additional income he could get through a ten-cent raise in the hourly wage rate or through an improvement in his employment security by a few weeks each year. To imagine that an income like this could make any real difference in the worker's attitude toward the enterprise and toward profit is just plain absurd.

At the same time, our profit-sharing plans assume that the worker must want his share of the profit in the same form in which the shareholder wants his dividend, that is, a payment in the years in which the profit is being made. Those are, however, the years in which the worker is likely to be fully employed and to receive a fairly good income, so that additional small amounts of money are of little importance to him. He needs additional income in the years when there is no profit and especially in the years when the enterprise operates at a loss, when the worker is likely to be unemployed at least part of the time and most urgently in want of additional income.

The Requirements of Effective Profit-Sharing

If a profit-sharing plan is really to give the worker a stake in profit, it must establish a meaningful relationship between profit, the worker's job and the worker's needs.

Concretely, this means first that the purpose of a profit-sharing plan has to be the improvement of the job. In most cases this will mean an improvement in security. For it is his job security that the worker con-

siders threatened most by his subordination to the principle of profit
ability.

While the worker's share should obviously be put aside in the years
in which the enterprise makes the profit, that is, in the good years, it
should be designed to help the worker in the years when he needs additional security, that is, either in the bad years or when he is sick, gets
old, etc.

*In addition, individual profit-sharing dividends will in the great ma-
jority of cases be entirely ineffective.* They will be too small to have
any impact. The major needs of the worker can be covered adequately
only in the mass; no one man, unless rich, can provide for them by
himself. A thousand individual savings of fifty dollars each will not,
for instance, protect any one member of the group against the risk of
unemployment, of sickness or of old age. But a reserve fund of fifty
thousand dollars might provide protection against any of these risks for
every member of the group. Individual profit-sharing dividends are
likely to be a waste, subjectively and objectively, psychologically and
economically. The individual should be able to withdraw his own share
—perhaps on a basis similar to the one on which the individual holder
of a life insurance policy can borrow from the company. But the fund
itself should be a community fund and set up to provide against the
common risks of the employee group.

Moreover, the specific purpose to which a profit-sharing fund is to
be devoted must be determined by the plant comunity rather than by
management's decision what it is the workers want or should want. It
is not enough to find out through a survey what the workers would
recommend. Management should confine itself to the decision to establish a profit-sharing arrangement and to negotiating the amounts to be
set aside for the fund. How to use the sum should be left to the
workers. The fund must be the workers' fund and their irrevocable
property.

Finally, administration of the fund must be the responsibility of the
employees. Management should be represented on the administrative
board, but only to render technical assistance, to advise and to speak
out against gross mismanagement or dishonesty. The controlling power
in the board belongs in the hands of the workers and their representatives. Such a board provides an ideal opportunity for workers and
union officials to acquire a managerial attitude, to learn to co-operate

with the enterprise and its management, and to obtain social prestige and satisfaction by exercising responsibility.

The profit-sharing fund must be *locally administered*. It must be the fund of a particular enterprise earmarked for the purposes of a particular plant community. If established on an industry-wide or nation-wide basis, it is bound to lose effectiveness and meaning.

The Use of a Profit-Sharing Fund

An obvious use of a profit-sharing fund would be to improve the income guarantee under a predictable income and employment plan. The minimum weekly payment we discussed is paid whether the worker works or not. But it is in the nature of an advance payment on work he is expected to do within the near future. To improve an income guarantee beyond that requires, however, funds which cannot be recovered and which can only come out of profits set aside by the enterprise during good years.

In practice, profit-sharing reserves would be used to increase the risk which the enterprise is willing and able to shoulder. Instead of limiting its guarantee to less than the predicted probability, the enterprise might, for instance, underwrite the prediction in full. The small risk involved would be covered by a contingency fund set aside out of profits. As the fund grows, the guarantee can be improved. No enterprise will ever be able to guarantee full employment come hell or high water. But in many cases relatively small appropriations out of the profits of good years will have a disproportionately large effect in improving the guarantee.

This is only one of the many possible uses. A profit-sharing fund might be set up to provide adequate severance and stand-by pay during technological changes. It might be used to supply sickness and death benefits or to supplement the worker's meager allowance under old-age insurance with a retirement pension.

It would be a mistake, of course, to cut the available sum into too many slices. But in different situations entirely different uses will be found for a profit-sharing fund. For example, one steel company in the South found that the greatest needs of its Negro workers—who comprise about two-fifths of the total force—were for housing, for a good school and for a decent hospital. A group of railroad workers living mainly in isolated mountain valleys considers their greatest need to be

a fund for the education of their children in bad times. The men believe that they themselves will somehow manage during a depression.
But they could not keep up the children's education when they are unemployed or working greatly reduced hours, and they want, therefore, to use a profit-sharing fund for their children's education rather
than for additional income.

The Benefits to the Enterprise

A profit-sharing plan properly designed and focused on the real
needs of the worker might convince the worker that profit is not hostile to his purposes, but fully compatible with them. The best profit-
sharing plan will not make the workers into missionaries for the profit
system and certainly not into admirers of the "profit motive." But it
might create an atmosphere in which a rational discussion of the function, meaning and necessity of profit becomes possible. It might change
the worker's attitude from one of profound resistance, in which his
ears are closed to all arguments—in which arguments can indeed only
help to confirm him in his profound hostility—to one in which the
worker is receptive to a discussion of the objective function of profit.
The very least we can expect from an effective profit-sharing plan is
that it will make the workers see that profits fluctuate, and that the big
profits of a good year are offset by the poor profits or by the losses of
a bad year. The realization that the "annual profit" is nothing but a
bookkeeper's fiction would by itself be a tremendous step toward the
understanding and acceptance of the economic system.

But the most tangible and immediate benefit for the enterprise is not
the impact of profit-sharing on the resistance to profit. It lies in putting
the burden of social security and benefits payments on a fluctuating
basis. It establishes flexibility of labor costs where the enterprise needs
it most and makes the worker benefit from the flexibility.

The demand for "benefits," that is, for guarantees of security, has
become as strong as, if not stronger than, the demand for higher wage
rates. For every dollar of wages paid, American industry as a whole
pays about ten to twenty cents in such "fringe benefits." And the demand is certain to become more insistent.

What is more important, once the principle of these benefits has been
accepted, industry will be asked to keep up its payments to the various
funds in bad times as well as in good times, and even if the worker is

not working. Life insurance, retirement pay, old-age pension, sickness benefits, etc., all require predictable premiums; their protection is, moreover, needed most when a man is out of work. But not even the strongest enterprise could possibly carry at the bottom of a depression a social-security burden of ten per cent of its peak wage-costs and stay solvent.

On the other hand, most enterprises could carry the burden if it were adapted to business volume and profits. In very good years, in other words, the enterprise could set aside considerably more than ten per cent, while in poor years it would set aside less or nothing. Under a decent accounting system such benefit charges—even today—are treated anyhow as if they fluctuated with profits. But only if this relationship is brought into the open and firmly established as a principle, will the enterprise obtain the full benefit of giving the worker a stake in profits.

The profit-sharing principle also offers the only way to allay the resentment of the worker against the high salaries of the top executives. It does not answer their complaint about the size of the differential between their incomes and those of the executives; this requires an understanding both of the management function and of the organization of the modern enterprise. But the worker resents, in addition, the fact that, in his opinion, the executive receives his high income in good years and bad, that, in other words, he leaves the worker with his low income to carry the entire risk of economic fluctuations. Moreover, the great majority of workers is convinced that the salary of the executive is, in some vague and mysterious fashion, taken out of the workers' pay envelopes, with the executives thus having a tangible interest in keeping wages and payrolls low. These two causes of resentment could be eliminated by applying the profit-sharing principle to all employees, including the executives.

All fixed salaries might, for instance, be limited to a multiple of the worker's average yearly income. The largest fixed salary might be set at ten times the average take-home pay of the fully employed worker, which at present would work out at twenty-five to thirty-five thousand dollars a year. However, the whole executive group would be entitled to a share in the profits according to the level of employment.

In dividing the executive bonus, the enterprise could then establish the ladder of money symbols of position and authority by simply giving the top executives a larger share than their subordinates, etc. This would limit fixed incomes to a sum which, while significantly higher than the worker's income, is still within reach of his imagination. It would give the executives additional compensation only when employment is high and when the workers also share in the profits. For if a profit-sharing plan for executives is to overcome resentment against high executive incomes, it must operate side by side with a profit-sharing plan for workers.

Obviously such an approach would be a mere palliative. But even to lessen the worker's resentment against the high executive incomes is worth while—and not for the sake of the enterprise alone. The social interest demands the use of money differentials as the symbols of authority and power in the industrial enterprise. Every society needs such symbols; for even the society of the angels is stratified by rank rather than egalitarian. To require of the executive that he work for nonfinancial, that is social, incentives is to misunderstand the function of the high salary, which is social rather than financial. Indeed, with our present near-confiscatory taxes on high incomes, executive salaries can be said to be almost entirely a nonfinancial, prestige incentive. And of all symbols of authority, money is socially perhaps the least dangerous. It is infinitely less dangerous than uniform or title, both of which breed arrogance, petty tyranny and the lust for power. Indeed money —and money alone—can be kept socially powerless. It can be taxed away, for instance. And contrary to the popular Europen belief, money as such—that is, mere wealth—is socially quite impotent in this country, as witness the embarrassed, uncomfortable and socially ambiguous position of the sons of the very rich, whose very wealth keeps them out of any career except that of philanthropist.

Yet the high salaries of the top executives are deeply and bitterly resented by the employees—and understandably so. Petty this resentment may well be. But it is not superficial; it reflects a real conflict between the ethos of our society and its structural needs. If we cannot heal this sore spot, we must at least try to soothe it.

The development of sound profit-sharing plans is of special importance in countries undergoing industrialization. It is no accident that

Soviet Russia has developed them further than any other country. In the early stages of industrialization the development of an income and employment prediction is almost impossible. Such a prediction presupposes a high degree of industrial and managerial maturity. At the same time, early industrialization is the period when the community needs of the workers are at their peak—needs that can only be satisfied through profit-sharing funds. The worker at this stage has not yet learned how to live in an industrial world. Having but recently arrived from the rural village, he is uprooted, deprived of his ancestral community, lost and bewildered. We do not have to go to the South African gold mines, to India or to Turkey to see this. The Southerner who came to Akron during World War I, the Southerner—white or Negro —who went to Detroit between the two wars, or the farm boy who goes to work in the new plants of the Deep South today, all provide an example of the social and cultural nakedness of the worker in early industrialization. Profit-sharing at this stage not only furnishes the funds for community needs. It provides the catalyst for the satisfaction of the greatest need: the formation of a community.

Finally, it prevents, at the very start, the formation of a dispossessed proletariat. It prevents the development of the worker's rejection of profit and profitability at the very time when the profit margin of the economy must be at its highest level, and when the economy must most emphasize the priority of profitability. It is in this period, therefore, that the worker will acquire his profound hostility to profitability unless he is given a meaningful stake in profit. The present attitude of the workers of the old industrial countries of the West, for instance, was certainly formed a century or so ago.

In the newly industrializing countries whose economic muscles are not strong enough yet to use income and employment predictions, profit-sharing is thus a major economic tool for the building of an industrial order. But it is an indispensable tool in the developed industrial economy as well. Income and employment prediction gives the worker the minimum of security he needs. But only if he has a stake in profit will he be able to accept the economic order of an industrial society.

CHAPTER 28

THE THREAT OF UNEMPLOYMENT

INCOME and employment prediction and a stake in profits would be sufficient to overcome the economic tensions of industrial society but for the depression psychosis in which the worker lives today. That the recurrence of large-scale unemployment would threaten every industrial society with political upheaval and social collapse has become a truism. Every industrial country has gone in for elaborate antidepression policies and has made the maintenance of high and stable employment the first goal of its economic policy.

Yet, we are today as far away from a working depression policy as we ever were. There are two major reasons for this dangerous failure:

First, the confusion between two entirely different kinds of depression: the depression caused by long term dislocation and the business or cyclical depression. The two require entirely different treatment.

Secondly, our whole thinking assumes that an antidepression policy must be carried out by the government. The prevention or cure of depression is indeed a responsibility of the government. But a government attempting to discharge this responsibility alone can only exorcise depression by conjuring up the threat of war. A genuine antidepression policy must be a national policy, to be sure. But it must be based upon, and carried out by, the enterprise.

Dislocation Depression and Business Depression

Our depression policy today is completely obsessed by the cyclical or business depression. Partly as a result of our recent experience, partly because of the profound influence of John Maynard Keynes, who summed up the special features of the Great Depression in a "general" theory of depressions, we have come to assume that all depressions are, like that of the thirties in the United States, business or cyclical depressions, that is, disturbances *within* an existing economic structure.

This, however, is untenable. A dislocation depression, caused by changes in the foundations of an economy and in its international economic position, is entirely different from a business or cyclical depression. To confuse the two diseases and to treat them as one, just because they both cause economic suffering and unemployment, makes effective treatment impossible. It is like treating alike constipation and appendicitis because both produce a stomach-ache. Just as a laxative will only make appendicitis worse, so will the application of measures appropriate to a business depression greatly aggravate a dislocation depression.

The major problem of the next decades may not be the business depression but the dislocation depression. The crisis from which Western and Central Europe are suffering is a dislocation crisis—the result of profound changes in the world economic structure caused by the industrial world revolution. The crisis of the British economy is similarly a dislocation crisis. And so, largely, are the economic difficulties of India, Malaya and Indonesia. The problem of the competitive position of the major economies and of their relationship is likely to be so dominant as to make the much-vaunted "Keynesian Revolution" of our economists look in retrospect like a ripple.

We know a great deal about the causes of the dislocation crisis; but so far we have little idea how to combat it. The traditional free-trade, multilateral concept has been proven to be unable to cope with a major international dislocation. It spreads the infection and tends to inflict upon the economy of the entire world the disease of one of its members. Its assumptions are those of a pre-industrial economy in which trade consists primarily of an exchange of raw materials and foodstuffs between countries of different climate and different geology. It puts the credit, prices and production of the domestic economy under the complete and unchecked control of the balance of international trade. This was justified in the eighteenth century, when international trade constituted the bulk of all monetary transactions. But it is destructive in an industrial age. It is ironical that the one country which officially professes and promotes the free-trade doctrine, the United States, is also the one country whose own economy contradicts every single major assumption of the free-trade economists.

But the only alternative to nineteenth-century free trade is even worse, certainly in the long run. Bilateral trade and autarky make economic dislocation permanent. Their very purpose is to solve the lack of balance in a country's international economic position by unbalancing the rest of the world. Bilateralism and autarky are restrictive not incidentally but by purpose and definition. Also, they can only work if they are being practiced by one country alone. The moment every country adopts them, they cease to give even the immediate relief to obtain which they are usually invoked.

Yet it is useless to hope that we can persuade any country not to fall back on bilateralism and autarky if hit by serious economic dislocation. It is not so much that these remedies promise some immediate relief, but that they are the only *action* which a country can today take against a crisis. Even if the free-trade medicine were effective, it would not be acceptable. It demands of government that it do nothing in a crisis that endangers the prosperity, if not the survival, of the country. No government can do nothing, however, and remain in power. Purely restrictive economic policies will continue to be generally applied to the dislocation crisis until we succeed in developing new principles which enable a government to counteract dislocation by expansion.

To overcome a dislocation crisis, we need new concepts of international economics and new tools and institutions. An industrial system apparently demands large, closely integrated and basically self-sufficient regional economic structures such as both the United States and Russia represent. It is not impossible that the Marshall Plan and Mr. Truman's call for an international program of systematic economic development in underdeveloped areas were the first steps toward such a new international economic system.

Certainly anticyclical, that is, Keynesian measures, can only make a dislocation crisis infinitely more serious. A country hit by dislocation is actually inflated—not in its credit structure but in its standard of living. It does not need more consumption; it needs more production and more capital investment. The Keynesian remedy of the "reflation" of consumption is the very worst thing for it; and the Keynesian medicine men who inherited their master's prescriptions without having his diagnostic skill are a real menace.

The Requirements of an Anticyclical Policy

But while the dislocation crisis may well be the major problem of the next generation, it is the cyclical or business depression of which the people are afraid. They demand of their governments a policy that will free them effectively of this fear. It is this demand that will put the greatest pressure on the political and the economic institutions of every industrial country.

A policy to overcome the threat of cyclical unemployment must counteract the conditions that make for cyclical depression. It must prevent the collapse of a depression into economic paralysis such as characterized the Thirties, and must overcome chronic mass unemployment. Finally, it must be able to counteract the fear of unemployment that haunts the Western World.

On all three counts government action by itself will be found wanting.

We are not dealing here with the "cause" of a cyclical depression. It does not at all concern us that we do not know whether the depression is caused by something in the nature of industrial organization or by something in the nature of "capitalism," whether its causes are monetary, overproduction, underconsumption, or sunspots. We do not even know whether there is such a thing as a "business cycle"; the evidence for the existence of a more or less regular cyclical up-and-down is anything but convincing.

But even if we really knew what causes it, we would still not be able to prevent a serious depression unless we could first prevent the preceding boom. Large-scale, chronic unemployment and the collapse into a creeping paralysis of confidence, imagination and enterprise are impossible unless there has been first a major boom; and they cannot be prevented if there has been such a boom.

A government that rests on popular support cannot counteract a boom. It is characteristic of the boom that it breeds unlimited confidence; everything that expresses doubt in the soundness of the structure or that threatens the enjoyment of the feast is rejected as groundless pessimism. It is also characteristic of the boom that nobody is willing to give up the prosperity he thinks he enjoys. At the most every group is willing to have the other groups make sacrifices, with the inevitable result that everybody enjoys unbridled license.

In the American boom after World War II labor was only too willing to continue ceilings on prices and on profits provided only that there would be no ceiling on its wages. Management was equally willing to see wage controls continue, provided only that there be no ceilings on its own profits and prices. No one agreed, however, to the continuation of rationing and the allocation of materials without which no system of controls could possibly have worked. In Socialist Britain pretty much the same thing has happened, even though all the controls have remained nominally in force. The only thing that the British controls could assure was a short delay in the start of the inflationary hayride.

Even a totalitarian government is probably incapable of resisting public pressure during a boom. Certainly the Soviet government has never been able to put on the controls in time, that is, before serious inflation had developed. Yet the Russian government should have been in an exceptionally good position to prevent booms—and altogether to prevent the sharp fluctuations from comparative ease to the extremes of austerity and privation that have characterized Russian life these last thirty years. Not only is the Soviet government largely impervious to popular pressures. Russian is not a developed industrial country, so that any threat of economic contraction can be counteracted by starting up industries which, while new to Russia, have already been developed in the West and can therefore be copied. Yet even with this major advantage, the Soviet government can hardly be said to have been successful in controlling or in preventing inflationary booms.

It is equally difficult, if not impossible, for the government of a well-developed industrial country to counteract a depression and to restore prosperity—except by policies which exorcise the depression only by invoking that other demon of our times, total war. We know today that the only reliable policy to restore employment, the only action that can be guaranteed to produce results, is the production of capital goods. Monetary measures may be sufficient to overcome a comparatively mild depression. But the original Keynesian remedy for serious depression—the creation of consumer purchasing power that underlay the New Deal policy in the Thirties—has proved itself incapable of "priming the pump" and of getting the economy going again. In fact, the Keynesians today have abandoned their master's remedy and now prescribe direct orders for capital goods in massive doses as the one therapy for a severe depression.

But what should the government order? This question is not unanswerable in an adolescent or immature economy such as that of Soviet Russia still is. It is always possible to develop new industries by copying the more advanced industrial countries. But highly developed industrial countries such as the United States, Great Britain, Canada, or Western Europe, seem in a depression to have a surplus of every known and every imaginable capital goods industry.

One popular answer to the question what these countries could and should do is Public Works. A depression is the right time to build highways and hospitals, irrigation dams and schools, air fields and post offices. Certainly Public Works projects should be deferred in prosperous times until lean years—however difficult the execution of such a policy would be in the face of public pressure and under our present year-to-year fiscal policy. But even at its most successful the Public Works program cannot be large enough to have any real influence on business conditions. If injected at the wrong time, it can convert a minor into a major boom and add to inflationary pressures. It can ease a depression. But it cannot fill the gap between a serious depression and prosperity.

In an economy not completely controlled by the government a Public Works program leads, moreover, to a decline of all other capital goods orders which offsets the stimulus of the government's orders. Even in a fully Socialist economy *lack of confidence* will effectively counteract a Public Works program through a contraction in the circulation speed of money, such as nullified so completely the New Deal's "pump-priming" program. Only in an economy that is both completely state-controlled and very close to the subsistence level, if not below it, will it be impossible for the economy to counteract the effects of a Public-Works program. In such an economy industry cannot curtail its capital program even if it loses confidence; and the consumer cannot restrict his purchases and thus slow down the circulation of money, as he is too poor not to spend immediately all the money he gets. In any other economy, however, a Public Works program cannot be the mainstay of depression policy. For the most important factor in the deep depression is not economic but psychological, that is, confidence; a Public

Works program, being clearly of an emergency nature, tends to create as much distrust in the future of the economy as it creates immediate jobs.

As a result, government in an industrialized country has but one weapon to fight a serious or chronic depression: an *armaments program*. It is at the same time the weapon that is handiest to government, most easy to apply and likely to be most popular, as it can always be justified in the name of patriotism and national security.

But surely a depression policy that depends upon war production is worse than no depression policy at all. It can only provoke an international armaments race. However desirable it may be for any country to be prepared and to be secure militarily, an international armaments race knows but one outcome: war. Even more dangerous, perhaps, is the fact that the use of war production to overcome an economic depression subordinates the foreign policy of a country to its internal economic needs and requirements. The more successful an armaments program is in its creation of work and jobs, the less possible does it become to stop or to reduce war production. Foreign policy will inevitably have to be conducted in such a manner as to justify a continued armaments program. Military security itself is jeopardized if the decision what arms to produce is subordinated to the number of jobs that is created by the production of this or that particular weapon.

Even if we overcame these two obstacles and found both effective government action against booms and a government depression policy other than the production of armaments, it would still be true that government action cannot be effective against the fear of a depression. For the very most that government could possibly ever do is to develop a policy of "full employment." And, paradoxical as it may sound, that does not give the protection against unemployment which the individual demands.

By its very nature the aim of government policy is a general one: "sixty million jobs" or "full employment." Similarly the measurements of its success must be general and abstract: the total number of unemployed, an index number of industrial production, national income, and expenditures, etc. But the worker's dread is highly individual and concrete. He is afraid to lose his job and afraid that he may not find another one. If his concern extends beyond his own security and that of his family, it takes in his fellow workers in the same plant or in the same town. "Sixty million jobs" or a national index of industrial production are mere abstractions to him and completely remote.

No government will be forgiven or allowed to continue in office if it fails to develop a positive depression policy. The penalty for failure is not only the dismissal of one particular government but may well be the destruction of the form of government through revolution or disintegration. Government is thus forced to assume responsibility. At the same time, no government really believes that it can discharge the responsibility. The citizen's dread of unemployment is matched only by the profound helplessness which all governments display in the face of this threat, and which breaks through even the most elaborate facade of economic advisors, voluminous statistics and Public Works programs.

Anti-Depression Policy in the Enterprise

We must find some organ that can effectively carry a depression policy aimed alike at the prevention of booms, at the creation of capital goods production, and at the assurance of job security for the individual in his individual job. Government cannot relinquish responsibility for the success of such a policy. But it cannot carry the full burden of a depression policy itself.

The actual attack on the cyclical depression will have to be made within the enterprise, in a free-enterprise as well as in a Socialist economy. It is the enterprise alone in which capital expenditures can be planned so as to act countercyclically and so as to give the individual worker a meaningful guarantee of his own job.

The starting point of such a policy would be the income and employment prediction. It is not too difficult to move from the prediction of future economic developments to an attack on the effects of the fluctuations themselves. This can be done by a policy of planning capital expenditures on a long-term basis—five to ten years. The enterprise would have to keep its capital budget separate from its operating budget. Major capital programs, major improvements in plant and equipment, large-scale replacement of equipment, etc. should then be deferred during a boom, to be undertaken during a depression period. The funds necessary for capital programs should be provided for as much as possible in good years; the programs themselves should be carried out in bad years.

These funds should remain free from taxation if they are actually spent on employment-making projects during years of unemployment. They should, however, be taxed at a confiscatory rate should the enterprise fail to use them during the periods for which they were intended.

Such tax privileges should provide enough incentive to induce at least the big enterprises to adopt a policy so manifestly in the interests of the economy as well as in their own. If this should not be enough, however, there would be the threat of a punitive tax on the profits of good years unless part of them were set aside for such employment-creating projects. And the granting of the tax exemption for employment-creating reserves should be made conditional upon their being earmarked for concrete income and employment guarantees for the employees.

Such a policy would prevent a run-away boom. The capital expenditure of business would not be added to the other inflationary pressures during a boom. The very fact that funds are actually withdrawn to be earmarked for future projects should have a marked anti-inflationary effect.

This policy would answer the question what capital goods orders should be given during a depression. Instead of having one program that would be unmanageable by its very size, we should have hundreds or thousands of individual plans for capital goods orders throughout the economy. Co-ordination of these projects by the government would be needed to prevent both a premature start on these projects and their abandonment during a depression because of lack of confidence. But the formulation and the execution of these plans should be left to the individual enterprises.

Above all, such a policy should have the necessary psychological impact. It would focus not only on the actual depression but on the fear of depression. It is the only policy that offers any promise of counteracting the depression psychosis of modern industrial society. It should serve alike to prevent the wild optimism of the boom in which all trees grow to the sky, and the pathological despair of the depression which sees nothing ahead but collapse and ruin. And its manic-depressive psychology, more than any economic factor, has been the worst and the most dangerous feature of the boom-bust cycle.

CHAPTER 2 9

"THE PROPER STUDY OF MANKIND
IS ORGANIZATION"

SO FAR the industrial enterprise has attempted on the whole to solve its problems of governmental and social organization by adapting pre-industrial principles. These principles were simply taken for granted and retained. In the pre-industrial business, whether trading partnership or workshop, one man or a small group of men were the "business." The others were there to make it possible for the partner or the master craftsman to be productive; they were helpers. We have attempted to project this concept onto the modern enterprise in which the producer is something entirely impersonal, the organization. But the enterprise is not the "long shadow of one man." If organized as such, it becomes unmanageable. The modern plant is not a very much bigger workshop. If conceived as such—and anybody who talks of "my workers" and of "our big happy family" consciously or subconsciously does just that—it becomes socially destructive. To the extent to which our actual industrial organization reflects the strictly personal structure of pre-industrial conditions, it can well be said to have no principle of order at all.

The attempt to organize the new on the principles of the old out of which it grew is a natural one. It is probably inevitable wherever the new institution develops through a gradual transformation of the old one, as did the enterprise. Indeed the development in the enterprise during the last fifty years strikingly parallels the early development of administration in the modern State. As with the enterprise, the emergence of the State meant a transformation of a personal function, Medieval Kingship, into an objective and impersonal institution. Where the medieval king had ruled, the modern State had to govern and to administrate. Where the king had discharged his kingly functions himself and directly, the State needed an organization; it needed both a government and a large human machinery, the bureaucracy. Yet, when the local governments of feudalism collapsed or were eliminated, the new tasks which devolved upon the central authority were at first handled as if they were different only in size from the functions of the king in the feudal system. As a result of thoughtlessness rather than because of any deliberate policy, the crown attempted to handle its new responsibilities by adding to the king's personal retinue, that is, to his court. One result of this was the institution of the "King's First Minister," such as Richelieu, through whose hands every detail of administration had to pass, and who was directly responsible for foreign policy, domestic policy and the conduct of wars, as well as for the supply of handkerchiefs for the king's bedchamber. The other result was Versailles—the last and desperate attempt to house all the king's servants under one roof and to maintain the court as an effective administrative body.

The parallel development in the enterprise is best illustrated by the experience of that pioneer and symbol of modern industry, the Ford Motor Company. For twenty years, until a new management took over just before Henry Ford's death in 1946, a tremendous industrial empire was ruled by a succession of "first ministers" who alone had the power to make a decision, and who alone knew what was going on. Practically the entire production was centralized in one plant, the River Rouge—the biggest concentration of industrial production under one roof and one of the marvels of the modern world.

This structure was not the result of an attempt to organize modern industry on a principle appropriate to it, but of the retention of pre-industrial concepts. As one of Henry Ford's oldest and closest associates put it, "Whenever Mr. Ford looks at the River Rouge, he sees the old bicycle repair shop where he started."

There has been no other Versailles, however; and the original is today an empty and rather depressing showpiece for tourists. Within a century the King's First Minister was replaced by the cabinet system, which delegates specific functions to specific officials, each largely autonomous within his own sphere, with a top executive—one man or a cabinet committee—responsible for basic policy decisions but free of administrative responsibility. Just as Versailles marked the peak and established a record in size that was never reached or surpassed, there will be no second River Rouge.

To stay too long on the old basis is dangerous. France has paid for Richelieu's success with three hundred years of governmental instability and administrative impotence. As for the Ford Motor Company, its management organization—or disorganization—resulted in a steady decline over the last twenty-five years from the position of leadership in its industry to third rank. Without the tremendous fortune amassed by Henry Ford in his early years, the company would probably have been forced into bankruptcy during the thirties. It still remains to be seen whether the new management can reverse or even halt the downward trend. The River Rouge may well, like Versailles, become a sightseeing attraction rather than an actually producing plant. Its manufacturing costs are high and inflexible. Its social climate is appalling. Even its union is so badly torn by strife, suspicion and internal hatreds as to be almost unable to function. And fear and insecurity pervades the management group, particularly in the lower and middle ranks.

But even in businesses that are much better managed than was the Ford Motor Company in the twenty years between the end of the "Model T" and Henry Ford's death, there are unmistakable signs that a new organizing principle is overdue. One is the all but universal atmosphere of tension and pressure in the management group. It is not fear for one's job nor competitive pressure that usually underlies this tension, but confusion and the inability to understand the rules of the game. Everybody "plays by ear," hoping that his neighbor has the score or knows the piece by heart; but the neighbor is forced to improvise just as much. Even the player who is a virtuoso on his instrument must feel anxious, frustrated and tense in such an ensemble. To hold the group together at all, discipline has to be tightened to the point of uniformity. It is no accident that we increasingly use army terminology when discussing industrial organization: "line and staff" is but one example. But tight discipline can only give the most temporary relief; in the long run it must increase the tension and frustration. This would be true even if the army pattern of organization with its focus on the one future moment of combat were not particularly ill-adapted to the needs of the enterprise.

Another sign is the growing concern with "organization." Company after company is going in for elaborate "organization studies" and "organization manuals." The literature on management organization is growing by leaps and bounds, especially in this country; and it seems to be increasingly dedicated to the proposition that *the proper study of mankind is organization.* In our schools, too, the discipline of business organization, though of the most recent origin, tends to take over the old established economic and political sciences, just as government administration, in this country at least, has usurped the central place in the study of government and politics that should properly be held by constitutional law and political theory.

The concern with organization is not, as the enemies of "bigness" often assert, necessarily pathological and a symptom of an inborn structural disorder. It is typical of all institutions which for their effectiveness depend upon the organization of human resources: the modern State, the Army, above all the Church. In the Catholic Church —the oldest and most successful of all institutions of the West—organization, especially the organization of the "management group" and the selection and training of tomorrow's leaders is the first and major responsibility of the men at the very top. No industrial enterprise has as voluminous an "organization manual" as the Church has in the Canon Law—nor, alas, one as clear, as consistent and as intelligent.

Yet the sudden clamor for organization bespeaks an acute disorganization. It indicates that the lack of the right principle is becoming a serious handicap and a source of trouble. Equally telling is the growing dissatisfaction with the "gadgeteering" approach to industrial organization which attempts to solve the problems of the enterprise by this or that technique. Indeed what is wanted by the people in industry themselves are not "principles of organization" but one clear and basic principle of order. They are like people who finally, after decades of patching up, building on and remodeling, cannot go on living in the old tumble-down shack and have to start building a new house from scratch.

But while the need for a new principle is increasingly recognized, the adoption of the one principle around which the industrial enterprise can be successfully organized will come hard. The principle is neither new nor difficult to understand. But it goes counter to the traditions in which the enterprise and its management have grown up. This principle is federalism.

CHAPTER 30

DECENTRALIZATION AND FEDERALISM

"DECENTRALIZATION" has become exceedingly popular with American business and is being hawked around widely as the cure-all for the ills of industrial society. It is, however, an exceedingly vague term. It is still widely used in its original meaning, as the functional delegation of authority and responsibility, that is, as the opposite to centralization. Another popular usage today applies the term to the geographic dispersion of productive units which may or may not remain under centralized authority. Or the term is used to describe a genuinely federalist constitution, that is, one that strengthens both the central and the local authorities.

Decentralization, in the original meaning of the word, is undoubtedly necessary. Functions have to be defined, authority has to be equal to responsibility, and decisions have to be made at the lowest possible rather than at the highest possible level. It is important to emphasize this concept of functional decentralization and to keep on warning the industrial enterprise against the dangers of centralization. Most of our enterprises are far too centralized; functional decentralization below the very top is still largely a pious fiction, whatever impression to the contrary the "organization chart" may give.

However, functional decentralization does not solve the structural problems of management organization and management function. It does not overcome the cleavage between operating management and top management and, therefore, does not give operating management the necessary understanding of top management problems. It also does very little to help in the problem of succession. The operating executive is still not being trained in top-management work and in top-management thinking, nor is he being tested for his capacity to perform the top-management function satisfactorily until he is actually at the top. The one specific problem of the enterprise that is made easier by functional decentralization is the pressure of operating and routine matters on top management. But that is, strictly speaking, not a problem of the structure of the enterprise, but one of methods, procedures and habits. Functional decentralization is an important tool of administration; but it is not the ordering principle we need.

Geographic dispersion had nothing to do with management organization originally. It aimed at bringing production closer to a source of raw materials or to a market, at cutting transportation or labor costs or at providing better service to customers. Other important factors were tariffs and restrictive laws on foreign enterprises—affecting only a comparatively small number of American enterprises but of vital importance to the European producers. These economic factors still largely determine decisions to move productive units or to expand by building a new plant in a different region rather than by enlarging an old one. An added impetus to geographic dispersion will come from considerations of military security.

By itself geographic dispersion will also have little effect on the organization of the enterprise. It makes excessive centralization a little more difficult; control exercised over the telephone by a head office five hundred miles away is centralization tempered by poor connections. But this is a purely accidental by-product; only too many enterprises—the typical railroad organization in this country, for instance—have succeeded in overcoming the obstacle distance sets to complete centralization.

Functional and geographic decentralization cannot solve the problems of management organization, as their advocates claim for them, because they attempt to solve mechanically a problem that is not mechanical but constitutional. They do not change the structure of the enterprise; they only change its procedures. The obstacles to a functioning management lying in the enterprise's structure are hardly affected by either functional or geographic decentralization. What the enterprise needs is a new constitution; functional and geographic decentralization offer only administrative reforms. These reforms are badly needed to be sure. But they do not go to the root of the matter.

The Federal Principle

What the enterprise needs is a principle that gives both the center and the parts genuine managerial functions and powers. This principle is *federalism*, in which the whole of the enterprise is conceived as made up of autonomous units. The federal enterprise and all its units are in the same business. The same economic factors determine the future of the whole as well as of all units; the same basic decisions have to be made for all of them; the same kind and type of executive is needed. Hence the whole requires a unified management in charge of the basic functions: the decision what business the enterprise is in, the organization of the human resources and the selection, training and testing of future leaders.

At the same time, each unit is a business by itself. It produces its own products for a distinct market. Each unit must therefore have wide autonomy within the limits set by the general policy decisions of the management of the whole. Each unit has to have its own management. The local management will be primarily an operating management; it will be concerned mainly with the present and the immediate future rather than with basic policy. But within a limited scope it will have also to discharge real top-management functions.

This new concept—of which in this country the organization of General Motors, of Standard Oil of New Jersey and of the surgical supply company of Johnson and Johnson are good examples—is also usually called "decentralization." But this term is dangerously misleading. Geographic dispersion is actually unnecessary to the new principle; the major units of the Johnson and Johnson Company, which is one of the most successful examples, stand in the same small town practically within a stone's throw from each other and from the central office. It could even be said that the new concept strengthens the center rather than taking power and authority away from it. It establishes both a functioning management for the whole and a functioning management for the unit. In effect, each management is the balance wheel of the other and keeps it going on a true course.

There are basic differences in concept and structure between decentralization and the new pattern. Under the new pattern each unit has a product and a market of its own. Its autonomy is therefore not just the result of a delegation of authority but derives from its own nature. Its management, to use a legal term, has original rather than derived autonomy. The top management of the whole can replace the management personnel of a unit. But it cannot do away with the authority and autonomy of the management of the unit short of abolishing the unit altogether. It must let the local management manage its own local business. This is not just another variant of decentralization, not just another administrative reform. This is a concept in its own right, the concept of a constitution based on the principle of federalism.[1]

Federalism relieves the top management of the enterprise from operating duties and sets it free to devote itself to its proper functions. It defines the functions and responsibilities of the operating people and furnishes yardsticks to measure their success and effectiveness in the operating jobs. Beyond that it bridges the gulf between top management and operating management. To be sure, the responsibility of the executives of the local unit for top-management functions will be limited. The area with which they deal is very much smaller; they necessarily operate within the policy limits set by the enterprise's top management. Also the top-management job is likely to be incidental in, rather than central to, the work of the local management— except in respect to the utilization of human resources in the plant, where the local people will have responsibility and authority fully equal to that of top management. But within these limitations the men in charge of the local unit perform genuine top-management functions.

In a federal organization local managements must also participate in the decisions that establish their own local business, and that set the limits of their own authority. Quite automatically they will be brought into the discussions and decisions on basic policy. They will come to understand the top management function and its problems. In this way top management decisions will become effective on the local level instead of being quietly sabotaged or misunderstood by the operating people, as is usually the case in the nonfederal enterprise.

The problem of the succession to top management is thus brought

[1] For a case study of a federally organized management see my *Concept of the Corporation* (1946), Chapter II, where I however still used the term "decentralization."

much nearer a solution. The manager of a unit receives a thorough education in top-management problems and functions while still in an operating position. He will be prepared and trained for top-management responsibilities. At the same time the management positions of the local unit provide an opportunity to test men in independent commands on a level where failure is not likely to endanger the entire enterprise and not even likely to destroy a man's usefulness. If the man is not qualified for further advancement, he may still contribute to the enterprise's success in his present or in another operating capacity.

The federal organization also supplies an objective criterion for the evaluation of executive performance and thus enables the enterprise to make the decisions on succession on a reasonably impersonal and reasonably objective basis. Judgment, instead of having to proceed from impressions and hunches, can be based on provable performance in an independent command. While not a "yardstick" in the exact meaning of the word, the criterion provides at least a fairly reliable compass bearing. To depend entirely on it would be folly. But in every concrete case it will have to be proven that the indications given by the compass bearing are not to be relied upon; why should a man not be qualified for a top position despite outstanding performance on the local level, or why should he be qualified despite shortcomings. While judgment will not be eliminated, personal likes and dislikes—not to mention prejudice and favoritism—should be bridled. The whole level of the discussion on promotions is likely to be raised. It should come to focus on the objective requirements of the job rather than on the claims to advancement individuals might have or feel they have. Above all, the men selected or turned down for a promotion will themselves be likely to view the decision as rational and objective and as based on generally understood and generally accepted reasons.

A federal organization also offers the best way to overcome the overspecialization and overdepartmentalization which the modern enterprise breeds. The general manager of a unit is not a department head or a technician. He is the head of an autonomous business, responsible for production and engineering, sales and purchases, accounting and personnel. He must see his unit as a whole rather than as a collection of departments to be a reasonably successful general manager. He will be forced to develop from "specialist" into "generalist" while, normally, still young enough to acquire a new way of looking at things.

Why Not Break up the Enterprise?

It may be asked why we need the large enterprise at all if we can organize it in autonomous units each of which represents virtually a business in itself. Wouldn't it be better to split up a federal business into independent businesses? What distinguishes such an enterprise from a mere holding company, the sole purpose of which is to control a large business with a small capital investment? What function does the enterprise itself fulfill; and especially what function does the top management of the enterprise fulfill?

The answer to this question was given one hundred and sixty years ago in the book that first developed and first applied the principle of federalism: *The Federalist*—especially in the letters that deal with the "Insufficiency of the Present Confederation" and with the "Necessity of an Energetic Government" (Letters XV to XXIII, almost all written by Hamilton).

Only one point needs additional stress. Hamilton could take for granted that his readers knew that the body politic needs a government. But it is not yet generally understood that an industrial system needs a management, and that there are management functions that have to be discharged. This necessity is grounded in the very nature of industrial production. We have no choice whether we want to discharge them or not, as the enemies of "bigness" want us to believe. Indeed, the campaign against the bigness of the industrial enterprise can have only one result, should it be successful: It must lead to the establishment of government agencies to discharge the management function; and these agencies will be not just big, they will be super-colossal.

The individual unit by itself will not, as a rule, be able to provide a top management—just as each one of the Thirteen Colonies was too small and too weak to provide a strong government of its own. The financial burden alone would be prohibitive, to say nothing of the problem of finding enough men of the caliber necessary for the job.

Organized and systematic work on the improvement of product and process, research in techniques, products and markets, would be almost impossible if the small unit were on its own, as would be the measures to give security to the workers. In many cases production is most efficient when a unit specializes on one product or on one market. But this is possible only where the individual product is part of an integrated "line," and where the individual unit is linked with other units engaged in the same business in the "common citizenship" of a federal union.

Altogether, the analogy between the federal organization of the enterprise and a holding company—or any other device of financial control—is a complete misunderstanding. The very purpose of a federal organization is to provide the one thing a holding company by definition fails to give: a functioning management. Because a federal organization alone can provide such a management, it provides the principle that can answer the needs of industrial enterprise and industrial society.

What Is Needed for a Federal Management Organization?

The federal principle can be applied only where all units of the enterprise are essentially in the same business. There must be a "common language and heritage" to make possible the "common citizenship." At the same time, the principle can be applied only where an integrated business, a true whole, is composed of parts which in themselves are integrated, and where a total product divides naturally into parts each of which is a whole in itself.

It is no accident that a company in the automobile industry, General Motors, was the first to develop a truly federal organization. No other product in general use is so much both a whole and a composite of parts. The components of a car—body, engine, steering gear, brakes, lights, etc.—are all very different though they all are parts of the same car. They have each a major market of their own in the demand for spares and replacement parts which, in the case of some accessories such as spark plugs or shock absorbers, accounts for half or more of total sales. Similarly a line of cars, such as Chevrolet, Pontiac, Oldsmobile, Buick and Cadillac, which covers the entire automotive market, is a whole. Yet each of the five cars is an entity in itself competing not only within its own price class with the cars made by other automobile companies but—especially through the secondhand market —with the other cars made by General Motors. The top-management job has to do with the future of the automobile business and therefore deals with a problem common to all cars, all parts and all accessories as well as with the relationship between them.

Johnson and Johnson, too, has a market for which all units produce; and each product is complete in itself. The case of Standard Oil is less simple. Here the major division goes by stages of production rather than by products. Exploration, crude oil production, transportation, refining and sale of the finished gasoline or fuel oil—all the stages in the production of petroleum products—are separate processes. The techniques as well as the equipment needed at each stage are different. Also, each unit has a market of its own and a source of supply of its own. The crude-oil-producing divisions, for instance, can—and do—employ independent exploration companies, and can—and do—sell their crude oil to outside refineries. In fact, there are many successful independent companies which confine themselves to crude oil production, to transportation, refining, or marketing. Yet each process is only a link in a chain; and the whole chain alone produces the final product.

Federalism is possible also when the production of one product can be organized in plants that supply an entirely separate territory. The obvious example are foreign or overseas subsidiaries. But within a large country, such as the United States, there exist several distinct territorial markets. A company with plants in the East and on the West Coast will keep both going even in a bad depression rather than supply California from the East. The freight charges to the West Coast are so high as to make it almost always more efficient and less costly to produce locally for the Western market rather than to ship from the East. A West Coast automobile-assembly plant manager exercises real managerial functions and runs what is in effect his own autonomous business.

Federalism is not universally applicable. If there is not the "common citizenship" of the same business between the units, there can be no real top management of the whole. Each unit would be a separate business. As such, it would require its own top management. In fact, there could be no management of the whole at all, though there might be people with management titles and management salaries.

If, on the other hand, the individual unit does not have a truly distinct market—based either on a distinct product or on the geographic separation of its territory—local autonomy is impossible. There may be a top management for the whole. But the local managements will not have a genuine management function of their own. Theirs will be only operating functions. Autonomy can only exist when the local management derives its power and function from structural necessity, that is, when the unit is a distinct business. When the power and function of the local management have to rest on voluntary delegation from the central management, there is no real autonomy and no real federalism.

There are many enterprises that cannot be subdivided into autonomous parts—most railroads, for instance. A railroad can go very far in regional decentralization—perhaps further than a manufacturing business. But the regional general managers will never quite enjoy the autonomy that can only rest on an autonomous and distinct product or market. On the whole, the majority of manufacturing and mercantile businesses is probably capable of federalization, the majority of public utilities and transportation businesses incapable of it. While the range of federalism is thus very large—much larger than most managements seem to realize—it is not all-embracing. The enterprises that are not capable of a federal organization can never go beyond functional and geographic decentralization, which may greatly relieve but can never solve the problems of a functioning management.

The Limitations of Federalism

Even when federalism is fully applicable it is not a panacea for the problems of management organization. In the first place, it only applies to the top group. It does not operate within the local unit. But the selection, training and testing of candidates for managerial positions has to start long before a man reaches the top level of the local unit.

Secondly, even federalism does not create the outside objective and disinterested body necessary to develop and to administer a policy of executive selection and promotion. It might even destroy what little there is of such a body in the present enterprise; for the Board of Directors in a federal enterprise is almost bound to cease to contain outsiders and to become composed entirely or predominantly of present and former executives.

Here, I believe, is perhaps the only area where legislation should intervene in management organization. We have imposed by regulation the independent audit of the enterprise's accounts by a qualified outsider, the certified accountant. We should impose upon the enterprise similarly the independent audit of its executive-personnel policies and management organization by qualified outsiders. This could be done through demanding of each enterprise beyond a certain size that it elect to its Board of Directors two men whose sole duty it would be to audit the enterprise's management organization and executive-personnel policies. These men would report to the public each year on the policies adopted, on the measures taken to assure a functioning management and to provide for continuity in management, and on the criteria underlying decisions on promotion within the executive ranks.

The difficult problem is to find a standard of qualification for these men. Obviously they should not be appointed by the government—theirs is a professional rather than a political function. Their qualifications cannot be established by an examination as in the case of the certified accountant. Technical skill or knowledge—all an examination can test—are of minor importance; wisdom and vision—both notoriously nonexaminable—the most important qualities required. One solution would be to leave it to each enterprise to select its own men, subject to its ability to convince a supervising agency, such as the Securities Exchange Commission or a Federal Registrar of Corporations, of their ability and qualifications—a procedure which, over the years, might develop a general set of standards for the new profession. Or there might be a committee composed jointly of distinguished businessmen and government representatives which would have the power to grant licenses to applicants it deems qualified—or, perhaps better, have the power to deny, subject to judicial review, licenses to applicants it deems unfit. But whatever the details, the enterprise—in its own interest—needs independent outside control of its executive-personnel policy fully as much as, fifty years ago, it needed independent outside audit of its books and accounts.

IS A COMPETITIVE MARKET NECESSARY
TO MANAGEMENT?

AS IMPORTANT as any internal factor for the development of a workable solution to the problems of a functioning management, may be the organization of the economy in which the enterprise lives. We have no final proof; but there is every indication that the problems are soluble only if the enterprise operates in a genuinely competitive market in which prices are established by consumer choice between alternative products. Certainly federalism can exist only in such a market; without it there can at best be functional decentralization.

The solution of the management problems requires an outside, impersonal yardstick of management performance. What has to be measured is not competence in a specialty but performance in making a business survive and prosper. The only yardstick—an imperfect one, to be sure—is performance in a genuine and effective market. Any other standard would not be objective and impersonal. It would be set by the very people whose performance it is supposed to measure. Or it would measure the wrong things: technical ability in a specialized function rather than general performance in the management of a whole, a business enterprise.

Much work and ingenuity have gone into the attempt to supply a substitute for market performance in the yardsticks of "socialist competition" which play so large a role in the Soviet economy. "Socialist competition" does indeed measure comparative productive efficiency. It can even measure technical competence. But it cannot measure managerial competence and performance. All "Socialist competition" must focus on the components of the job: the rate of speed of an operation, the amount of waste, the number of man-hours needed. But it cannot measure the efficiency of the whole. Also,

"Socialist competition" must take for granted the existing job: the product as it is, the existing process, the existing organization. But the most important function of management is to adapt product, process and organization to change, to foresee, to innovate. By its emphasis on past performance as the only measurement, "Socialist competition," however, is likely to discourage concern for the future on the part of management.

In support of this I would like to refer not to a Socialist economy but to an enterprise which by the nature of its business cannot apply any yardstick except that of "Socialist competition," even though it operates in a free-enterprise economy: the American Telephone Company. The telephone business being unavoidably a monopoly—for otherwise telephone service can simply not be rendered—admits of no test of performance in a competitive market. Instead, the American Telephone Company has developed standards of performance which are probably very much finer and more reliable than any of the standards of "Socialist competition" developed in Russia. They have also been used much longer. But every one of these standards refers to purely technical performances: the number of calls per operator, the time needed for the completion of a long-distance call, the number of billing clerks needed for a thousand customers, the number of lines out or order at any time, etc. Every managerial employee of the company, down to foremen and supervisors—from Seattle to Key West—competes against all the others in terms of these standards. But there is not a single standard of managerial performance.

The American Telephone Company is probably the most management-conscious of all our large enterprises. It is organized in autonomous companies, each with its own distinct territory and its own autonomous management; by all outward signs it is completely federalized. The management is also extremely conscious of the fact that it lacks any but technical standards. Yet it has not been able to develop standards of management performance. And because its standards have to be technical rather than managerial, it has been forced to keep its executives in technical work until they are at or very near the top. The reason is neither shortsightedness nor lack of effort; it is simply that the telephone business cannot operate in a competitive market.

By "competitive market" I do not mean that abstraction so dear to the theoretical economist and so utterly meaningless: "perfect competition." A "competitive market" does not necessarily exist because the productive resources of the economy are privately owned, and is not necessarily absent when they are nationalized. A "competitive market" could exist even in a regulated economy where the government, through monetary and credit policies, establishes the balance between consumption and capital accumulation. The only requirement for a "competitive market" is that the consumer have a real choice between alternative ways to satisfy the same want, and that this choice determine—or at least significantly affect—both the size of the market and the price of the product.

The telephone company therefore does not operate in a competitive market. In the United States the telephone is a necessity; the demand for it is largely independent of price, and probably even of quality of service. The one factor seriously affecting it is the general level of business over which the Telephone Company has no control. At the same time, telephone service in a given area can only be rendered by one enterprise, as all experience has shown. Similarly, an electric power company is not in a "competitive market" as far as the supply of electricity for domestic lighting is concerned. But in supplying electricity for domestic appliances it is at least partially in competition with other suppliers of energy and fuel: coal, gas, bottled gas, kerosene, etc. And there is a truly "competitive market" for industrial power, as the industrial users can build their own powerhouses and thus determine both the size of the market and the price.

The one system that by definition excludes the "competitive market" altogether is the one that we, following the Russian example, call today a "planned economy." Essential to a planned economy is the elimination of all traces of the "competitive market," and the complete transfer of all power over the size of the market and the price of a product from the consumer to the planners, that is, actually, to a new top-management group in control of all industry. Whether a planned economy can function at all except under steady and mounting inflation and under great and universal scarcity for all goods does not concern us here. But it certainly cannot have any outside, independent yardstick of managerial competence and performance.

At the same time, a planned economy depends more on the proper discharge of the top-management function and makes infinitely greater demands on its top management than any other form of economic organization we know. We might say that a planned economy rests on the proposition that management can be selected so as to be perfect and infallible. Such supreme confidence in human perfectibility may be forgiven people who, like most advocates of a "planned economy," have never seen a management in action and have little idea how imperfectly and how fallibly it operates. But surely it is somewhat rash to expect managerial perfection from a system that, by definition, must operate without an adequate criterion of management competence and management performance.

All evidence we have, indeed indicates that the one genuinely planned economy, the Russian economy, is in a perpetual management crisis. The recurrent "purges" of industrial managers, of Ministers and Commissars in charge of industries—who correspond to the chief executives of our large corporations—even, of the chief members of the Planning Commission itself—point both to a lack of a reliable yardstick and to failure in performance. There is, indeed, a striking parallel between the basic and irreparable weakness of the Russian political system of dictatorship and the basic weakness of the Russian economic system of planned economy. In both there is no orderly succession. It is not possible to prepare, train and test tomorrow's leaders, to establish criteria for legitimate succession or to get rid of an unsatisfactory leader except by force and purges. Both lack, above all, a constitutional principle. Just as any constitutional principle of government requires the outside check of an impersonal and incorruptible law, so does a constitutional principle of management organization—such as federalism—require the outside check of an impersonal and uncontrolled "competitive market."

In all our voluminous discussion about the market, its role in the solution of the problems of a functioning management is hardly ever mentioned. Yet is is certainly as important as any economic function the market may fulfill. In an industrial society it is probably the most important function of the market and the one for which there is no substitute.

EIGHTH PART: The Principles of Industrial Order: The Self-Governing Plant Community

CHAPTER 32

COMMUNITY GOVERNMENT AND BUSINESS MANAGEMENT

THE economic principles—income and employment prediction, profit-sharing and depression policy, and the principle of federalism—make possible an attack on the political and social problems of industrial society. But they do not solve them. They neither make management legitimate nor do they give the member the status and function of citizenship in the industrial enterprise.

These problems have their origin not in the structure of management but in its very function. No matter how management is organized, where it is recruited, and to whom it is accountable, its first responsibility will always be to the economic performance of the enterprise and not to the welfare and interests of the enterprise's members. It will always and of necessity see the enterprise under a management angle of vision.

Nor can these political and social problems of the enterprise be solved by changing the behavior of management, by getting the "right kind of people," by training them properly, or by stirring up their "social consciousness." It is of course highly desirable for management to contain men conscious of their social responsibility and skilled in the leadership of men. But they will still be managers, charged with an objective economic function and responsibility. They may be most popular personally and most effective in their own human relations. But they would be grossly remiss in their duty did they not always put economic performance first—and they would also enjoy no respect within the organization. The attempt, so popular today, to solve the political and social problems of the enterprise on the basis of personality, rather than on that of principle, cannot succeed. It can only lead to "Enlightened Managerial Despotism"; and all Enlightened Despotisms have ended in revolution.

We need a principle that expresses the fact that the interests of the enterprise and of its members are different interests. They differ in character: the one is exclusively economic; the other a mixture of the political, the economic and the social, with the social predominating. They also differ in direction: the one looks to the production of goods, the other largely to the production of status and the function of citizenship.

We do not only have divergent interests and objectives; we have two distinct institutions. The plant community is indeed contained in the enterprise—as the enterprise is contained in society. But it is no more a creature of the enterprise than the enterprise is a creature of government. Its existence does not rest on the needs and purposes of the enterprise but on the needs and purposes of the members as human beings. Management can neither make the plant community nor abolish it; it is spontaneous and irrepressible in every enterprise.

If the interests of enterprise and members were in conflict everywhere, an industrial order would be impossible. The only possible organization of the enterprise would be a class war that would go on regardless of the organization of society and would rage just as violently under Communism and Socialism as in a capitalist society. But while different, the two interests are in essential harmony in the most important area: the social area.

Because the enterprise has to fulfill at one and the same time two separate and divergent functions, it must be organized on a pluralist basis. Because divergence and conflict within the enterprise can be embedded in a strong foundation of harmony, because one and the same policy in the social sphere will satisfy both interests simultaneously, a pluralist organization will be possible and mutually fruitful. The enterprise needs a management responsible for economic performance and endowed with full authority to discharge its responsibility. It also needs a self-government of the plant community to discharge its social responsibility—subordinate but autonomous and endowed with authority over those functions that primarily pertain to the social life of the plant.

The autonomous self-government of the plant community cannot be the governing organ of the enterprise. Its functions are not only limited; they are also strictly subordinate. Management must remain the governing organ of the enterprise, and economic performance its governing rationale. Indeed, the self-government of the plant community can only be justified if it strengthens management and makes it more capable of managing, and if it furthers the economic performance of the enterprise. But at the same time the self-government of the plant community has to have its own organs and officers. Its legitimacy lies not in approval by management but in election by the plant community. And in matters pertaining exclusively to the social life of the plant community, its authority must be original rather than derived—just as management enjoys original and autonomous authority over all matters pertaining to economic performance.

The Scope of the Community Government

The relationship between management and the self-government of the plant community will not be like the relationship between two suns, each revolving in its own orbit and separated from the other by light-years of empty space. The plant-community self-government will indeed have its own function, authority and responsibility. But it will, on the whole, not deal with independent functions and will be forced to work with management—in co-operation but also in conflict.

There is one area only which is purely social, one area that is entirely incidental—even irrelevant—to economic performance. It comprises those functions of community life that are separate from job and work in time and space: transportation to and from work, parking, the cafeteria, recreation activities such as sports clubs, hobby clubs, picnics and parties, and educational activities.

There is another area in which the enterprise has no interest other than that the job be done. Here belong vacation schedules, most shift assignments and often assignments to particular crews. All the enterprise is interested in is that the right number of men with the proper qualifications report to shift and crew; who they are, specifically, does not matter.

In these areas the community government should be entirely on its own. Nor are they unimportant areas socially. To be sure, they do not loom large in the order of the universe. But what they lack in importance they make up in the intensity of the feeling they arouse. This goes particularly for cafeteria, recreation and education activities, picnics, etc. Here the workers meet as members of a community. Precisely because they have nothing to do with the job, and because participation in them cuts across lines of authority and departmental specialization, these activities are endowed with an impact for exceeding their weight. They also bring in the individual as an active participant, if not as a leader. They allow the display of the very abilities and qualities for which the work-situation offers the least outlet. For this reason management control of these activities is resented keenly. The worker feels about it the same way the Sudeten Germans in pre-Hitler Czechoslovakia felt about the regulation that only Czech speech would be understood by the stamp-sellers in the post offices and by the switchboard girls in the telephone exchanges. The Sudeten Germans had their own public schools, their own state-supported universities, their own state-supported theaters and opera houses—in short, full cultural autonomy in all the objectively important matters. But they were only conscious of the petty pinpricks of discrimination in their everyday contact with the Czech rulers. Resentment against these pinpricks was one of the main props of Hitler's campaign among the Sudeten Germans.

The transfer of responsibility and control for the objectively petty, but emotionally highly intense, community activities such as cafeteria, recreation, shift assignment, vacation schedule, etc., would thus remove a source of particularly intense irritation and antimanagement feeling. It would also give the community government a sphere of authority that is by no means unimportant to the members.

But it would certainly not make a major difference in the internal structure of the enterprise. All areas that go beyond these "easy" functions are, however, in some degree affected with an economic interest and require co-ordination between community government and management.

The concrete list of functions that are properly within the jurisdiction of the community government will differ from plant to plant. In general they will include six major categories, varying from matters where the economic interest is only incidental to matters where it predominates.

The first category would include safety and health matters—clearly employee matters primarily. Indeed, they have so little direct bearing on economic performance that they should be turned over to the plant community without reservations.

Then there are the functions where management has a legitimate and profound interest in the basic policy but not too much concern with its detailed administration. Included here would be guaranteed income and employment prediction, profit-sharing funds and other security benefits. In their establishment, management clearly has to take the lead. In their administration, the main responsibility should be that of the plant community, with management confined to technical advice and assistance and to veto power in case of dishonesty or gross mismanagement.

Another category includes most of the personnel-management functions: placement and assignment of job, training, absenteeism and turn-over, plant discipline and plant rules, transfer of workers between different departments and occupations, etc. Here management's interest in both policy and execution is fully equal to that of the plant community. They are functions to be handled jointly throughout.

Problems such as promotion within the ranks, wage differentials, job definition, job description, time and motion study, standards of output, incentive pay and the decision whether a cut in the work force should be made by laying off men or by spreading the work, also concern equally both sides. They will have to be decided jointly; indeed, they are being decided so today wherever a union contract is in force. But unlike the other problems of personnel-management, they are essentially conflict issues. While the administration of the policies agreed upon should be as much a joint affair as the administration of any other personnel-management policy, the policies themselves will have to be decided by negotiation and compromise rather than by co-operation.

The community government has an entirely different function in the vital area of technological change. Its job here is primarily one of communication. The worker also may have to be retrained. There may be a problem of reabsorbing him should his job be eliminated, or of compensating him should it be impossible to find work for him. But the most important, the most needed, service is to inform the worker of the meaning of the proposed change, and to inform management of the reaction of the workers to it. To establish communication on technological change would be one of the greatest contributions to the psychological security of the worker and to the economic performance of the enterprise. Only an organ of the plant community can perform it.

Finally the community government may operate directly in the interest of the enterprise's economic performance by promoting greater productivity. Though always put first in our discussions of labor-management co-operation, this may actually come last in time. It presupposes a predictable income and employment plan, the intelligent use of profit-sharing and a lessening of the resistance to high corporate salaries. It also aims at enlisting the self-government of the workers for a purpose that goes beyond its original function of organizing the social structure of the plant community. To be successful, co-operation on increased productivity must be based on an understanding on the part of the workers what the management function is, and why the enterprise is governed by economic performance. This can only come as a result of a considerable experience in community government. Otherwise co-operation to raise productivity might be denounced by the workers the moment a boom is over—whereas it is needed the most in times of slack business.

The Organization of the Community Government

There must be *one* central organ of the community government responsible for all the functions—just as there is one top management. To attempt to organize a plant as if it were a Boy Scout Troop, in which everybody has to have a function and a title, would seriously interfere with efficient production. It would destroy the usefulness of the whole concept and could only lead to a frittering away of its social effects. That all the committees for joint work in the community areas which exist today, have had so little effect on the social climate of the plant community is as much a result of this frittering away of energies as of the resistance of management to the principle of community self-government.

This organ of self-government must be close to the employees. The unit which it represents must be small enough for the individual employee to be able to participate actively. It must be a truly local government. A general committee responsible for all matters of community self-government in an enterprise employing twenty-five thousand men in nine plants would be meaningless. It would be too far from the concrete problems to be effective, and too remote from the concrete worker to be *his* self-government. The individual plant—in very large plants even the individual department—will have to be the unit of self-government.

What should be management's relationship to the community government? It should be based on the fact that to be effective this government has to be a *self*-government. The closest analogy within the enterprise is the relationship between the top management of the whole and the managements of the units in a federally organized enterprise. The one difference is that the worker by virtue of his position and function cannot be given managerial responsibility and experience in the sphere of economics and can obtain it only in the social sphere.

Management's function should be the setting—jointly with the community government—of clear standards of performance rather than supervision over the community government or interference with it. In those functions that touch so closely on economic performance as to require a management right to interfere, management should rely upon a power of protest or veto rather than exercise a right of approval and sanction.

Above all, it is absolutely necessary that the existence and the powers of the community government not rest on management's good-will but be grounded in a legally binding obligation. Community government is not a substitute for the union. On the contrary, to be strong and independent, community government must be anchored in the union contract.

The autonomous self-government of the plant community introduces a new *principle* rather than startlingly new practices. In practice, such matters as safety or health have been put under joint committees of management and workers in a great many industries with satisfactory results. Internal discipline has become a matter for joint handling through the grievance procedure. The assignment of shifts and of jobs is everywhere determined by the union agreement if not dictated unilaterally by the union. Lay-offs and promotions follow rules set by the plant community rather than by management. Even hiring, in a very large number of industries, has ceased to be under the exclusive control of management; in some industries it has passed under the exclusive control of the union. Nowhere, however, has the principle been adopted that the management of its social life is the community's own responsibility. But it is precisely this principle that is important and likely to have a decisive impact on the problems of enterprise, management, plant community and union.

The self-government of the plant community—subordinate to, and limited by, the enterprise's need for economic performance, but autonomous within its limits—is the answer to the enterprise's demand for a "managerial attitude" of its members, and for acceptance on their part of the economic rationale of the enterprise. It satisfies the members' needs for citizenship, recognition and opportunities; it alone can solve the problem of the "split allegiance" between enterprise and union, as well as the problems of union function, union cohesion and union leadership.

At the same time it will not undermine management's authority and power. On the contrary, it is likely to increase them and to bring about the acceptance of the governmental authority of the enterprise as a legitimate authority.

CHAPTER 33

"MANAGEMENT MUST MANAGE"

WE found three major demands which the enterprise must make on the plant community. It must demand of the worker the "managerial attitude." It must demand of the worker an understanding of the economic rationale of the enterprise and an acceptance of the yardstick of profitability and productivity. And it must obtain out of the plant community a steadily increasing supply of trained and tested people to fill the positions in the "industrial middle class." All three demands are met by an autonomous self-government of the plant community; indeed, only the autonomous self-government of the plant community can fulfill them.

The managerial attitude can only result from managerial experience. Indoctrination, propaganda, training courses or books can never give it. They are very useful things for someone who has the experience. Without it, however, they are bound to be ineffectual.

A very nice illustration of this is given in one of the recent studies of the National Planning Association on the *Causes of Industrial Peace.*[1] This study tells the story of a highly trained labor economist in high government office, a friend of the union leader and a student of unionism—in other words, a man with a great deal of theoretical knowledge and training—who was put in as the company's labor relations manager when the union was first recognized. But it was not until he had taken over the job that he began to understand what is involved in labor relations.

Then, in his own words, "he took a very intensive post-graduate course in economics." He learned, for instance, that the profit margin on a $75

[1] NPA Case Studies No. 4, "Hickey-Freeman Company-Amalgamated Clothing Workers of America," by Donald B. Straus, Washington, D.C., January, 1949.

suit was around $2. He also learned that each suit had some 200 operations performed upon it and that if you increased the rate on each operation by just one penny you could easily wipe out the company's profit. But the most valuable lesson in his post-graduate course was this: those figures in a theoretical discussion are lifeless. The same figures when you are responsible for making the decisions can become very terrifying realities. The result of this "post-graduate" experience was to make Dr. Stone a very cautious and often meticulous bargainer.

In the modern enterprise the worker is necessarily without any experience in the *management of the enterprise's business*. The rank-and-file job-holders—whether of production, technical or clerical jobs—obviously cannot be given authority and responsibility for decisions regarding the enterprise's business. They cannot be organized on a decentralized basis. The very definition of these jobs is that they take orders rather than give them.

Attempts to give managerial experience through advisory boards, such as the "junior board of directors" pioneered by the McCormick Spice Company in Baltimore, can be effective if the members of these boards are themselves in genuine, though subordinate, management positions. For other employees they would be meaningless play-acting. They might give some knowledge; they can never give a genuine experience such as can only come from being actually responsible for a decision that really affects the work and the job. All attempts to give the workers this experience through placing worker-representatives on the Board of Directors or into top management must prove similarly futile. Whereve i tried—in Germany, Austria or Czechoslovakia after 1918, in France and Great Britain today—they have failed. Even if the worker's representative knows enough to be able to take a real part in the decisions, the problems on which he participates will be far too remote from the workers' own problems and from the workers' own jobs to be meaningful to him, let alone to the workers whom he represents.

But the worker can be given *managerial experience in the government of the plant community*. To be sure, this is managerial experience with very different problems; but the important point is that it is experience in the making of real decisions, in the development of effective policies and in the handling of conflicts and compromises. It is also experience with problems of the plant as a whole. It is experience which is as easily accessible to the worker as experience in the management of the enterprise's business is inaccessible to him. And unlike the management experience, which the worker can acquire in the union, it is not "anti" experience but is focused on the satisfaction of worker needs in the enterprise and in harmony with it.

The number of men who at any one time can acquire firsthand this managerial experience is necessarily limited. But the effect should permeate the entire plant. There will presumably be considerable rotation in office. Also, the governing organ of the plant community will have to work through local representatives who will carry the spirit and the attitude of the governing organ throughout the plant, and who, in order to be effective, will have to be kept closely informed on decisions. Finally the members of the plant-community government will inevitably be the men best qualified to make "public opinion" in the plant, so that their attitudes should speedily be reflected throughout the whole plant. It is amazing, for instance, how the managerial experience of the members of the plant government at the American Cast Iron Pipe Company in Birmingham, Alabama, is reflected throughout the entire plant and its thousands of workers. The members of the community government are the men whom the workers respect and to whom they look for leadership. The worker is willing to listen to them; he is eager to adapt his thinking and his attitudes to their thinking and their attitudes. If they adopt a "managerial attitude" based on their own managerial experience, the whole plant adopts a "managerial attitude" based on their example.

It is for this reason also that the plant-community self-government seems likely to be able to overcome the major obstacles to successful communication between enterprise and workers. If management tells the workers that the enterprise is in economic difficulties and that greater productivity and efficiency are required, it is almost certain to be dismissed as mere propaganda. If management, however, can convince the members of the plant self-government of the seriousness of the economic situation, the worker will be willing to listen.

The self-government of the plant community should give the workers an immediate and effective experience of the economic realities. It will bring out clearly and directly the relationship between the worker's needs and desires, and profitability and productivity. It will actually give them a sphere in which they *make* economic decisions.

The governing organ will have to have a budget which it itself will allocate. Today the expense of the community life of the plant is, by and large, buried in the general expenses of the enterprise. Not one worker in a million knows how much it costs to keep the plant safe or to run a decent cafeteria. If he knows the figures, he does not believe them. The enterprise today gets no thanks for its activities on behalf of the community; it often increases the resentment against itself and management. I strongly urge that the self-government of the community be left to decide what to spend these sums on and how. The amount to be made available by the enterprise for the social activities of the plant should be set by contract and should be paid directly to the worker—either as an "extra" fifteen or twenty cents an hour or as a lump sum of so many hundreds of dollars a year. The self-government should itself develop the specific program and purposes, should get its program approved by its constituents and should collect the money from the worker.

Finally, the autonomous self-government of the plant community would seem to be particularly well equipped to satisfy the enterprise's demand for able and trained candidates for promotion. The men serving ir. the plant-community offices receive a training as good as any that can be given to a foreman or to a junior member of middle management. Their training is not primarily in production and certainly not in engineering or in specific skills. But they learn to see the plant as a whole. They learn what management is all about. Above all, they are bound to acquire skill and understanding in the management of men—the very skill and understanding most members of middle management lack the most, and the one which it is most difficult to give to a man in a production job.

Management Authority and the Plant Community

Whatever the benefits that an autonomous self-government of the plant community might bring the enterprise, they would not be worth the price of a weakening of management's ability to function. Yet the immediate objection will certainly be that an autonomous plant government destroys management's authority. It will even be said that it makes it impossible for management to manage.

It is undoubtedly management's duty to manage; and management's proper function must be preserved. Its authority must be strengthened;

for management in this country today has been weakened in many areas to a point where it cannot efficiently discharge functions it is responsible for discharging. But *what* is management to manage— everything? The government that claims everything for its province, is likely to be considered without title to govern anything.

Management's first responsibility is for the economic performance of the enterprise. The governmental power of management is a necessary power because it is human beings who produce. But the social organization of the plant society is properly a management responsibility only insofar as it affects the economic performance of the human organization. Basically the two things are separate. Where the social organization is either purely incidental or irrelevant to economic performance, assumption of responsibility for it on the part of management seems not just superfluous; it must weaken management's proper authority.

Wherever managements attempt to manage the social life of the plant —and in the absence of an organ of self-government management has to assume this burden by default—resentment and resistance are created. The men feel that they are being treated as children.

A good example is that of one big oil company which has built up a complete system of sickness, retirement and death benefits for its workers. Investigation showed that the worker himself put other things, for instance job security, far above these benefits—and a minute fraction of the money spent on these benefits would have given almost complete job security. A substantial number of workers actually resented the company's policies. A worker loses all his accumulated claims if he leaves the company's employ or is discharged for cause. This seemed eminently fair to management, as the benefits are financed entirely by the company. But to the workers these provisions seemed a subtle bribe to keep them in the company's employ however dissatisfied they might be. Some even suspected that the threat of dismissal and of a loss of benefits was being used to force workers to "toe the line," and to keep their mouths shut rather than voice a grievance. The resentment was so strong and so general as to be the major reason why the workers joined a union—and a particularly militant one. Yet management had never even suspected it.

Management cannot even make the right decision on most plant-community matters. Because of its mistakes in these matters, its judgment and competence in the economic sphere may become suspect in the plant.

Recently the president of a fairly large company sent out a personal letter to employees to tell them that business, after several years of unprecedent wartime and postwar activity, had begun to fall off. He stated the economic facts frankly and clearly, and warned that budgets might have to be cut and men be laid off. He outlined the measures the company planned to counteract the slump. A few weeks later an outside research organization made a survey in the plants. It found local management, supervisors and workers almost unanimous in their belief that top management had shown so often that it did not know what the *social* problems of the plant were, that there was no reason to believe that its judgment was any better on the *economic* problems of the enterprise—if indeed the falling off in business were not directly the result of management incompetence. What makes this such a convincing and typical example is that each man interviewed began by quoting specific policy decision directly affecting him, which proved that management did not know what was going on. The lack of respect for top management was not based on ideology or on general principles but on concrete experience of management's remoteness from the social organization of the plant.

But today we do not really have to ask the question whether it is to management's interest to manage the social life of the plant community, or whether management is capable of it. Management today, as a rule, no longer has the authority for these decisions. All it has is the privilege of being blamed when something goes wrong. In most of the areas that are likely to fall under the jurisdiction of the plant government, management has been forced to share its power with the union, if not to leave to the union altogether the determination of policies and rules. But along with the financial burden, management has retained the full responsibility for the administration of these policies and rules. Since every one of the rules represents a "concession" that is bitterly and publicly bemoaned by management, management will never get the credit for their fair and successful administration. Whatever goes wrong is management's fault, however.

An extreme example is the administration of the internal rules of the railroad workers' unions. Management has accepted the seniority rules of the unions as the sole basis for the assignment of "runs"; management has no more to do with the setting of these rules than the Man in the Moon. At the same time, management has no authority or control over the "crew-callers" who actually assign crews to runs. These men obtain their jobs on the basis of seniority in the clerk's union irrespective of background, training or experience; they can rarely be removed or disciplined for incompetence or mistakes. Yet management is fully responsible for their mistakes; every railroad pays hundreds of thousands of dollars each year for mistakes in "crew-calling." As this is being written half a dozen railroads face strike threats arising out of unsettled disputes over "crew calling." These disputes convince the men both that management is out to wreck the union, and that management is incompetent. Yet—worst of all—every railroad management would consider the suggestion that it turn over "crew-calling" to the unions as an attack upon its "management prerogatives."

It may be argued that management by itself can discharge the responsibility for the social structure of the plant community. It may also be argued that management would be stronger if it had full authority in this area. But it cannot be argued that management is strengthened by accepting responsibility when it no longer has authority. It is the most elementary political rule that any government will lose power, respect and integrity if it accepts responsibility without commensurate authority. If authority without responsibility turns into tyranny, responsibility without authority turns into ridicule. Today's management does not have the sole authority. By relieving itself of the full responsibility it could only gain in strength and prestige.

So far our argument has been negative: the self-governing plant community does not weaken management. There is an even stronger positive argument: the self-governing plant community strengthens management. Withdrawal from those functions which are only incidental to the economic performance of the enterprise would endow management with a new authority in respect to all the functions relevant to the enterprise's economic performance. Today the assertion of management's authority is always open to the charge that it rests on nothing but management's desire to dominate. Because management today gives orders in so many areas which have little to do with the enterprise's economic performance, all its orders are suspect and resented. If management establishes clearly that it will not give orders in those areas which concern the worker's social life rather than the economic performance of the plant, its orders, requests and decisions should carry with them the assumption that they are indeed based squarely upon the economic necessities and in the common interest.

At the same time, through the plant government the problems of the enterprise will be brought daily to the attention of the most influential members of the plant community. Most of them will not come up as conflict issues but as data relevant to a joint decision. They will come up not as abstract principles but in relation to concrete, specific and immediate concerns. They will thus be understandable; and there will be willingness—if not a desire—to understand them. That the management representative will often have to say that this or that decision, while plausible, would not work, or that this or that goal could better be reached by some other means than that proposed, will in itself be helpful. In every such case the management representative will be forced to talk concretely and specifically on a concrete and specific point rather than in vague and meaningless generalities about "management prerogatives." The translation of the general into the particular, which is precisely what the worker cannot do for himself, will thus be done for him.

At the same time the plant government creates a channel for the communication of the nature of the management function to the workers. Understanding of management's problem and respect for its job cannot be communicated directly from management to worker. All that can ever be communicated directly is that picture of the "boss" entertaining other bosses at the golf club which plays so prominent and so dreary a part in our company magazines. All the worker can ever deduce from it is that the boss has it pretty easy and gets paid for what other people would be willing to pay for, had they only the money and the time.

But the men in the self-government of the plant have themselves to perform management functions. They are in a position where they are almost forced to come to an understanding of the work and functions performed by management. They will not necessarily come to like the "boss"; nor is this either a desirable or a necessary goal. But they will come to understand his function. Even if they do not acquire respect for the people actually in management—and they will of course

learn to distinguish between competent and incompetent managers—
they are bound to acquire understanding and respect for the management function itself. This is infinitely more important than "love" for
the boss which, after all, caters only to management's vanity and does
not help it in any way in its performance.

The best example is probably the experience of the one American
company that has actually introduced effective worker self-government
in the plant community, the American Cast Iron Pipe Company in
Birmingham, Alabama, a company employing several thousand men,
both white and colored. What makes this example so interesting is
that this company started out some twenty-five years ago on an entirely different tack. At the death of the founder who had built up
the business, the workers became the owners of the capital stock of
the company. The idea of worker ownership, however, simply did not
produce results. The workers themselves are the first to admit that
they were not much interested in it. Some of them even realize that
financially they might have benefited more under a straight profit-
sharing plan; with the ownership of the business vested in the workers,
the company has not been able to raise capital on the outside and,
therefore, had to plow back the bulk of its profits into its expansion
programs.

But over the years the company has developed a system of worker
self-government. Starting from the realization that individual profit-
sharing dividends were not what the worker needed, and that the use
of profits for collective purposes of the plant community required an
organ of the workers, the company has developed a system of workers'
councils—one for the whole plant, one for the special problems of the
colored employees—which are the governing organs of the plant community.

This has not led to any weakening of the position of management.
It has on the contrary greatly strengthened management. The workers
now themselves understand that the business needs a professional management. They understand that this management must have full authority over all matters affecting the company's economic performance.
They understand why this management must be paid adequate salaries.
They have even come to understand why the enterprise must operate
at a profit and why it is to the interests of the workers to have maximum efficiency and maximum profitability. The usual attitude on such

matters as disciplining or lay-offs has become completely reversed. It is now management which tends to intervene on behalf of a worker whose discharge for a breach of discipline or plant rules is recommended by the workers' council; it is management which usually recommends that men should not be laid off in a temporary business setback.

This company is no utopia. It has its troubles and conflicts—including a rather tense union-management situation. But it has succeeded in gaining understanding of, and acceptance for, the management function.

CHAPTER 34

THE WORKER AND HIS PLANT
GOVERNMENT

THE need for a responsible self-government of the plant community runs through all our work in the study of human relations in the industrial plant. The central finding in this work has been that the employee needs and demands the *actual experience of responsible participation* in his own job and in those affairs of the plant that concern him directly.

A few illustrations—largely taken from my own experience—show this clearly.

During the last war one of the big aircraft companies suffered a sudden drop in morale and output throughout the plant. This was all the more perturbing as this company—perhaps alone among the aircraft companies in the region—had managed to build a high *esprit de corps* among its workers. Management was caught completely unprepared by the sudden outbreak of workers' dissatisfaction and of open hostility—with a "quickie strike" apparently not too far off. The cause for this change in the social atmosphere was found to have been a management decision to hire trained professionals to run the Red Cross, the Blood Bank and the fund-raising campaigns of the plant hitherto run by the workers. Management was motivated purely by a desire to help. It felt that the responsibility for these campaigns and drives put too heavy a burden on the volunteers who had been carrying it. It also felt that the campaigns themselves would be more successful if handled by professionals.

To the workers, however, these campaigns had been something of their own. They had started them by themselves. Leadership in them gave a scope of action and responsibility to some of the most responsible and most ambitious workers. It gave them prestige, a standing in the plant and a standing in the community. They knew that the campaigns lacked the professional finish; but they wanted to overcome the difficulties and weaknesses themselves. Management's action, therefore, appeared to them not only a vote of nonconfidence. It appeared a petty interference in affairs of the workers which were in no way management's concern. It took months, after control had been turned back to the workers, before the damage done by management's well-intentioned action was repaired.

The experience of one of the large power companies points the same moral. Originally each of the two adjoining big cities served by the company had had its own independent power system. There are still some different policies in force in the two areas, among them different life insurance programs.

In the one area the program was notoriously inefficient. The workers did not receive sufficient protection and paid high premiums. Yet more than eighty per cent of the workers in the area were enrolled in the plan. The other area had one of the most up-to-date life insurance plans with low premiums and high protection. Less than forty per cent of the workers, however, took advantage of it even though the company paid a substantial share of the premium, whereas it did not contribute at all to the premium in the first area.

Management for a long time had felt very critical of the life insurance program in the first city. It finally called in a firm of insurance experts to find out how the adequate insurance program in force in the other city could be extended to cover all workers. Much to their own and to management's surprise, the experts came to the conclusion that the notoriously inefficient program of the first area should be made to cover the entire system—if necessary even without improvements in coverage and premiums.

The workers in the first area were deeply attached to their inefficient program, though they knew very well that it was inefficient and expensive. But unlike the other program, it was their own. A group of workers twenty-five years ago had themselves picked the insurance company, had arranged for the program and had written the contract. All the agents were fellow employees who looked after the insurance business in their spare time. That the company did not contribute to the premium was in itself a factor in the success of the program as it made the men feel all the more proud of it.

In the other city, the program was considered just another company-sponsored activity. The company had negotiated the contract and the insurance company had sent its own employees to act as agents. It was, of course, financially a much more attractive program. But its sole attraction was financial, whereas the other program gave the workers social and prestige satisfactions far beyond the financial.

The best evidence is in the contest on "My Job" which General Motors ran in 1947, and in which 175,000 workers entered individual essays. In two General Motors plants in which the recreation programs are entirely organized and run by the workers themselves, recreation activities were among the major sources of job satisfaction—outranking even security, supervision or pay. But in plants where the recreation programs were under the control of management, the satisfaction was very much smaller. There were signs of dissatisfaction, if not of resentment, in those plants where management not only sponsors but actually runs, the activities—even though among those were the plants with the most comprehensive programs.

The autonomous self-governing plant community is also the only way to satisfy the individual's demand for opportunity. It creates the opportunities for advancement outside the economic value system which the society of the plant today so conspicuously lacks. The positions in the community government, whether at the top, that is, in the governing organ of the plant community, or in the department or division, would carry prestige. They would give the worker a new dimension for the fulfillment of his ambition, the display of his abilities and the acquisition of social prestige. A man who serves for any length of time on the council of the plant community is a big man in the plant and in the town. He has known responsibility for large affairs. He has been given tangible proof of the esteem in which his fellow workers hold him, and of their belief in his integrity and competence.

The autonomous, self-governing plant community is not a social panacea.

But it overcomes the gulf between the groups in the enterprise. It establishes communication. It makes it possible for workers and middle management to see the enterprise from the angle of vision of top management, and for top management to see the enterprise from the angle of vision of the worker and of middle management. It makes impossible the maintenance of the belief in the "slot-machine man" and brings all groups in the enterprise face to face with the others as they really are.

The self-government of the plant would consist of workers. At the same time it would work closely with management. It is inevitable that all the issues of the plant, all the things the workers wants to know, all his questions, complaints, doubts and bewilderments, would come up for discussion. They would come up in the normal course of business and always in connection with concrete decisions, that is, in a form in which they can easily be understood. This applies not only to the areas formally within the scope of the plant-community self-government but with even greater force to the areas outside. What the worker wants to know about his job and what he does not know about it, what the worker wants to know about the product and what he does not know about it—all these problems of integration of worker and process, worker and product, and worker and team would come out in the open. The problems of placement and of fitting the job to the man, the organization of the group into a work team, the authority and function of the supervisor would similarly come to the surface. This would not automatically solve these problems—in fact, some will be very difficult to solve. But it will create the political and psychological conditions necessary for their solution; and otherwise they cannot be solved at all.

I saw only recently a telling demonstration of the difference between a situation where the plant community itself makes the decision and one where management retains the decision-making power. A company in Indiana decided to develop a better placement method. Another company in the same city—a plant of about the same size and engaged in very similar work—heard about this and decided to follow along. Both companies decided that it takes about six months after a new man has come into the plant before he can be placed successfully, and that only the foreman, together with the man himself, can work out the right placement. Both hired the same man from a State University as their consulting psychologist. And both companies came out with pretty much the same placement manual. In the one company the new placement method works; in the other it is about to be given up as a total failure. In one it is stanchly supported by foremen and workers, in the other it is sabotaged and resented by them. In the one company the problem has been solved; in the other it has become a running sore.

The only difference between the two companies was that in the one the plant community decided, while in the other it was merely consulted. The difference was there right from the start. In the one company management called a meeting of the foremen, explained its idea and asked the foremen to elect six of their members to think through the problem and work out a manual. It did the same with the workers with ten years or more service in the plant. Finally, it asked the union to nominate a few shop stewards to the committee. In the other company similar meetings were called; but instead of asking foremen and workers to elect their representatives, management appointed a number of men, leaving out the union altogether.

In the one plant the outside consultant was hired by a foreman-worker committee and worked for it. In the other plant management simply hired the same man. In the one plant the committee did all the work, brought in other foremen and workers to hear their opinions, tested out its own ideas and finally wrote the manual. In the other plant the personnel department did all this, with the committee acting in a purely advisory capacity, etc. It was the plant that left the work to the committee that came up with a workable plan; in the other plant foreman and worker interest evaporated long before the work was done and the final plan was very largely a copy of the manual developed by the committee in the first plant. And even though the foremen in the second company know very well that the new methods work successfully next door, they have nothing but contempt for it in their own plant; it is "another one of those gadgets management thinks up to make more paper work for the foreman." As for the workers in that plant, they consider it a sinister management conspiracy. In the first plant the union is solidly behind the plan, in the other—organized by the same local of the same union—the union considers any application of the plan a breach of the contract and cause for a justified grievance.

The most telling result is the difference in the social standing of the foremen and workers who participated in the work. In the one company they have become leaders—expressed, for instance, in election to all kinds of offices in the foremen club or in the plant's athletic association. And they talk about the plan to anybody at the drop of a hat. In the other plant they pretend that they never even heard of it.

Equally striking is the difference in the effect on management's attitude toward its workers. In the one plant management talks about the other things it intends to ask the plant community to do, and about the intelligence, enthusiasm and loyalty of the men. In the other management has convinced itself that there must be something seriously wrong with its foremen and workers, and that they are all in need of psychological treatment.

This tendency to explain the failure of a human-relations policy in the plant where management attempts to run the plant community itself, as evidence that the worker is emotionally unbalanced, is perhaps the most serious result of community government *for* rather than *by* the plant community. It must lead to a concept of the worker as both emotionally ill and moldable by psychological techniques, that is as remote from reality as the concept of the "slot-machine man," as mechanistic and as destructive. Unfortunately, it is only too often the conclusion which management draws from the failure of its attempts to create a "constructive attitude" in the plant by doing things for the worker.

It is, of course, always easier to blame trouble on the emotional maladjustment of the other person than to admit that one's own behavior and policies fall short of perfection. There is no doubt that there are as many maladjusted people among the employees as there are in any other group. There is as legitimate a place in the plant for a psychiatrist or clinical psychologist as there is for a plant doctor. But the main reason why so many employee-relations people in American industry today have come to the conclusion that the roots of the social problems of the plant are outside the plant and in the worker's personal maladjustments, is precisely that their human-relations programs have failed because they were management programs *for* the employee.

No program based on the conclusion that the employee is a neurotic can possibly do anything but harm. It has given up respect for the employee as a human being. It has given up the conviction that the interest of the enterprise as well as the needs of the individual demand the fullest utilization of each employee's abilities and ambitions. Instead, it considers these abilities and ambitions as psychopathic symptoms which have to be "deflected into innocuous channels." Instead of aiming at making the plant into a place where normal people—including the whole range of "normal" deviations from the norm—can find the fulfillment they need as men and citizens, it sees in any manifestation of this need a sign of emotional illness. And the only reaction of the plant to such an approach on the part of management is violent resentment.

This may seem a gross exaggeration. But unfortunately it is the direction which a good deal of the human-relations work in this country has been taking. It is inevitable for human-relations work to degenerate into this caricature of itself if it is based on management control of the plant community. The only basis on which human-relations work can be effective is the responsible participation of the community in the actual decision.

The Industrial Middle Class in the Plant Community

So far our discussion of community government has emphasized the rank-and-file worker, whether manual or clerical. But the application of the principle of community government to the industrial middle class promises to be even more productive.

The individual member of the industrial middle class—foreman, technician, engineer, salesman, accountant, designer, plant manager, etc.—either discharges managerial authority or performs professional duties. But the scope of his authority is so small and he is so dependent on management's decisions and policies that he cannot be given a genuine managerial experience or attain the view of the whole of the "managerial attitude." His job cannot be organized on the federal principle; often, he cannot even be given authority through decentralization. The scope and responsibility of the typical supervisory, technical or even middle-management job is too narrow for meaningful authority.

Socially, the member of the industrial middle class is often worse off than the rank-and-file worker. He has no communication with top management; he has also little communication with the other members of his own group. Often he does not work together with them but with the rank and file. Considerations of prestige and authority forbid him to join the community of his subordinates; even if he would want to, he would not be readily accepted. He is isolated; he is caught between the top management on which he depends for job and promotion, and the rank and file—including the union—on whom he depends for performance.

He is even more restricted in his opportunities than the rank-and-file worker who, at least, has the union and the informal social organization of the plant in which to find leadership and recognition. The supervisor or the technician has only the necessarily narrow and purely economic opportunity of a promotion. His only chance to assert himself is often by "throwing his weight around" and by compensating himself for his lack of genuine authority and status by bullying his subordinates. But the petty white-collar despot who takes it out on those that cannot hit back is hardly an asset to the enterprise; he will only create inefficiency, if not sabotage and bitterness.

But while individual members of the middle class cannot be given meaningful and independent authority, the *group* carries tremendous responsibility and tremendous prestige. It can be given very real authority if it is organized as a self-government.

The self-governing organ of the industrial middle class has to be separate from the self-government of the rank and file. In many cases it will be management's organ for dealing with the community government of the workers. Unlike the community government of the rank and file, that of the middle class does not need a basis in a contract between management and union. It derives its standing from the delegation of managerial power to it which makes it a part of the management structure. It need not be very highly organized—though it has to be a good deal more formal than mere periodic meetings of the management group or the appointment of a few committees on specific problems. Its constituency will be quite small in all but the very largest enterprises; it will number in the hundreds rather than in the thousands.

But the main difference between the two is that the community government of the middle class will have less jurisdiction over social matters and much more over managerial matters pertaining to economic performance. Its three main functions will be: communication with top management; the personnel-management problems of the middle group themselves—selection and training of men for supervisory and technical jobs, their training in the job, their rotation between departments, etc.—and the representation of the enterprise before the community government of the rank and file, especially in rank-and-file personnel-management matters. Every one of these functions has a social aspect. But they have at least as much to do with the efficient utilization of the enterprise's human resources, that is, with economic function. It would, therefore, be as appropriate to talk about the community government of the industrial middle class as the means to extend the principle of federalism beyond the top-management level, as it is to consider it as an application of the principle of autonomous community self-government. And the industrial middle class, indeed, both participates in the government of the enterprise and is subject to it. It both enjoys the prestige and satisfactions of the managerial position and suffers from the social isolation of the cog in the mass-production machine.

It will be said against the entire idea of plant self-government that the employees will not be able to manage the social life of the plant community as efficiently as the trained professional put in charge by the management. It will also be said that a good deal of the work is purely technical and therefore not capable of discharge by a workers' self-government, in which political considerations, factionalism, personal ambition, if not outright demagoguery, will inevitably play a large part. The argument misses the point. There is no reason to assume that the plant community will dismiss the safety engineer or the doctor and attempt to have technical or professional work done by untrained men. It is the direction and decision, not necessarily the execution, that will be in its hands. There will certainly be incompetence; there may also be dishonesty. But that argument holds good against any self-government anywhere. It is not the aim of self-government to produce the best possible government (which is an illusion anyhow), but the most responsible government and the one most willingly accepted and supported by the citizens. Above all, the choice is not between a form of organization that does the job well and one that may do it badly. The choice is between one that does not and cannot do the job at all, and one that will do at least a part of it. For the main job is not technical; it is to create a functioning plant community. And that can only be done through an autonomous self-government of the plant community.

CHAPTER 35

PLANT SELF-GOVERNMENT AND THE UNION

THE establishment of the plant community endows the union with a new role: it must take an active and constructive part. Union participation is absolutely essential for the success of the plant's self-government. Self-government must stand on a firmer foundation than management's pleasure. Otherwise it will degenerate into rank paternalism and into a "company union," and will rightly come to be regarded by the plant as a device to buy off the worker with honeyed words and empty titles. A plant government that rests on management's good intentions alone will be unable to oppose management. It will be like that Russian parliament called by an absolute Czar that was dissolved the first time its vote went contrary to the Czar's wishes. At best it will be an advisory body; it cannot have any real authority or enjoy any real respect.

But the only firm foundation for the plant government is in the union contract. What is in the contract is no longer a promise that can be revoked at will. It has legally binding form, and it has a strong champion willing and able to fight.

The only alternative to union participation in the plant government is union hostility and opposition. If the union does not regard the plant government as its very own, it must regard it as an attempt to undermine, if not to "bust" the union. The plant government then becomes the greatest spur to the union to intensify the war for the exclusive allegiance of the worker. The first casualty in this war would be the plant self-government itself.

This needs all the more emphasis because of the tendency of many managements today to use the device of community self-government to fight the union or at least to "neutralize" it. This can only destroy the community self-government. It must destroy the worker's trust in the one effective principle of social order in an industrial society. And it must make the union both stronger and more hostile to management and enterprise. This policy makes about as much sense as an attempt of a maiden aunt to break up the happy marriage of a favorite nephew by being extra-nice to the "poor boy" and extra-nasty to the young wife. Even if she succeeds in breaking up the marriage, she will have made mortal enemies of both the nephew and his wife. Any management attempt to use the self-government of the plant community as a means to pull the worker away from the union and toward exclusive allegiance to management, is bound to have the same result.

Fullest union participation in the self-government of the plant community is also in the direct interest of enterprise and management. The foremost problem of the enterprise in its relation to the union is that of the "split allegiance" of the worker. An autonomous plant government will not eliminate the conflicts that underlie and justify the rise of the union. To expect it to establish the millenium of sweetness and light is a complete misunderstanding—above all a misunderstanding of the nature of power and of the function of conflict. But in the self-governing plant community the conflicts would be firmly embedded in common ground. In the normal day-to-day relationship management and the members of the enterprise would be joined in a common task and a common purpose. The conflicts would lose none of their sharpness. But they would lose their bitterness. They would cease to be the focus around which all relations are organized. Today the conflicts embitter all relations, just as a few drops of bile will embitter a whole dish. But if contained within a functioning plant community, the conflicts would become the subordinate rather than the dominant element in the relationship. Instead of the competition for the allegiance of the worker against each other, management and union would both share in a new and strong allegiance of the worker to the enterprise.

Union participation in the plant's self-government would greatly strengthen management's position in its dealings with the union. The local union leaders would almost be bound to be men who either serve or have served in the community government. They would not therefore be any more pro-management or any easier to deal with. But they should have an understanding of management's problems and of the concrete problems of the plant, the lack of which adds so much to the bitterness of the union-management relations today. In most cases the local leaders, however adamant on conflict issues, would also have respect for the men in management with whom they have to deal and would be respected by them in turn.

At the same time the union would become a broad channel of communication between the enterprise and the workers. The position and function of the union official in the shop—the shop steward or union committeeman—would be changed entirely. The shop steward undoubtedly performs important management functions; indeed in many plants he carries more managerial authority and power than the official representative of management, the foreman. He in effect sets or approves standards, determines discipline and decides disagreements between workers and between worker and foreman. Yet today he exercises this managerial power primarily *against* management and *against* the enterprise.

In a functioning community self-government in which the union participates, the shop steward would become the local agent of the self-government, acting both as a liaison between the workers and their leaders and between the governing body and the workers. He would not be an agent of management. Yet he would no longer exercise his authority against management but in conjunction with it. There is probably nothing that would do as much to restore the position and prestige of the foreman and to make his job manageable and meaningful again as such a change in the role of the shop steward. Indeed, wherever we have taken the smallest step toward bringing the shop steward into the management of community tasks—for instance, in joint work on safety in some Standard Oil refineries, in a joint attack on the causes of grievances in some of the steel companies, or in a suggestion system—the improvement in the authority and prestige of the foreman and in his ability to act as the "first line of management" has been phenomenal.

Another new union task is bound to grow out of union participation in the plant self-government: the bringing together of the industrial community of the plant and of the local community of city and town. In several industrial cities, especially those of middle size—Akron, Ohio; Windsor, Ontario; or Flint, Michigan—the union has already become a major factor in civic life and the link between town and plant. But in these cities today the union exploits its strategic position in order to mobilize the community against the enterprise and against management. It uses its social and political power mainly to create political pressure for union demands. It does not yet attempt to give the local community the understanding of the industrial plant that it so badly needs, and usually completely lacks; nor does it try, on the whole, to integrate the industrial worker into the local community. There are some notable exceptions. The two New York garment workers unions, for instance, are leading members of their communities in the best sense of the word—and without giving up any of the objectives of unionism or any part of their strength. But on the whole most unions use their tremendous power in the community not only narrowly but most shortsightedly as a weapon of pressure.

Yet in the industrialized city the union has an opportunity unmatched by that of any other group or institution. American management has lately become conscious of the importance of "community relations," of the need of the local community to understand what the plant is and what goes on in it, as well as of the need of the plant to be accepted by the community. Yet direct communication between management and the community is practically impossible. There is ample room for co-operation on matters of common interest, such as, for instance, plant location, transportation or parking. But management is too remote from the ordinary citizen to reach him. And its very job and authority create a wall between it and the community.

We know on the other hand from a good many studies—such as those of Dr. Claude Robinson—that the town's opinions about a plant, its policies and its management are created almost entirely by the plant's workers. The enterprise can gain knowledge and understanding on the part of the community in which it lives only through the members of the plant, and especially through their own group organization, the union.

The union is as close to the community and as much part of its life as management is remote and isolated. The union can participate in all community affairs, organized or informal. Its members are the citizens, the congregation of the churches, the parents of the school children, and also the patrons of the taverns and betting parlors. The union—and the union alone—can convey to the local community the experience of industrial life and with it a basis for understanding and knowledge. That the local community acquire this experience is a vital need of the industrial enterprise. It is also a vital need of an industrial society. Today the industrial plant is a mysterious, if not rather frightening, place to those who do not actually work there. Such a split must create a permanent tension in our society.

The local community also needs the active participation of the union as a member. Only worker participation in the local government can restore the life and vigor of local institutions in the industrial city or town. Without it they must become either mere local branches of a central government or the tools of cynical and corrupt machines. The worker must participate as a responsible and proud citizen—that is, in the interest of the whole local community rather than for the sake of purely selfish and immediate gains. And the only organ through which he can participate in his capacity as an industrial worker is normally the union.

Playing a strong role in the community is also in the interest of the union itself. It is one of the strongest bulwarks against the real danger of a nationalization of the union movement. It creates support and understanding where the union needs it the most and usually finds it the least: in the middle class. Perhaps nothing has done as much to gain public acceptance for the union in the United States as the close contact between members of the middle class and union members or union leaders in the churches, Protestant, Catholic or Jewish. The earnest and unselfish work of unionists in church affairs explains, for instance, the enormous prestige of the Automobile Workers Union in Windsor, Ontario. At the same time—a lesson which union leaders might well take seriously to heart—the attempts of a few union men in Detroit, just across the river from Windsor, to use their prominent position in the churches to enlist the prestige and power of organized religion for union ends, is probably more responsible for the prevailing anti-union attitude of the Detroit middle class than management propaganda or any other factor.

The Union and the Family

Above all, the union alone can bridge the gap between industry and the family. It cannot close the gap—no institution can do that. Even the New York Garment Workers unions have not been able to do it. Yet all adult members of a garment worker's family are likely to work in the same industry and to belong to the same union; and as the garment workers belong to one or two racial and religious minorities, Italian Catholic or Eastern European Jew, they have been both a closely knit and a sharply isolated group. Where the family, as in industrial society, has ceased to be the productive unit, it is inevitably separated from society. It can at best be a "corresponding member" or enjoy "guest privileges." But the unions can at least give the family an understanding of the menfolk's work and world, and pride in it. That the American union movement as a whole understands this opportunity—however little it may have done about it so far—is one of its most distinctive as well as one of its healthiest traits.

To serve as the channel between industry and the local community, and as the bridge between industrial society and family, may well be the socially most important tasks of the union. In them it may find its positive and constructive function, as distinct from the antifunction of the tribune's veto that is its first and foremost function in the plant. But to discharge these functions, the union must participate actively, if not enthusiastically, in a plant-community self-government. Without such positive role and responsibility within the plant the union will normally be forced to subordinate all its activities and all its opportunities outside the plant to the needs and expediences of the industrial warfare against management and enterprise within the plant.

Can the Union Work in the Plant Community?

But for the union it will be very difficult to accept this new responsibility, even though it brings new power and prestige. No union could, indeed, decide to stay outside of a functioning community self-government. To allow a strong organ of the employees to develop and to function without union participation would be political suicide. But the union may well prefer to fight against the establishment of a community self-government. If it is forced to agree to it, it may attempt to destroy it from within through sabotage.

At first sight there would appear to be little reason for such an attitude. The union undoubtedly stands to benefit tangibly from participation in the community government. Indeed such a community government is the only means to resolve some of the most difficult internal problems of the union. It would immeasurably strengthen the local roots of the union. It would increase the participation of the members in union affairs, and their interest in them, and thus prevent that dry rot of member apathy which has proven itself the worst danger to established and successful union movements. It would help to restore the union function as the symbol of the worker's own opportunities that is so important a factor in the allegiance to the union. It would solve most of the problems of union leadership and would provide the unions with an abundant supply of well-trained and tested leaders. It would also greatly decrease internal tensions, extreme factionalism and the pressure for the "political strike." Above all, it would make virtually impossible the suppression of unionism through nationalization. It would create a multitude of strong union cells each with a life of its own which no government could take over for its own purposes.

Yet participation does entail real risks for the union. It tends to strengthen the local organization at the expense of the industry-wide or nation-wide organization. The more successful the community government becomes, the greater the danger that the union will disintegrate into a loose federation of company unions. Community self-government threatens to deprive the union of its "anti" function and therewith of its very reason for existence. Can a union co-operate with management in nine-tenths of all matters and yet fight management successfully over the remaining tenth? Or will such a union become a puppet of management altogether?

Even greater are the obstacles in basic attitudes and basic beliefs. Participation in the community government requires an acceptance of management as necessary. For a European union this will be most difficult; but it would also be a bitter pill for most American unions to swallow. It requires an acceptance of the survival and prosperity of the enterprise as in the union's interest. In addition, the union has to admit—if only to itself—that, while independent and existing in its own right, it is the junior and more limited institution. In brief, the union has to give up its belief in unionism as a "sacred cause." In their practice the unions have long abandoned this belief; but they cling all the more strongly to it in their creeds.

At the same time the unions would have to realize that the economic issues around which most of them have built their entire organization are only a part rather than the whole of the relationship between enterprise and worker. And while the unions hotly attack the belief in the "slot-machine man" when expressed by management, they themselves—with conspicious but few exceptions, such as the New York Garment Workers unions—are as much wedded to it as any management.

Finally, the union leaders would have to give up the habits, the patterns of thought and action, and the conventions of a lifetime. This may be the highest hurdle of them all. Indeed, our only hope lies in the fact that the union leaders of today are, by and large, old, and that a new and younger generation may prove more flexible and less habit-encrusted.

These are very formidable obstacles. We should indeed not be surprised to find more resistance to the principle of the community self-government among unions and union leaders than among managements. Even those who would be willing to support the new principle may hold back for fear of being branded "management men" and "traitors to their class."

Yet the interest of society demands that the union participate in the community government. We have therefore to make it possible for the unions to overcome their own fears and hesitations. There is very little we can do to overcome the difficulties in union attitudes. We can only trust to the pressure of the membership, which is certain to support a functioning community government enthusiastically, and to demand equal support from their union leaders. But we can at least attempt to answer in advance the tangible—and justified—fears that the community government will make the union a "company union" and deprive it of its independence, of its security and unity, and of its "anti" function.

In effect, this means the universal recognition—anchored in law—that union membership is normal and desirable. This does not necessarily mean the "closed shop," in which only men already members of the union that is operating in the plant, can be hired. But it certainly means the "union shop," in which any new employee has to join the union within a few weeks or months, and has to remain a member as long as he is employed. Only a union that has this assurance that its right to existence and its right to represent the workers cannot be undermined by management, can be expected to be willing and able to participate in the community government.

This raises, however, the big question of the safeguards on union control over the citizen. It also creates new and difficult problems of society's protection against union monopoly and union restrictions.

As far as the union itself is concerned, union participation in the plant self-government raises the question where the union would find a sphere of action beyond the purely local level of individual plant and individual enterprise such as it must have to survive and function. And where would it have a meaningful sphere of anti-action? Finally, even fullest union participation in the self-governing plant community will not solve two problems vital to society: that of a rational wage policy, and that of the strike.

The final topic in this discussion of the principles of industrial order is therefore the question of the union as a citizen.

CHAPTER 3 6

A RATIONAL WAGE POLICY

SOCIETY must demand a wage policy that is in the interest of the
entire economy. The unions, on their part, must put their own political
aims first in their approach to wage-bargaining. If the unions are to
participate in the self-governing plant community, this need for an
exclusively political wage policy will become even greater. The wage
area would thus seem to offer the only sphere of meaningful and
emotionally potent anti-action, as also the only sphere of national
or industry-wide action.

Most of today's discussion of a rational wage policy assumes—if
it does not expressly assert—that the determination of wages should
be taken out of the arena and be handed over to an impartial arbiter.
In effect, a "rational wage policy" seems to demand compulsory
government determination of wages according to objective economic
criteria.

The union position as summarized, for instance, in Arthur M.
Ross's *Trade Union Wage Policy* assumes, on the other hand that there
is nothing objective or rational about wages, and that the only criterion
applicable to them is the balance of power.

Both positions are untenable. We know, indeed, what a rational
wage policy should achieve. It should give the worker the highest possible wage over the business cycle that is compatible with
the highest possible employment over the business cycle. It should
give the enterprise a predictable wage burden that would combine
flexibility of labor costs over the business cycle with efficiency for
each wage dollar spent. It should give the economy a maximum of
stability. It should provide a wage burden neither so high as to make
impossible the proper provision for the costs of the future, nor so
low as to deprive the economy of the consumer purchasing power

it needs. It should not push up the break-even point of industrial production to a level at which even a minor set-back could produce widespread unemployment. But at the same time it should establish the principle that wages should go up in definite relation to an increase in productivity and efficiency.

But none of these is clear, objective or measurable. All attempts to arrive at objective yardsticks of the "right" wage have been utterly futile. The objective and impartial determination of wages is sheer illusion; government wage determination can only convert the struggle over wages from one between private parties into a struggle for control of the government, which must in the long run undermine if not destroy free government.

But it is equally impossible to allow wages to be set by pure power-play.

A solution must satisfy both demands. This requires first that we learn to distinguish clearly between two entirely different stages in the determination of wages: the bargaining over the wage burden and of the factors relevant to it, and the setting of concrete wage rates. It also requires that we distinguish between two different levels of wage determination: industry-wide and local. The first is the proper level for the determination of the wage burden; the second for the determination of wage rates.

Wage Burden and Wage Rates

All wage negotiations today focus on wage rates. This traditional focus, however, makes no sense at all. Wage rates per hour or per piece are not what the enterprise is interested in. It is interested in wage costs per unit of production. Wage costs per hour and per piece are also not what the worker is interested in. He is interested in income. Whatever its historical roots, the wage-rate focus long ago ceased to be anything but a stumbling block for both parties.

The major question for society, enterprise and union is what the wage burden on production should be. How much of the total cost should go for labor costs? How much of the total income should be the worker's income? Wage *rates* are not the first but the last question to be considered.

If the first stage in wage negotiations were to aim at producing agreement—or at least compromise—on the wage burden, the negotiations themselves would deal primarily with the factors that are relevant to the determination of the wage burden. What these factors are is fairly obvious. The list includes, first, general considerations: the "going wage"; the standard of living considered normal by the society—what in this country we are apt to refer to as an "American standard of living"—the cost of living, or more precisely changes in the cost of living which affect the purchasing power of the wage. It includes considerations of basic economic theory and policy, such as the effect of a certain wage policy on the national economy, etc. Finally, it includes a good many factors which are pertinent to the industry itself: its productive efficiency and profitability; the degree to which it offers steadiness and security of employment; the special skills required; the safety hazards; the incentives proper to the operation of the industry; and finally the competitive situation of the industry and its economic outlook.

But while we can expect a considerable measure of agreement on what factors are to be considered relevant, we could not—and should not—expect agreement how these factors are to be interpreted and weighed. Anyone expecting sweet harmony to rule bargaining sessions over fundamentals is bound to be sadly disappointed. But we can expect results that are actually more important to society. Such negotiation should limit the range of disagreement. On a few issues disagreement will remain total disagreement. The more theoretical the argument, the more violent, probably, the disagreement. On the one question that is wholly theoretical—the effect of basic wage policies on the economy—there is certainly going to be absolutely no agreement between the "purchasing power" theory of the union, and the "capital accumulation" theory of the employers.

But the more concrete the problems are, the more will disagreement tend to be disagreement on emphasis or on timing rather than disagreement on principles. We may even reach a point—actually reached by the New York Garment Workers unions—where questions of economic fact regarding the situation of the industry are settled by a joint union-management group of experts before the negotiations start and are rarely disputed at all.

More important: the atmosphere would be changed. Today the two sides only meet to battle out a concrete contract. Both think for the day only. Both use—or abuse—arguments on basic policy to gain an immediate advantage. The union, for instance, will stoutly maintain that the cost of living is of first relevance to wages as long as the cost-of-living index goes up. It will equally stoutly maintain that it has nothing to do with wages as soon as the index starts going down. The United Automobile Workers Union has done just that during the last few years and without changing leadership or negotiators. Management will emphasize "ability to pay" during lean years, such as the thirties, and will refuse to admit its relevance in the boom years of the forties, etc.

The moment, however, negotiations focus on the factors relevant to the wage burden, both sides have to take a stand on policy and stick to it. They may still disagree just how relevant cost-of-living or ability to pay are; but they will find it hard to proclaim one factor to be supremely important one year and refuse altogether to consider it the next. The new focus would force both sides to develop what they now completely lack: a long-range economic policy with respect to wages. It should act as a brake on the tendency to exploit an immediate advantage at the expense of long-time relations; at the least, it would make demagoguery much less attractive. It might even lead to the acceptance by both sides of the principle of automatic wage adjustments following changes in cost of living, productive efficiency or profitability.

But the major gain would be that the basic factors are discussed away from the pressure, the publicity and the emotional tension of the contract talks—that, indeed, most of them will be battled out at a time and at a stage where the discussion is fairly theoretical and deals with a hypothetical future rather than with immediate application.

Such a reformulation of the concept of collective bargaining would give the enterprise a predictable wage burden—something it needs as badly as the worker needs a predictable income. It would be of even greater value to the union. It would make its opposition function meaningful not only to the union member but to the citizen. It would give the union an industry-wide arena in which it has a legitimate and vital function. It would establish the authority of the national officers without interfering with the authority or independence of the local officers. Above all, it would give the union movement a long-range basic policy.

However, the negotiations over the wage burden can only be successful if they are separated from the negotiations over wage rates, that is, over the concrete contract. Also, they can only succeed if they are carried out on an industry-wide basis, that is, separate from the con-tract negotiations of a concrete enterprise. At the same time, however, we must stay away from nation-wide negotiation of wage policy.

Today negotiations over the general, the wage burden, are im-mersed in the negotiation over the specific, the wage rate. I don't think that anyone who has ever witnessed the amazing performance that goes today by the name of "collective bargaining," can consider it very productive of anything but bitterness and confusion. In fact, I have not been present at any bargaining session at which the one side did not argue basic economic theory only to be answered by the other with an argument on minor wage iniquities in one department of the plant. Granted that wage negotiations must have some of the unreality of a mock trial. Granted also that both sides are as inter-ested in impressing their respective constituents as they are in gain-ing a settlement. Granted finally that wage negotiations are inevitably a contest of power as much as a bargaining over economic issues. Yet the fact remains that not even the purposes of a mock trial are being served if the two sides talk past each other all the time. Indeed, com-pared to the typical wage negotiations, those famous absurdities, Mr. Pickwick's trial and the court scene in *Alice in Wonderland*, are marvels of sanity and of clarity.

If all negotiations are conducted on the level of the industrial enterprise—the prevailing pattern in this country—the confusion is, however, inevitable. Also, negotiations company by company are bound to produce the wage pattern that is least in the interest of society, enterprise and union alike: the pattern set by the "wage leader." The position which General Motors, for instance, occupies today in the automobile industry's wage pattern, or which the wage negotiations of U. S. Steel occupy in the steel industry is a thoroughly unhealthy and demoralizing one.

On the other hand, it would be very undesirable to have wage negotiations conducted on a nation-wide basis. This level is so far away from the plant as to make the discussion necessarily a very abstract one. The argument will focus on national income figures and national product, which, however important, are practically un-translatable into the terms of the individual enterprise, which is, after all, where the wage burden has to be earned and paid. Also, a wage policy determined nationally will inevitably strengthen monopolistic tendencies. It will tend toward wage rigidity and might easily degenerate into a supercartel.

Superficially, national wage determination might seem attractive to the union, especially as the political power of the union, that is, its command over the vote, might be decisive. In the end, however, the union movement would lose incomparably more than it could gain. The final decisions would be in the hands of a small group of national leaders. Even though nominally associated with individual unions, these men could never think or act in terms of an individual union—let alone an individual local—but only in terms of that abstraction, the union movement. The federation of unions would thus become the only effective organ of the labor movement, with the individual union reduced increasingly to the status of an administrative unit. Wherever that has happened—and the complete ascendency of the Council of the German Trade Unions before Hitler over individual unions and locals is one example—the union movement has disintegrated swiftly.

The proper level for what for want of a better name might be called the "general agreement" is therefore the industry. But the proper level for the *bargaining over actual wage rates* and wage contracts is the individual enterprise. This is particularly true if we are going to adopt predictable income and employment plans and profit-sharing plans, which will necessarily vary from enterprise to enterprise—and in the large federally organized enterprise even from unit to unit.

These local negotiations aiming at agreement on concrete wage rates may not, outwardly, look too different from negotiations as they are being conducted today. But the very fact that they are conducted against a background of a general agreement on the wage burden appropriate to the industry and on its determination, is bound to change their character fundamentally. Almost certainly the starting point of the local negotiations will be the general agreement. Both sides will argue that it does not apply to the concrete circumstance of the enterprise. But this in itself changes the tenor of the discussion. It limits the range. It substitutes specific arguments about facts for the "horse-trading" of excessive claims and counterclaims so general today.

The Four Issues of Wage Policy

The approach outlined here—and it is no more than a first approach —is not offered as a panacea. But if successful, it should focus collective bargaining increasingly on the four problems on which union and management hold legitimately opposing views, and on which there can be compromise but never real agreement.

The first of these is the basic theoretical question whether production or income come first. The argument between the adherents of the "capital accumulation" theory and those of the "lack-of-purchasing-power" theory is logically as senseless as the argument whether chicken or egg came first. Politically, however, it expresses in very clear form the basic differences between the aims, purposes and responsibilities of the two sides. It is, therefore, deeply relevant to collective bargaining.

The second basic issue is that of the relationship between above-average or below-average productive efficiency of a given enterprise and its wage burden. If a company operates at a rate of efficiency significantly below the average for the industry, management is bound to maintain that this is the result of exceptional circumstances rather than of management ineptitude, if not that it reflects low worker productivity. Management, therefore, is almost certain to consider low productive efficiency a cogent argument for a lower than average wage burden. Management must argue that an average wage burden in an enterprise with lower than average productivity could only further increase the company's already threatened competitive position. If productive efficiency, on the other hand, is higher than average, the union is bound to maintain that this reflects greater productivity per worker which must be expressed in above-average wage rates.

The third issue likely to become very difficult also arises directly out of the problem of productivity. Who should receive the benefits if productivity increases? The union will contend that the entire benefits should go to the worker in the form of higher wage rates. Management will contend that the entire benefit, or at least a very large share of it, should be divided between the enterprise and the consumer, that is, should be distributed in the form of higher profits and lower prices.

But the most stubborn fight will, probably, be over the issue *when* the benefits of increased productivity should be distributed to the worker. Should higher productivity be first achieved before wages go up? Or should the enterprise prefinance the rise in productivity? The union will contend that to expect the worker to produce more before he is being paid more, puts the burden of economic progress on those least able to carry it. Management will contend that to increase wages first is a gamble that no one, least of all the worker, can afford to take. Both sides have a case; but this is precisely why the fight is likely to be so hot. In fact, this issue underlies some of the most difficult and most bitter wage conflicts.

The existence of these basic conflict issues will make certain that collective bargaining will not become a statistical "fact-finding" process but will remain what it should be: a live conflict between the parties representing different interests and aiming at different purposes. But if we could succeed in focusing collective bargaining on these basic and real issues, we would already have made the biggest step toward a rational wage policy that would balance the interests of the enterprise, the interests of the worker, the interests of the union and the interests of economy and society.

CHAPTER 37

HOW MUCH UNION CONTROL OVER THE CITIZEN?

THE problem of union control over the citizen is not a problem of morals. It cannot be solved by giving advice to the union. Nor can it be dismissed with the argument that the union, representing the "common people," will always do the decent thing. It is a problem of power. To enable the union to function, we have to give it broad powers and have to make union membership practically general. But if society is to survive, these powers have to be limited, controlled and regulated. The conditions under which a union is granted its powers and the limits of these powers have to be set; and their exercise over the citizen has to be controlled. This requires legislation.

Access to union membership is increasingly becoming the pre-requisite to a livelihood. By controlling it, the union therefore controls a basic right of the citizen. Hitherto, we have maintained that the union is a private and voluntary association and therefore the sole judge of its membership requirements. But it can no longer be main-tained that the union is either private or voluntary. It is endowed with considerable governmental authority and it possesses necessarily great coercive powers. With the adoption of the new principles of indus-trial order, the public and compulsory side of unionism is going to become even more prominent.

If there has been any recognition of this so far, it has expressed itself in attempts to prevent the union from attaining security. Not all these attempts have been as childish as the union-shop provisions of the Taft-Hartley Act which try to halt union security by red tape—about as intelligent as an attempt to stop a flooded river by requiring of the waters that they get a stamped permit in triplicate, and about as successful. But any attempt to solve the problem by denying union security is bound to be altogether futile and to do harm. The starting point must be public recognition of the desirability of union security and legislation that makes it easy to obtain. At the same time we need a clear statement of the rights of the union to deny membership as well as a statement of the rights of the citizen to demand membership.

This should not be difficult. For centuries we have been developing basic rules for similar situations, such as admission to the Bar or to the practice of medicine. We only have to follow the precedents.

In the first place, expulsion should be allowed only for three specific reasons: nonpayment of regular dues, conviction on a criminal charge, and gross moral turpitude.

There is a fourth reason: conduct grossly unbecoming a union member and likely to disrupt the organization of the union and of the plant community. But this needs considerable further definition. A union should undoubtedly have the right to expel a man who makes constant trouble, for instance, by coming to work drunk every morning or by picking fights. But expulsion for such reasons must be preceded by several express warnings. And it must be provided by law that this right of the union to get rid of the undesirable must not be abused. Specifically, the union must be forbidden to deny admission or to expel for reasons of race, creed or political convictions. It cannot be allowed to deny admission or to expel for opposition to the incumbent union leadership, for agitating against the incumbent union and in favor of another union, or even for agitating against a union altogether. Certainly expulsion for any political or social activity outside of the plant, as a private person or as a citizen—unless it be criminal or grossly immoral—should also be forbidden.

Secondly, the union should be enjoined by law to establish a procedure for disciplinary action which gives the accused member ample opportunity to defend himself, and which meets judicial requirements of fairness, clarity and objectivity. Such a procedure is lacking today in many unions, where expulsion proceedings have all the characteristics of a kangaroo court.

Finally union decision on admission and expulsion should be made subject to judicial review, just as similar actions on the part of the Bar or the medical profession can be taken to the courts.

These provisions are not likely to be considered oppressive by the union movement even though there will, of course, be a show of opposition against any proposal to impose limitations on union power. There is, however, one provision that will be met with considerable skepticism—and not only on the part of the unions. That is the rule that no union be allowed to refuse admission or to expel because of a man's political conviction or party membership. We have reached the point where it is, by and large, accepted, even on the part of the most hidebound craft unions, that race and creed must not debar a man from union membership—however much the actual practice of some American craft unions in respect to Negro membership contradicts their professed ideal. But it has become increasingly common for unions to deny membership to Communists or to make membership in the Communist Party a ground for expulsion. And in this the unions have the overwhelming approval of American public opinion.

Any union must have the right to declare Communists ineligible to hold office in the union—just as any union should have the right to declare redheads or all people whose last name begins with a "P" ineligible to hold office. The right to hold office in the union does not derive from the rights of the citizen. Nor is refusal to grant access to union office a denial of any basic right of citizenship. Indeed, any union that wants to maintain its cohesion and integrity had better declare Communists to be ineligible to hold union office.

But this is something entirely different from denial of access to union membership to Communists. As long as the Communist Party is not outlawed, the union cannot be allowed by its own act to outlaw it. That this is an inescapable conclusion will be seen at once when we raise the question whether any union should be allowed to deny membership to Catholics or to Baptists or to people who were born on the Pacific Coast. There is no doubt that public opinion would consider unbearable such a ban on the part of a strong union in control of the workers in its industries, and would demand legislative or judicial action against the union. As long as the Communist Party is not outlawed by government, denial of union membership to Communists is no different from denial of union membership to anybody else. In brief, union policy on admission to, and expulsion from, membership is not entirely "private" and the union's own affair. It is, to use a legal phrase, affected with the public interests. For this reason the union must not be allowed to deprive minority groups of their citizenship rights as long as the law guarantees them these rights.

Monopolistic Restrictions on Union Membership

The second problem are the monopolistic restrictions on union admission which block access to a craft or trade. There is first the practice, common among some of the older craft unions, of charging high admission fees to new members. The main purpose is either to preserve a monopoly of a lucrative trade for the sons of members or to make membership in the union a marketable asset. Sons or close relatives of old members can come in without paying any admission fee or for a greatly reduced fee; or new members are allowed to come in without payment of the fee if they buy a membership card from an old and retiring member. There is absolutely no justification for the high admission fee. It is neither in the social interest nor necessary for the functioning of the union. It should be outlawed without any concession or exception; admission fees should be generally limited to the prepayment of the dues for a few months.

Much more general and much more damaging is the actual and potential abuse of apprenticeship restrictions. In the long run a union which monopolistically restricts the number of apprentices digs its own grave. The apprenticeship restrictions of the shop-craft unions in the American railroad industry, for instance, which have effectively limited the number of skilled mechanics, have been a major factor in the switch from the steam locomotive to the Diesel locomotive, which requires much less shop repairs and shop maintenance. Railroad after railroad has closed down its locomotive shops, and has dismissed permanently its shop craftsmen. But the fact that Nemesis overtakes a monopolistic union in the long run is little consolation for the harm these practices do to economy and society. Apprenticeship restrictions —the number of apprentices, the time of apprenticeship required and their training—should be made subject to governmental control. I personally would feel that no restrictions on the number of apprentices should be permitted—for exactly the same reason for which we do not permit the Bar Association to restrict the number of law students, or the Medical Association to restrict the number of medical students. But certainly any union restriction on the number of apprentices should be made subject to the anti-trust laws, and should be declared illegal if its intent or purpose is in restraint of trade. And though less important, union attempts to establish an apprenticeship requirement where there is no skill to be learned or—the much more common case—to preserve an apprenticeship requirement even though the craft has lost its skill and character, should be subject to invalidation under the anti-trust laws.

Closely allied to union restriction on apprentices are union restrictions on technological improvements, on new tools, new materials and on new processes—what is known in this country as "featherbedding" and in England as "ca'-canny." These restrictions, at least in this country, are important primarily in two kinds of industries: industries in which technological progress threatens to displace traditional skills, such as building; and industries with a long-term trend of shrinking employment, such as the railroads. But it is precisely in these industries that restrictions on technological progress do the most damage to the industry as well as to the economy. They tend to prevent the growth and development of an industry that could become a mainstay of the economy and a major employer, or they prevent the recovery of an industry vital to the economy. There is a genuine problem of technological unemployment in these industries. But the attempt to solve it by restrictive union rules can only make things worse.

The solution is not simply to outlaw "featherbedding," as has often been proposed. Certainly it should be forbidden. But at the same time the ban should be made dependent upon the development of a fair and reasonable method of handling technological unemployment by the employer: adequate severance pay, adequate retirement pay for older men made technologically obsolete, retraining, and a policy of systematic reabsorption of the men through careful planning in close co-operation with the union.

Union Seniority and Worker Security

The development of economic security policies for the worker, such as a predictable employment and income plan or a profit-sharing plan, creates additional problems of union control. Under such plans there would be constant pressure on the union to restrict the benefits to a group of "insiders" and to keep away "outsiders" by making union seniority the absolute qualification for participation in these benefits. There will be pressure against the employment of new people except at the very bottom of the ladder. There will be renewed emphasis on jurisdictional and craft lines. There may be an increase in the competition between unions and in their mutual exclusiveness. In short there will be a real danger that union policy will freeze economy and society. It may tend to cut down the individual's chance to move within the economy and to get a new job elsewhere, and to penalize anybody who leaves his job or loses it. Absolute and exclusive union seniority would threaten to bring about a new system of bondage in which the individual would again be tied to the job—by a golden thread to be sure, but tied nonetheless. There may again be a fixed status which the individual cannot change easily. And it would be a completely irrational status: status by accident of employment.

That an enterprise that has laid off people cannot hire outsiders until it has offered employment to its former employees, is standard practice today, followed even by nonunionized companies. Even though it clearly increases the odds against the man who has lost his job elsewhere, it is fair and equitable. But we must not accept policies that would convert the successful enterprise with a good employment prediction or high benefits out of profits into a closed corporation at all times. This would destroy social mobility. It would almost inevitably produce hereditary castes; at least every other system that has given exclusive benefits to a self-governing group without any public control of its policy of admission, has developed into a system of closed hereditary monopoly privileges.

We must make it possible for a man to transfer from one plant to another without losing his seniority altogether. We must make it possible for a man to take his accumulated benefits along when he changes jobs. We must make it equally possible for a man to transfer within his trade and craft from one union to a competing union without losing his seniority and with it all his claims to security and benefits. Finally, we must make it possible for a man to transfer his skill from one craft to another and not to be excluded from employment only because in the place where he grew up a particular skill was considered to belong in the jurisdiction of the Photoengravers whereas in another city it is under the jurisdiction of the Lithographers, or because he has been driving a taxicab where he now wants to drive a truck. And what applies to union restrictions on mobility and competition should apply equally to company policies having a similar effect. The customary provision that makes an executive's pension rights dependent on his not going to work for a competitor, for instance, seems to me to be contrary to the public interest. While not violating the letter of the antitrust laws, it certainly violates their spirit.

But we must also not destroy the stability of the union structure or of the plant community by outlawing seniority or craft jurisdiction. They fulfill a necessary purpose. We are therefore faced with a problem of balance. We might allow a man to transfer from plant to plant or from union to competing union provided his accumulated seniority is suspended for the first year, or provided he takes a cut of one-third or so in his accumulated seniority. We might allow a transfer from one craft to another on the basis of a simple examination to be administered jointly under an impartial chairman by officials of the man's old union and officials of the man's new union, etc.

But the techniques which we might develop are not important. Most important would be that society shall not be forced by union inactivity and resistance to legislate the balance. In this area the unions themselves should definitely take the initiative. Legislation will have to be resorted to if the unions do not themselves develop workable policies. But legislation would also be a very crude way of meddling with a delicate mechanism. It would be like trying to fix a wristwatch with a shoehorn. It has been done, I am sure, but it is not recommended by the best watch makers. It is in this area, therefore, that the union leaders have an especial responsibility but also a real opportunity. The more important it becomes to belong to a particular plant community and to a particular union, the greater the security and benefits accruing therefrom, the more important will it be for the union to develop policies that will keep open the access to all workers.

CHAPTER 3 8

WHEN STRIKES BECOME UNBEARABLE

OF THE major problems of the union as a citizen, the strike problem is likely to be eased most by the adoption of the principles of industrial order outlined earlier. The positive and constructive function which the union acquires under these principles should eliminate a good deal of the pressure for the "political" strike. It should make it possible for the union leader to function without having to roar all the time like the outraged father in a Victorian melodrama—the role that John L. Lewis knows so well how to play. The new opportunities in the plant community would offer satisfaction in constructive work for the demands for recognition and advancement which find an outlet today only in factional feuds within the union. In addition, the new concept of collective bargaining with its separation of wage burden from wage rate—especially if combined with income and employment prediction and with the policy of giving the worker a stake in profits—should greatly reduce the number of strikes in which wages are the actual or apparent issue.

But the strike would still remain vital to the union. Perhaps we might eventually reach a stage under which the "right to strike" became a pure symbol like the veto power of the British Crown over acts of the Dominion governments: a right that is stanchly upheld but never invoked. But in the foreseeable future strikes will continue. Society will have to find some way to reconcile the union's need for the strike with society's demand that no private group have the right to threaten the national welfare by concerted action.

There must be no general ban on striking except during national emergencies such as a war. To abolish the right to strike would be to abolish genuine unionism. It would be the first step toward the nationalization of the unions and toward the total state. Also, whatever government intervention there is in strikes, must be exclusively in the national interest; the government must not throw its weight either on the side of the union or on the side of the employer. That the government's power under the Taft-Hartley Act to stop a strike by injunction so clearly strengthens the hand of the employer—even though it is to be used only when a strike threatens the national health, welfare or safety—is a grave blemish and explains much of the union resistance to the Act.

But society could and should impose the rule that the strike is an extraordinary appeal to force rather than an everyday tool. The parties should thus be expected to agree in advance to arbitrate all disputes under an existing contract. Indeed, the general extension of the system of the permanent impartial umpire, which has worked fairly well in every industry that has tried it, would be highly desirable. In the absence of an agreement on arbitration, the interpretation of the meaning of an existing contract and of the rights and obligations of either party under it, should be left to the institution that is specifically designed to settle disputes over the meaning of contracts, that is, the ordinary courts. And work stoppages, whether strikes or lock-outs in order to enforce the terms of an existing contract or an interpretation of their meaning, or to change the terms of the contract, should not be allowed.

Such a ban would actually strengthen the union and the union leader. Today they are helpless against unauthorized "wildcat strikes" and actually have to condone, if not to support, them. An example is the strike of the British Railway Workers in June, 1949, against Sunday work rules that were in complete agreement with the contract. And the strike at the Ford Motor Company at the same time actually was intended to undermine the authority of the union leaders by forcing them to support a "wildcat strike" against the provisions of an existing contract at the very moment when delicate negotiations for a new contract were about to start.

The real problem is, however, the legitimate strike that endangers the public health, safety or welfare. There is no way to unravel this knot; it has to be cut. No government can allow a strike that endangers society. No attempt to give the workers in "essential industries" a special status can solve the problem, if only because every industry is potentially "essential." The government—any government —must have the right to judge which strike is likely to endanger the common weal. It must have the right to take legal action in such a strike to get the workers back to work.

At the same time, this government action must not degenerate into intervention on the side of management as it is likely to do under the Taft-Hartley Act. Whenever the government bans a strike on the ground that it would endanger the national welfare, it should also take temporary control of the enterprise. The profit which the enterprise is to receive during this period of government seizure should be fixed at the lowest annual average rate of profit for the last ten years. If the company showed a loss in any one year during the last decade, its return during the period of government seizure should be zero. If there is an actual loss during the period of government seizure, the burden should be borne by the company.

At the same time, the workers of a seized plant would be expected to work at the old rate if the strike is ostensibly over a demand for higher wages. If a strike were called to resist a company demand for a cut in wages, it would be advisable to demand of the workers that they work at the lower wage. In either case the differential between the wage paid and the wage demanded by the workers should be accumulated in a trust account pending settlement.

In other words, both workers and company would bear considerable risk. Certainly neither side would gain an advantage; in fact, both would have a strong incentive for settling the strike. As for the company, the economic effect of government seizure would be almost equal to the effect of a strike. And while the workers would face a smaller economic loss than what they are likely to incur during a strike, they would also be much less likely to obtain the victory which a strike in an essential industry, with its strong public pressure for an early settlement, might have brought them.

These last two chapters have dealt exclusively with limitations and restrictions on the union's freedom of action. Yet they are not "restrictive" in the sense in which all legislation on union behavior has traditionally been restrictive. They are based on the assumption of a powerful, generally accepted and secure unionism. Their aim is not to penalize the union or to hold it down; on the contrary, it is to enable the union to perform its vital social task. What we are aiming at is, in other words, genuine regulation rather than restriction.

Only one thing could convert such regulation into punitive and restrictive measures: blind union opposition to any attempt to define the limitations of union power and the conditions of its exercise. It is such opposition that has turned into restrictions the earlier attempts to regulate the enterprise. Most union leaders in this country realize today—though they will hardly admit it publicly—that they owe the Taft-Hartley Act to their refusal to co-operate in the writing of a genuinely regulatory bill when the Act was under discussion in Congress in 1946. A demand for unbridled license in the exercise of social and political power will always produce punitive restrictions. It is perhaps not too much to hope that our union leaders—or at least the younger men who are about to succeed them—will understand that it is in their hands to decide whether the American union movement is going to be restricted or whether it is going to be encouraged and strengthened through the proper regulation of its functions and power.

CONCLUSION: A Free Industrial Society

TO BE livable, any society today must be a free society. In the age of the total state, freedom has become indivisible—just as peace is in the age of total weapons. The comfortable combination of personal liberty and security with autocratic government—the *"Rechtsstaat"* of the European Humanist who did not want to be bothered with politics—is no longer possible. There is no halfway point between free society and slave society.

Whether industrial society will be free or slave will depend primarily on the relationship of the State to enterprise and plant community. If the central government is in complete and direct control of enterprise and plant community, freedom is not possible. It is precisely this control that makes the modern tyranny a "total" tyranny; there is no resistance against such a State and no meaningful sphere of privacy, let alone of freedom. At the same time, the autonomous enterprise and the autonomous plant community are the firmest basis on which a free society could be built. Indeed, free society today requires the autonomy of enterprise and of plant community.

Free society is threatened by the lack of responsible participation of the citizens in their own government. Without their participation free government will decay from within. A government to be free requires more than this or that right, this or that restriction on government power. It requires *citizens*: men who take responsibility. Responsible participation in government requires, however, an active local self-government. The national government is too remote for the citizen to take a direct and personal part in it. Only in the local community can the citizen acquire an experience of government.

The modern welfare state in particular must become both bankrupt and tyrannical unless local self-government is strong. As long as the benefits flow from a central government, the individual will remain convinced that they cost nothing. He will not understand that everyone of these benefits constitutes a charge on the production of the community, and that increased benefits can only be obtained by increasing productivity and efficiency. The very wealth of an industrial economy which makes possible these benefits is also the greatest danger to its prosperity as well as to its freedom.

It is futile to argue that the way out is to get rid of the welfare state. What good would be our ability to produce wealth such as no age has ever dreamed of, if we could not with it satisfy man's hope for security against the physical risks of existence? But let us not confuse the "welfare state" with the "hand-out state." If the member of society does not learn that the satisfaction of his hopes depends on increasing output, increasing productivity and increasing efficiency, that, in other words, it depends on *his efforts*, the promise of the welfare state will end in misery and slavery. The people will not be willing to abandon their hope of security. The worse things become, the more they will cling to it. And they will force themselves into a tyranny the sole purpose of which will be to enforce the equality of misery.

The benefits of the welfare state may have to be planned nationally; but they must be administered locally. Government should set the standards. Government should provide subsidies to those groups that are not rich enough to provide security equal to the national standard; and it should obtain the funds for these subsidies from those groups which are wealthy and able to carry more than the average burden. But the program itself should be a program of the local self-governing community.

In an industrial society the only meaningful units of local government are enterprise and plant community. The decay of the traditional local governments, especially of town, city and county, is indeed primarily the result of the shift of focus to enterprise and plant community. Only in a society where enterprise and plant community are autonomous local self-governments, and where they carry and administer social security, will freedom be strong. After having discussed the *functional* requirements of industrial order, we therefore now have to ask the question: What are the *political* requirements of an industrial society; what is needed to make it possible for industrial society to remain a free society?

The Rights of Property in a Free-Enterprise Society

The major political problem of a free-enterprise system is that of the rights of property in the industrial enterprise. A free-enterprise system faces no particular political difficulty in establishing enterprise and plant community as autonomous units. In fact the system is based on the assumption of the autonomy of the enterprise. Both the problem of union independence from the government and that of preventing union domination of the government in the interests of one group, should be materially eased by the establishment of the autonomous self-government of the plant community. But the right of the investor in the enterprise, "the right of the capitalist," is a major issue. If the legitimacy of management within the enterprise depends on the establishment of the autonomous plant community, the legitimacy of management in society, the legitimacy of its economic power, depends on the solution of the problem of the "capitalist."

In our discussion we usually confuse two entirely different things: the legal rights of the investor and the function of the capital market. The capital market is not "capitalistic." It has no more to do with "capitalism" or any other "ism" than other mechanisms such as banking or retailing. It serves an objective function. It insures the flexibility and mobility of the economy. It is necessary that the successful enterprise distribute its profits, its contribution to the risks of the economy and a large part of the reserves against its own risk. Otherwise the economy would soon become monopolistic, with a few big businesses getting bigger all the time. It is equally necessary that old industries decline and new industries come up. This continued process of aging and renewal is the basal metabolism of an economy. If it is blocked, the economy will die of self-poisoning. The only way to protect the economy against its own waste products is a mechanism that forces industries and enterprises to compete against each other for capital. In fact, *the competition for capital is at least as important to keep an economy a competitive one as the competition for markets and between products* on which our economic thinking has traditionally focused.

There is, however, nothing in the function of the capital market that would require the giving of an ownership right to the investor. All the investor has to be given is a claim to a share in the future income. The investor himself has made it unmistakably clear that he is not interested in ownership; indeed, that he does not want it. He has abdicated his legal right of control and he resists all attempts on the part of management to make him take an interest in the enterprise, let alone participate in its affairs.

The only purpose still served today by the legal fiction of the investor's ownership is to make it possible for one man or for a small group of men to obtain managerial control of a huge enterprise by buying a minute fraction of its stock—absolute control in some cases rests on ownership of less than one per cent of the stock. This is partly possible because of the wholly desirable dispersion of stock ownership in the population, as a result of which some of our largest companies have almost a million individual stockholders every one of whom owns only a few shares. It expresses also the apathy of the stockholder and his refusal to exercise his legal rights of ownership even to the extent of voting his stock.

It might be said that in a great many cases the enterprise has benefited from such control by a minority stockholder. But the fact that it is an able and aggressive man who is likely to take advantage of the discrepancy between the legal and the actual situation, does not make the practice any less of an abuse or any more justified. It only shows that our present concepts cannot be maintained or defended.

There is absolutely nothing in the nature of investment that either requires or justifies ownership rights, that is, rights of control. A future age may well regard the idea that control of a productive organization of human beings can be bought and sold for money, in the same light in which we today regard the buying and selling of human beings under slavery. However much of a fiction the investor's ownership has become, the principle will continue to provoke profound resistance. It grounds the political and social authority of the enterprise in an investment of money. But investment entails no political or social responsibility. All it entails is an economic risk. No case can be made out for endowing investment with political and social rights; all it is entitled to is an economic reward. The political and social, that is, the managerial function, can be based only on the objective function which the enterprise discharges as the economic organ of society.

The best solution would be simply to legalize the *de facto* situation. The investor in the large enterprise should not acquire any legal title of ownership, but only a claim to economic rewards. We should definitely exempt from this rule investment in subsidiary companies—following the precedent of their treatment under the income tax laws. We should also specifically exempt the investment of the founder of a business who has himself developed it from small beginnings into a prosperous company. But his heirs certainly should not be entitled to inherit his ownership title. Money can be inherited and can be bought and sold, but power must go only with responsibility.

Finally, we should limit the application of the new rule to the large enterprise. We could either set an arbitrary size limit: investment in a company employing more than five or ten thousand people may not carry ownership rights. Or we might prefer to limit the rule to companies with securities: notes, bonds, preferred shares or common shares, in the hands of the public. Either would create a few absurdities; the second alternative would, for instance, leave the Ford Motor Company under ownership control despite its size. But on the whole, either alternative should work equitably. And neither is likely to discourage investors.

This does not mean that we should abolish the legal concept of ownership altogether and convert the large enterprise into a corporation of the public law, comparable to a university or to a hospital chartered by the State. In fact, the change could be made without any change whatever in our legal concepts. Instead of forty million shares each carrying a completely spurious claim to a microscopic share in the ownership, there would be forty million certificates of investment each carrying a perfectly genuine claim to a share in the profits and to a share in the assets in event of liquidation. In addition, there would be certificates of ownership—or "shares," in our present terminology —which would carry the full legal title and which would be vested in perpetuity in the Board of Directors. The device of the "share without voting rights" is already used widely. In many cases the sole voting power in the company is vested in a "voting trustee," with the investors receiving only certificates of a claim to profits but no vote. And in the Ford Motor Company, for instance, the bulk of the shares —given by Henry Ford and his son to a charitable foundation—has no vote though it participates in the income on the same basis, share by share, as the voting shares held by the Ford family.

Such a change in the legal construction of the rights of the investor should go hand in hand with a reorganization of the Board of Directors which would make it a more effective organization and make it the organ that expresses the new and tenable basis of management's authority and power in economic function instead of in property rights. The Board should contain representatives of the investor; for after all he has a real interest in the conduct of the business. Management should be represented too for the same reason. But there should not only be, as has been said before, a number of full-time "management auditors" whose duty it would be to prepare and enforce policies of management organization and management succession. There should also be representatives of the plant community and of the communities in which the enterprise operates. Such a Board would have the power to appoint a management or to remove it. It would have the final say on all major capital expenditures. But it would not be supposed to act, as under the absurd fiction of today, as the actual governing organ of the enterprise, but primarily as a supervisor and maker of policy.

To abolish the legal fiction of the shareholder's property right would not change much, if anything, in his actual position. But it should remove the profound conviction that the enterprise exists to make profits for the shareholder—a conviction greatly strengthened by the traditional rhetoric of management. It would put the shareholder politically on the same footing as the bondholder. It is much more important, actually, for the enterprise to earn the interest on its bonded indebtedness than to earn a profit on its shares; if it cannot pay its bond interest, it goes into bankruptcy. Yet the bondholder is not a "public enemy." In fact, if bondholdership has any connotation, it has a favorable one. The bondholders in the United States are primarily big institutions, such as insurance companies and banks, whereas the shareholders are increasingly middle-class or working-class individuals. Yet bondholdership is associated in our minds with the "widows and orphans," whereas shareholdership is associated with "Wall Street" and the "tycoons." Finally the divorce of ownership control from investment should make it possible for the employee of the enterprise to understand that the enterprise must try to satisfy the demands of the shareholder not because he owns the company but because otherwise the enterprise will find it difficult to obtain the capital it needs to create jobs and to make these jobs attractive and secure.

The Problem of "Bigness"

There is a second problem a free-enterprise society has to solve: what is popularly known as the "problem of bigness."

The term is actually grossly misleading. It implies that we can do something about bigness in an industrial society. Actually, the modern industrial enterprise has to be big—for technological reasons, for managerial reasons and in order to supply a mass market efficiently. It implies that bigness is socially destructive. But a resolution of the basic economic problems of an industrial society is not possible except in the big enterprise. Research, on which our material progress has come to depend, is too expensive to be carried by any but the big and strong. The big enterprise alone can sustain the weight of war production and can convert fast from peace to war production and back. It alone can adopt long-range policies. Finally only the big enterprise can afford a management. Indeed, it is the basic weakness of the campaign against bigness that it considers bigness a cause whereas it is an effect. And it is above all an effect of the need for a management which is grounded in the very economic and technological nature of modern industrialism. If the big enterprises do not provide managements for industrial society, government will have to do so. We have no choice between big and small. All attempts to get rid of bigness represent not much more than sentimental nostalgia, and are doomed to fail. We have only the choice between a great number of competing big enterprises and one "supercolossal" big government.

The slogan of "bigness" also implies that the big enterprises enjoy such preponderant competitive advantage as to be immune to economic changes and invulnerable. Actually, the turnover among the very biggest enterprises is fully as great as among the smaller ones. To be sure, a few companies have supplied the bulk of the automobile market in the United States for a long time. But they are not the same companies today they were twenty-five years ago. Then Ford alone had sixty per cent of the market. Today Ford has less than twenty per cent. General Motors—supplying twenty per cent in the earlier period— now has forty. And the Chrysler Company, which did not even exist a quarter-century ago, sells today twenty per cent of all American passenger cars. The same is true in practically all industries. Indeed, the development of Ford is typical; in most major industries in this country the leading company of today has a conspicuously smaller share of the market than the leading company of twenty-five years ago. The market has been growing faster than even the biggest company.

But there is a real problem: the *problem of smallness*. It is vital to a free society—and to a functioning economy—that it be possible for small enterprises to exist side by side with the giants, and especially that it be possible for new enterprises to come into existence and to grow. What matters is not whether the enterprises are big or small, but whether there is a steady self-renewal of the economic cells. The problem is not one of size, but one of the basal metabolism of industrial society.

We need thus a policy that creates favorable conditions for the new, young and growing enterprise. These conditions cannot be obtained by combatting bigness, that is, by a purely negative action. They require positive measures in favor of smallness and youth. Today, however, our governmental policy—whatever its protestations—penalizes and persecutes the small, and especially the young and growing, business. The way in which we regulate business imposes a load of papers and forms which the small business cannot carry. Our fiscal policy does not make any provision for the risks and dangers of economic infancy and growth. To expect the young and growing enterprise to be able to carry the full burden of our taxes is very much like expecting a small boy to be able to make a forty-mile forced march with an infantryman's full pack on his shoulders. Especially vicious is the refusal to recognize that the young and growing business faces such extraordinary dangers and is exposed to so many childhood diseases that it must be allowed to build adequate reserves out of profits and to write off its losses over a fairly long period. In addition, we need a determined policy—and perhaps even some new institutions—to reopen the capital market to new ventures. Today our tax policy, in cahoots with our central-banking policy, effectively debars the new venture from access to risk capital.

A positive, energetic and courageous policy of encouraging the new and the growing enterprise is the best safeguard against the evils of bigness and of overly concentrated economic power. If we adopt such a policy, we need not fear bigness or monopoly; we will have provided the forces that will enable the economic body to take care of these problems by itself. It is also the only safeguard. Any other policy would at best doctor superficial symptoms.

The Political Problems of Democratic Socialism

The political problems of Democratic Socialism are a good deal more difficult than those of a free-enterprise system. There is a real problem of the flexibility and mobility of the economy under government ownership. There is a real problem of the relationship between government and the trade unions. Finally, it is much more difficult for "Democratic Socialism" to establish and maintain the autonomy of enterprise and of plant community.

Once the government owns industry, it will become very difficult to maintain the "basal metabolism" of the economy, the decline of obsolescent and the rise of new industries. Would any government be willing to let a major industry in its direct control and ownership decline or disappear, or will it maintain an outmoded or obsolete technique in order to preserve the "people's investment"? In a free-enterprise society, industries that have outlived their usefulness lose their ability to attract capital and eventually go bankrupt and disappear. But if the government is the owner, is it likely that any industry, however obsolete, will be allowed to die of capital starvation or to go bankrupt?

Even more serious is the question of new industries under socialism. Our "planners" seem to have tacitly assumed that there will always be an unplanned and more advanced economy available whose industries can be copied. But if Democratic Socialism becomes general or if a Socialist country aspires to be a fully developed industrial country, it will have to produce its own new industries. Yet not one of the major industries in existence today would have been started in a planned economy. In their early days the electrical industry, the chemical industry, the automobile industry, the aluminum industry, the rayon industry—to name only a few—were dubious ventures. Their technology was primitive, the capital investment required was very great, results were very uncertain. Would any government have been willing to gamble on the poor prospects these industries held out? Would it even be justified in taking such a gamble with the public's money?

In a Socialist society the need for competition is actually much greater than in a free-enterprise society. *If it is not a "free-enterprise"*

economy, it must all the more be a "competitive-enterprise" economy.
For the restrictive forces are bound to be much stronger. We may
even say that "planning" has much less scope in a Socialist economy.
To make Democratic Socialism work, it will be necessary to get rid
of the present concept of planning altogether, and to return to the
economic concepts of earlier Socialism, which focused on government
determination of a few basic controls such as that of credit, rather
than on the determination of production and consumption as does
modern planning. Actually, the ideas of planning are not Socialist at
all in origin, but derive from the war economy of World War I. Their
merger with Socialism during the last twenty-five years is likely to
prove the greatest stumbling block to the realization of the dreams of
the Democratic Socialists. Democratic Socialism actually needs a free
and unplanned capital market or some very good facsimile thereof. If
the decision which industries to supply with capital and which industries to starve of capital, is left entirely to the government, the economy
is bound to become rapidly immobile and frozen.

As soon as Democratic Socialism is established, the labor unions are
in crisis. They are suddenly in the management. They can either maintain their traditional role as a special pressure group against enterprise and society and use their political power to enforce the demands
of one group in society on the rest. Or they can become an arm of
the government-management and lose their function as the specific political organ of the workers. In practice, as we have seen in any country that has tried Democratic Socialism, the unions are torn between
those two tendencies and usually end up by making the worst of both.

If the unions take over the government, society will lose its economic
productivity and efficiency and with that its ability to survive economically. One result of this will be increasing resentment against the
unions on the part of society. In the end government will be forced by
public opinion to suppress unionism by nationalizing it. But this would
also be the end of Democratic Socialism and the beginning of a totalitarian regime. If, on the other hand, the unions become a part of
the management and give up their function, they will lose the allegiance
of their members. "Wildcat" strikes and rebellion against their leadership will become general and the members will be drawn increasingly
to demagogic groups—Communist or Fascist—that promise to restore

"honest unionism" and denounce the incumbent leadership as hirelings of management. In the end, too, government will have to suppress unionism to prevent openly subversive and revolutionary forces from gaining control of the workers.

Democratic Socialism should therefore be even more concerned with the maintenance of a truly autonomous union movement than is a free-enterprise system. One requirement is probably that the union movement in a Socialist State cease to be associated with any one political party, if not that it abandon political activity. In a State that owns its basic industries the unions can neither be allowed to be a part of the government nor to be a part of the opposition—in their own interest as well as in that of economy and government. But the major requirement for the survival of unionism under a Socialist form of government is that management and the plant community are autonomous and not under the direct control of the government. Only then can the union movement maintain its opposition function without being at the same time in opposition to government itself.

The ability to establish and to maintain the autonomy of management and plant community is the touchstone of Democratic Socialism. If either enterprise or plant community become directly controlled by the government, a free society is impossible. It would lead to the suppression of unionism. It would also lead to complete government control over the private citizen.

It might not be too difficult for Democratic Socialism to establish an autonomous self-governing plant community. But it will be very difficult indeed for it to tolerate a truly autonomous management, let alone actually to establish one. Management must be nonpolitical. It must discharge its objective function according to the best interests of the enterprise. It cannot be a civil service by the very nature of its job. Where the government is the owner and has full legal title, the temptation to assume full control will, however, be very great. It can only be overcome if the enterprise is established as an autonomous unit, if, in other words, the government puts the same restrictions on its own property ownership that I recommended for the investor in a free-enterprise society.

In addition the independence of management under Democratic Socialism must be grounded in the convictions of the community. Management must enjoy a professional standing at least equal to that of lawyer or doctor, whose independence is based on popular respect for professional competence and integrity rather than on laws. Perhaps it must even have the standing of a genuine "aristocracy," such as the Confucian scholar in China, the Senatorial Class in Republican Rome, or the "gentlemen" in eighteenth- and nineteenth-century England, whose title to rulership was grounded in its responsibility and accepted as such by the people.

Whether the experiment in Democratic Socialism will succeed is therefore still very problematical. Its greatest danger are the very doctrines and illusions that propelled it into power. Every one of these illusions will be dispelled almost as soon as Democratic Socialism starts operating. One example is what has been happening in Great Britain during the last five years. But the danger is great that this will not lead to a rethinking of the basic problems, and to a reformulation of the ends and means of Democratic Socialism. It may instead lead to a grim determination to cling to the illusions which could only lead to collective persecution mania and totalitarian misery.

In this country there is a tendency today to regard Democratic Socialism as an aberration that must inevitably lead to a totalitarian regime. Certainly a free-enterprise society, *as the term is understood in this country*, is much easier and much less risky. But we better realize that some form of Democratic Socialism—or at least an approximation to it—is the only form in which a good part of the world today can have a free industrial society. The motives behind Democratic Socialism in Europe and in the formerly colonial world are not understood in this country. The tremendous dislocation crisis from which Western and Central Europe and the formerly colonial areas suffer as a result of the industrial world revolution, requires a degree of social discipline and a concentration of effort very similar to the requirements of a war economy, and likely to be attainable only under a very strict organization of resources. If Democratic Socialism makes a virtue out of necessity, it is still a necessity.

But more important than the economic motives behind the drive for Democratic Socialism are the social and political motives. What Americans mean by "free enterprise" is so radically different from European "capitalism" and even more from "capitalism" in the formerly colonial raw-producing areas that nothing but confusion can result in an attempt to try to project American concepts on Europe and European concepts on America. Indeed, to call the American system "capitalism" is utterly ludicrous, considering what the term means elsewhere.

The difference is not primarily one of wealth and resources or one of technology. It is one of social climate. One fact alone makes American reality totally untranslatable into European terms. In this country *one out of every eight workers—other than farm hands—has a direct investment in industrial securities.*

Much more important, even, is the fact that this country does not know, and has never known, a "ruling class" in the European sense. By the same token this country has never known an "industrial proletariat" in the European meaning of the term. Instead, the organizing concept of American society has been that of social mobility—up and down—which denies the existence of "classes."

Other factors enter. What is called "materialism" in the United States —actually a grossly misleading term for an attitude which values material goods as symbols of success but does not value possession as such[1] —produces uniformity in the material style of life. There is no "upperclass" dress, furniture, automobile or architecture in this country; but there is also no "lower-class" style. The classes differ in the size and in the number of possessions, not in the basic mode of living. Hand in hand with this material uniformity—though noticed much less often— goes the most bewildering multiplicity and variety in the cultural institutions, such as schools and churches. In Europe, on the other hand, the unity—not to say uniformity—of the cultural tradition goes together with large variations in the material style and mode of living.

Finally, in the sharpest possible contrast to Europe, let alone to the East, social envy is absent as a motivating form of *group* action. It exists to any extent only among a dispossessed minority such as the Negroes; and its manifestations, for instance in Richard Wright's novels, come to the American as a terific jolt, whereas they are accepted as a matter of course in Europe by both Right and Left.

However illusionary the beliefs and doctrines of traditional European Socialism, it reflects therefore genuine social and political tensions. This is even truer of the formerly colonial areas of Latin America, India,

[1] In all American fiction and folklore I recall not one miser!

China, etc. In addition, European industry has on the whole proved incapable of producing genuine managers, that is, governors of the enterprise who put the interest of the enterprise above their own proprietary interest. There are exceptions: the people who run Imperial Chemical Industries and Unilever in Great Britain, Rathenau in Germany, the Philips group in Holland. Lately, conscious efforts to build a management have been made, especially in England. But on the whole the European industrialist has followed the pattern of the French *"propriétaire,"* with his emphasis on the preservation and enlargement of the family fortune, and on the barring of all "outsiders"—including the very people who actually run the business—from a full share in the economic fruits, the social prestige or the political power of the "capitalist." One reason for this has been the unhealthy domination of Continental industry by the big banks. Another undoubtedly is the power and prominence of the industrial combination which concentrates the managerial decisions in the hands of the anonoymous bureaucracy of the cartel or trade association.

It is a dangerous illusion of the European Left that a management will come into being automatically as the result of the expropriation of the private owners; indeed, nationalization is likely to make more difficult the development of a genuine management. But there can be little doubt that the European "capitalist" has failed, on the whole, to provide management. Yet modern industrial society requires a management; indeed, the need for a management is the greatest need of all countries today, far outranking their needs for dollars, raw materials, technical "know-how" or machines. The failure to produce a management has therefore rendered the European private owner powerless to oppose nationalization on the grounds of function; he can only appeal to the right of property or, purely defensively and negatively, try to show that private ownership is the lesser evil.

The point of this analysis is not that I favor Democratic Socialism. I regard it with the gravest misgivings—if only because of its legacy of illusions, utopian dreams, intellectual arrogance and perfectionism. It lives in a pre-industrial world, the world of 1850 rather than that of 1950—a world full of fabled monsters who, if they ever roamed the earth, have long become extinct. It has absolutely no concept of modern production. On the one hand, it believes that a mere redistribution will magically double or triple the available goods. On the other hand, it conceives in typically pre-industrial fashion of the amount of goods and services as completely static, and as a result fails to see the possibility of creating wealth through increasing productivity. I am opposed to its profound conviction that there is something immoral in competition. Above all, I am opposed to the basic assumption of the Socialist that a government servant is necessarily wiser, less selfish and more honest than a private citizen simply because he is a government servant.

My point is that Democratic Socialism represents not strength but weakness. It is not only the reaction to the barrenness of the Conservative tradition of Europe. It is above all the European Left, that is intellectually utterly bankrupt. All it stands for is opposition to the past. It is both frightening and pathetic to see how completely the British Labor Government, for instance, has in five years run through the entire intellectual capital of the Fabians that it took fifty years to amass. But for this very reason it is very important that Democratic Socialism succeed in developing on its own lines a workable and adequate policy for a free industrial society. The danger is very great that Democratic Socialism will fail; but then the forces that are behind it will be greatly tempted to abandon their belief in freedom in order to retain their illusions of Socialism. And if Democratic Socialism should fail to cling to its belief in democracy, this country may find itself isolated in a world hostile to it, and to our most cherished ideals. We have to realize that we have almost as much of a stake in the success of Democratic Socialism—precisely because it is so very weak—as the countries that are actually engaged in the experiment.

The free industrial society that emerges from this analysis is certainly very different from what we have traditionally considered to be "Capitalism." It is also very different from what we have considered traditionally to be "Socialism." *An industrial society is beyond Capitalism and Socialism. It is a new society transcending both.*

In this country we are very close to this new society, judging by actual institutions and practices. Nothing suggested in this book would constitute a radical or a revolutionary innovation. In fact, in some areas—management organization, for instance—the principles developed here would only codify and make general the best of current practice. In others—the income and employment prediction or the self-government of the plant community are examples—the principles, while new, only bring out the actual, though still partly hidden, trends. But in thinking, belief, and spirit these principles are indeed still very new and radical. The major obstacles to a free and functioning industrial society do not lie in institutions. They lie in the blinders habit has put on our imagination. We do not need "social engineering"; we need courage and vision. The real challenge is one of leadership—both to our managements and to our union leaders. The time is ripe for courageous and imaginative leadership—but it will not wait for us very much longer.

This is an anti-utopian book. It aims throughout not at the ideal society, but at a *livable society for our time*. This is a more modest aim than the quest for the perfect society that will shine as a beacon through the ages. It is at the same time a more ambitious undertaking. It requires concrete, feasible and effective policies, policies that can be done and that will do.

This book is concerned with political action. Such action will not cure the depravity of this age of concentration camps, police tortures and absolute weapons. It will not overcome the profound spiritual crisis of Western man. It will not jar us out of our frightening moral numbness. Political action is no substitute for the great Prophet who shall call this generation to repentance, for the great Saint who shall turn our vision back to the source of all light, or for the great Poet who will sing again of the greatness and dignity of Man. But it was not a politician but a great Saint who said: "Before men can be Christians they have first to become citizens." If political action cannot exorcise the manmade demons that haunt our world, it can, at least, give us the weapons to fight them, and with them courage and hope where today we walk in fear.

Epilogue to the 1962 Edition

TEN or twelve years are not a long time in history, but they are a very long period in current events, which is, of course, the subject of this book. And the dozen years since this book first appeared (two months before the outbreak of the Korean War) have been years of rapid change.

A good many of this book's "predictions" have come to pass sooner than the author himself would have imagined, and much sooner than his critics, a dozen years ago, would have thought possible. This is particularly true in the field of labor relations. An annual income guarantee, for instance, seemed utopian in 1950. Something very much like it is today a near-reality in those union contracts providing for Supplementary Unemployment Compensation, for organized re-training, or for a systematic balancing of the number of employees against technological changes in the industry (this last was stipulated in the San Francisco dock workers' contract signed in 1961/2 and also in contracts for glass blowers throughout the country).

Similarly, to relate wages to the cost of living and to productivity seemed a naive thought then; it became reality in the automobile industry contracts only a short time after the book was published. Finally, we increasingly realize, as I predicted, that "fringe" benefits (such as retirement pensions or health insurance) will have to be financed out of profits rather than considered a charge against costs. Today in a good many major benefit plans (that of American Motors, negotiated with the Automobile Workers in 1961, is one example, that of the Champion Paper Company another), this has been carried out.

More important, it is now generally accepted even within the labor movement itself that the trade union is not a primary but a secondary institution, which depends for its existence as well as for its effectiveness on management and on management's performance. The most discussed book on labor relations in 1951 was *A Philosophy of Labor*, by the Columbia University historian Frank Tannenbaum (New York: Knopf), which put forth in the most eloquent terms the labor movement's traditional thesis, according to which the trade union is the basic and indeed the central institution and community of an industrial society. Ten years

353

later, in 1961, the most discussed labor-relations statement was that of a group of leading American labor experts from Princeton, the University of California, and M.I.T., who had begun a world-wide survey of economic development and industrialization in the belief that labor relations and trade unionism were its central factors and, much to their surprise, had come to the conclusion that these were relatively unimportant and that the central and determining factor was the development of management and managers.

And when *The New Society* had talked of a national wage policy in which the interests and needs of society would mark the limits within which collective bargaining could be allowed to operate, this was not only considered utopian but, by many people in both management and labor, a rather reactionary attack on the unrestrained freedom to bargain in the market place. That we need such a national policy—though it is a very difficult thing to define, let alone make effective—has by now been generally recognized. This realization underlies, of course, the labor policy of the Kennedy Administration. And the professed tendency of this policy to be neither "anti-labor" nor "anti-management," neither "pro-labor" nor "pro-management," but instead "pro-nation," enjoys public support, no matter how severely various steps taken under it may be criticized.

Another area where predicted events then considered most unlikely to happen have become reality is in our understanding that mere legal title cannot begin to solve the basic problems of an industrial society. The disillusionment with nationalization of industry as the "magic wand" has become so general that (unthinkable only a few years ago) nationalized industries can be returned to private ownership without mass uprising of the workers. Indeed, the workers in the British steel industry, in the German Volkswagen automobile company, and in the industries owned by the Austrian government seem to have been the strongest supporters of a return to private ownership—if only because it is so much easier to fight management when it represents the "wicked capitalist" than when it represents the "public" or the "nation."

However, other things which this book expected have not come to pass. One example would be the failure of European socialism to dominate Europe's governments. European socialism has proved as sterile, as devoid of new ideas, as frozen in obsolete attitudes as I originally stated (to the great scandal, by the way, of most of the book's reviewers). But it had seemed to me that this would not keep the European Social Democrats from capturing control of government, or at least from having to be included in a government coalition. By and large this did not happen. By now it seems likely that the European non-Communist left will not be able to obtain power until it has succeeded in ridding itself of the obsolete and sterile slogans of yesterday.

These are, however, not the really important things that have happened. The really important things—as usual in an attempt to analyze and to predict—are changes which the author when writing the book fully saw but failed to perceive, fully recognized but failed to understand. What makes predicting the future so certain of failure is not that the unexpected always happens. It is that the expected always means something so very different. The most disappointed man is always the prophet whose vision has come true, the pioneer who has reached the new frontier, the explorer who has found the new continent.

Four developments belong here: the dynamic developments of the last decade in our industrial society. The first is the dramatic resurgence of Europe, its tremendous jump into economic growth and leadership after forty years of stagnation and timidity. The second is the explosive "revolution of expectations," the sudden demand for economic and social development throughout the whole world, especially among the totally underdeveloped, the pre-industrial, the formerly colonial areas in Africa and Asia.

The third development, equally important though entirely different, is the emergence of a middle-class employee—the "knowledge worker"—as the largest and most rapidly growing group in the working population of the industrially developed countries, especially the United States. In *The New Society* this group was clearly seen but not perceived. The book still divided the industrial world into two groups, "workers" and "managers," though emphasizing again and again that the characteristic group was a different one of technical and professional employees. Today it is quite clear that this third group is the most important. It is a group of "workers" though it will never identify itself with the "proletarian," and will always consider itself "middle-class" if not "part of management." And it is an independent group because it owns the one essential resource of production: knowledge. And yet it is employed and can make its knowledge effective only through access to the industrial organization. It is this group whose emergence really makes ours a "new" society. Never before has any society had the means to educate large numbers of its citizens, nor the opportunities for them to make their education productive. Our society, however, cannot get enough educated people, nor can it really effectively utilize any other resource but the educated man who works with his knowledge rather than with his animal strength or his manual skill.

And finally, perhaps as a result of the three preceding developments, management is no longer something one has to emphasize and feature. That it exists, that it has an essential role and function in society, that it is a distinct group with its own knowledge, its own area of authority and responsibility, its characteristic behavior and problems, is obvious today. We have discovered management. In fact, there has been something like a "management boom" all over the world, in Europe as well as in Japan, and especially in the developing countries (but also in the Soviet Union). In India, for example, management was not even mentioned in the first Five Year Plan (adopted at the time *The New Society* first appeared). The emphasis was on capital investment and the balance of payment. The second Five Year Plan already mentioned management, though in a subordinate capacity. But whatever success the second plan had was derived from the totally unexpected emergence of substantial numbers of managers and entrepreneurs outside of the plan, in the private economy. And in the third Five Year Plan, adopted in 1961, the development of managers is a central task, and one to which considerable energies are being devoted.

This is typical of what has been happening all over the world. "Management" was something the United States tried hard to transplant to Europe through the Marshall Plan. At first the transplant did not take root. Today Europe is full of management magazines, management associations, institutes for advanced management development, and so on. Some of the most advanced of the new management techniques (for instance Operations Research, i.e. the application of systematic, primarily mathematical methods to management problems) have been taken up much more enthusiastically by the Europeans than by their American counterparts.

These are very important changes and in many ways they create conditions quite different from those *The New Society* assumed and discussed. But at the same time they make more important, rather than less important, the analysis this book tried to present; the problems and opportunities it attempted to point out; and the conclusions it reached.

What was then still largely an American situation and an American concern—or at least one confined to the old industrial countries of the North Atlantic—has, as predicted, become truly international, and, indeed, truly supra-national. The problems in Japan and India are similar to those in the United States or in Germany. They are not too different in the new industries of Brazil or Rhodesia. Judging by what information we háve, they are very much the same in the Soviet Union. And, one suspects, they are the same (only infinitely more difficult) in Communist China.

The opportunities, too, have become much greater. This is particularly true with respect to the emergence of the "knowledge worker." He, more so than the manual worker of yesterday, needs the "managerial vision"; indeed without it he is ineffectual and frustrated. He cannot obtain social status and function from membership in a protest group of the "exploited," the proletarian class of nineteenth-century socialism. He needs the status and the opportunities of a full member of industrial society. And, as all our experience shows, the only way to obtain an effective organization of "knowledge workers" and full performance from them is by letting them manage their own plant community. All the talk about "creating a campus atmosphere" for "researchers" simply means that they have to be given this responsibility for running the plant community precisely because it is so important that we obtain high performance and output from such high-quality and high-cost human resources.

Similarly, the emergence of management as a central function in our society makes all the more urgent and important understanding of this function—by managers as well as by their fellow-citizens. It is necessary for a society to think through what power and authority management can legitimately claim and must claim, in order to perform. At the same time we must guard against the tendency to let management claim more authority than its performance requires. Management's grounds for authority need to be clearly defined, for modern industrial society will only operate properly if management is seen as a central but limited organ.

What I am trying to say is that the past twelve years have seen an unfolding of the trends and ideas which this book originally tried to describe and to present. A good deal of what was then future expectation has become present reality. The essentials, however, remain the same, as do the main purpose and theme of this book: In the industrial society of today we have a distinct, a "new" society, and one which it is our job as citizens to understand. It cannot be understood by applying to it the slogans of yesterday, or indeed any slogans at all. It requires to be looked at in its own terms as something which, like any creation of Man, is both a problem and an achievement.

INDEX